Spiritual Care in an Age of #BlackLivesMatter

*Examining the Spiritual and Prophetic
Needs of African Americans in a Violent America*

EDITED BY

Danielle J. Buhuro

FOREWORD BY
Chanequa Walker-Barnes

CASCADE *Books* • Eugene, Oregon

SPIRITUAL CARE IN AN AGE OF #BLACKLIVESMATTER
Examining the Spiritual and Prophetic Needs of African Americans
in a Violent America

Cascade Books
An Imprint of Wipf and Stock Publishers
199 W. 8th Ave., Suite 3
Eugene, OR 97401

www.wipfandstock.com

PAPERBACK ISBN: 978-1-5326-4808-3
HARDCOVER ISBN: 978-1-5326-4809-0
EBOOK ISBN: 978-1-5326-4810-6

Scripture quotations marked (NLT) are taken from the Holy Bible, New Living Translation, copy-
right ©1996, 2004, 2015 by Tyndale House Foundation. Used by permission of Tyndale House
Publishers, Inc., Carol Stream, Illinois 60188. All rights reserved.

Scripture quotations marked (NRSV) are taken from New Revised Standard Version Bible, copy-
right © 1989 National Council of the Churches of Christ in the United States of America. Used by
permission. All rights reserved worldwide.

Cataloguing-in-Publication data:

Names: Buhuro, Danielle J., editor. | Walker-Barnes, Chanequa, foreword.

Title: Spiritual care in an age of #Blacklivesmatter : examining the spiritual and
    prophetic needs of African Americans in a violent America / edited by Danielle J.
    Buhuro ; foreword by Chanequa Walker-Barnes.

Description: Eugene, OR: Cascade Books, 2019. | Includes bibliographical references.

Identifiers: ISBN: 978-1-5326-4808-3 (paperback). | ISBN: 978-1-5326-4809-0
    (hardcover). | ISBN: 978-1-5326-4810-6 (ebook).

Subjects: LCSH: Pastoral counseling. | African Americans.

Classification: BV4011 S75 2019 (print). | BV4011 (epub).

Manufactured in the U.S.A.   SEPTEMBER 16, 2019

To the gentleman who raised me as his own,
my father, 'Poppy',
who early on lived African American Spiritual Care into my life.

THANK YOU, CALVIN WILLIAMS!

Contents

Foreword / Chanequa Walker-Barnes xi
Preface: Why This? Why Now? / Danielle J. Buhuro xvii
List of Contributors xx

Introduction / *Lee H. Butler Jr. xxiii*

PART 1: Caring for the Victims of Violence and Social Justice Activism

1. From Viral to Voyeuristic: When Police Brutality Videos Turn into Black Death Tourism; Self-Care for Black Trauma / *Danielle J. Buhuro 3*

2. If They're Black, Call 911: Addressing White Persons' Biased Illogical Paranoia / *Danielle J. Buhuro and Jamie D. Hawley 9*

3. Brown Lives Have Never Mattered: The Demonization of Immigrants, Refugees and Asylum Seekers Is Not New / *Mariela Gonzalez 15*

4. When the Movement Gives Back / *Julian DeShazier and Damon A. Williams 23*

5. Domestic Violence and Pastoral Care in the Age of #BlackLivesMatter / *Sharon Ellis Davis 37*

6. See Her: Creating a Culture of Safety in the Black Church for Young Women and Girls Living in a Prison Nation / *Liz S. Alexander 48*

CONTENTS

7. Creating Circles of Peace: Mindfulness as a Pastoral Response to Health, Education, and Violence in the Black Community / *Marsha Thomas* 58

PART 2: Caring for Body and Soul in the Black Community

8. Rethinking Interpretive Tools for a Liberating Spiritual Care / *Afri A. Atiba* 71

9. Breaking Bread and Breaking the Silence in Black Churches: Let's Talk About Mental Health / *Rochelle Johnson* 81

10. My Mind's Made Up: Barriers to Accessing Mental Health Services for the African American Community / *Charlene Hill* 92

11. Give Us What Magic Johnson Got! Spiritual Care for Black Lives Living with HIV and AIDS in the Era of #BlackLivesMatter / *Michael Crumpler* 102

12. When Life Doesn't Seem Worth Living: Congregations Engaged in Suicide Intervention and Prevention During the Era of the #Black Lives Matter Movement / *Delois Brown-Daniels* 114

13. #BlackHealthMatters: Addressing Food Oppression in the Black Community / *Danielle J. Buhuro* 127

PART 3: Caring for African American Marriages, LGBTQIA Partnerships, and Families

14. Finding a Mate the Same Hue as You: A Systematic Review of Mate Selection Barriers among African Americans, Spiritual Resources, and Therapeutic Interventions / *Heather C. Lofton* 135

15. The Talk: Black Fathers, Black Sons—Letters to Survive / *Jamie D. Hawley and Derrick Floyd* 148

16. Changing the Subject: Creating Caring Communities for Women Impacted by Abortion / *Karen Walker-McClure* 160

CONTENTS

Part 4: Caring as Chaplains Within Institutional Settings

17. Why CPE? / *Ardella Gibson* 171

18. . . . And the Truth Shall Set You Free: The Critical Need for CPE among African American Clergy in the Age of #BlackLivesMatter / *Amber Coates, Mariela Gonzalez, Michael Smith, Terrance Thomas* 179

19. A Manifesto: Black Spiritual Care in American Hospitals / *Karen Hutt* 186

20. Pastoral and Spiritual Care to African Americans in the United States Armed Forces / *Joseph Yao-Kotay* 194

Bibliography 201
Index 215

Foreword

CHANEQUA WALKER-BARNES

SOMETHING WAS HAPPENING IN Saint Louis. My social media connections to racial justice activists across the country had my Twitter and Facebook feeds lighting up. I started digging, searching first for Saint Louis, and then for Ferguson, swiping my screen down to refresh the feed repeatedly. Eventually I came across the threads of a few people who seemed to be on the scene. A local rapper using the Twitter handle @theepharoah, had witnessed the shooting outside his apartment window and was live-tweeting: "I JUST SAW SOMEONE DIE OMFG." Police had shot a Black teenager. They had left his body on the street in plain view, unidentified until a woman made her way toward the crowd, looking for the grandson who had been on his way to see her. Finally, there was a name: Michael Brown.

The next part of the story was remarkable: the people stayed with the body. Quietly, they watched as the coroner's office finally showed up at the scene. Then, when Michael's body had been loaded into the coroner's van, they followed, walking en masse to the police department. There too they waited calmly for someone to come outside and explain why Brown had been shot when, as the word had already spread, his hands had been up. Watching the photos and videos that were being spread via Twitter, I recognized their somber poses, their insistence on staying with the body, their demand for accountability for a life lost. It was a historic African American mourning ritual.

Dying and mourning have always been serious business among people of African descent. The sacredness attached to death and funerals is a remnant of African cultures that survived the transatlantic slave trade, European colonization, and cultural assimilation. Thus, West African traditions of honoring the family and the deceased with elaborate memorials and visitation continue to be important rituals among Blacks in the United States. In many Black families, the time between death and burial may extend up to two weeks now to raise the funds needed to provide a befitting memorial or to allow geographically dispersed relatives the time needed to make travel arrangements to pay their respects. In predominantly Black neighborhoods across the country, people still observe the tradition of pulling over to let funeral processions pass.

A particularly relevant aspect of African American mourning rituals is the importance of how—and by whom—bodies are handled in death. In *Passed On*, Karla Holloway notes the significance of the question, who's got the body? in African American mourning and burial practices. Who's got the body? is the question that my older relatives continue to ask when someone has died. Even more than Sunday morning worship, death in America remains highly racialized. African Americans have a long distrust of White morticians and funeral homes, and thus overwhelmingly turn to Black funeral homes for burial services. Who's got the body? is shorthand for, Who will be handling the person's body in this last ritual? Will they treat them with dignity and respect, regardless of the person's standing in the world? Will they approach their embalming, dressing, and positioning as a sacred, intimate act? Will they take care to make sure that the deceased is presented in a way that honors the best of the person and their family?

Asking who's got the body? is also a way of finding out where and when people can "sit with" the body and the family of the deceased prior to the funeral, to ensure that they are not left alone.

As the crowd returned to the Ferguson Police Department the day after the shooting and waited for an official word, they seemed to be saying, "We've got the body. We will make sure that 'Big Mike' is treated with dignity and respect. We will make sure that the police handles this case in a sacred way that honors the best of him and his family. We will make sure that his family is not alone." They were doing the "different kind of memorializing" that follows death that occurs from racialized violence against Black bodies, one that requires public lament. Quickly, though, it became clear that Missouri officials interpreted their grief as threatening, their mourning as rebellion. Instead of compassion, they stonewalled. Instead of assurances of accountability, they provided militarized police and unreasonably instituted curfews. I recognized the meaning behind the official responses as easily as I had recognized the crowd's: they were fanning the flames of an already tense scene into a riot.

It was August 9, 2014, my seventeenth wedding anniversary. Normally, I would have been celebrating and deliberately avoiding all media. But it was not a normal year. Five weeks earlier, I had been diagnosed with breast cancer. Still recovering from a hysterectomy, I would be undergoing a double mastectomy in four days. Later that evening, I would gingerly get dressed and make my way to dinner. But at home, there was little more that I could do than watch as the shooting and subsequent protests unfolded in Ferguson, and as many of my ministry friends made their way to Missouri to support the protestors. I felt helpless. I wanted to join this historic movement in voice and in action. Eventually, I figured out a role befitting both my physical limitations and my expertise as a theologically trained clinical psychologist. I could amplify what was happening in Ferguson to my clergy-filled network and encourage them to act within their own contexts. I could respond to the protestors' requests for financial assistance and emergency supplies to sustain their work. And through the power of social media, I could reach out directly to activists on the ground to remind them to care for themselves in the thick of the battle, and to let them know that I was praying for them by name.

It turns out that I was not alone in my struggle to figure out my role. In Ferguson and later in Baltimore, social media has also provided a bird's-eye view on the struggle that Christian clergy have had in discerning the nature and scope of our role in the contemporary Black Life Movement. Unlike its twentieth-century forebears, this modern civil rights movement is not dependent upon charismatic, highly educated, male religious leaders. Indeed, its leadership is largely composed of a diverse array of millennials—those born between the early 1980s and the mid-1990s. The movement that began in Ferguson has been birthed and sustained through the labor of young African Americans who know firsthand what it means to be profiled, both by law enforcement and by middle-class Black churchgoers. They tend to value equality and relationality over hierarchy and protocol; they are distrustful of institutions and those who wield institutional power; they eschew the politics of respectability; and they reject the idea that leadership is the birthright of a particular gender identity, sexual orientation, ability group, social class, or generation.

Clergy stumbled over how best to approach this group. Some grew frustrated at the lack of a clearly identifiable spokesperson and lectured the young activists about their need to establish structure and hierarchy, failing to recognize the problems embedded in such patriarchal understandings of leadership. Others expected that as in prior movements, the young activists would do the groundwork of organizing protests and then move to the background to allow older, more prestigious, and properly religiously credentialed leaders to assume the role of spokespeople. Some learned the hard way that these young activists would not hesitate to boo internationally recognized civil rights veterans offstage for attempting to use protest events to raise money for their own organizations. Neither would they hesitate to drop a shame-inducing freestyle in the face of prominent clergy who they believed were using community organizing gatherings to further their own political and ecclesial ambitions.

Other religious leaders, however, found ways to serve alongside, and even behind, the protestors without attempting to usurp their leadership. Womanist queer theologian and United Methodist elder Dr. Pamela Lightsey traveled to Ferguson in the midst of the August 2014 protests as an amateur journalist to document firsthand what was happening while marching in solidarity with the protestors. Her livestream and Twitter feeds quickly became trusted sources of information about "what was really happening in Ferguson" for people like myself who deeply distrusted the mainstream news coverage. Rev. Traci Blackmon, pastor of Christ the King United Church of Christ, went to the apartment complex where Michael Brown had been shot to minister to those who had watched helplessly as police left his body in the street for over four hours. She was a steady presence among the protestors, one who gained trust through her willingness to be led by them. When hundreds of Black Lives Matter riders were suddenly stranded without housing after traveling to Ferguson from all over the country, Rev. Starsky Wilson, the senior pastor of Saint John's United Church of Christ, arranged for them to use the church as both lodging and headquarters. Wilson, whose participation in the movement has continued long past the initial protests, would later be elected cochair of the Ferguson Commission, an independent body examining the social and economic conditions underlying the protests. For each of these figures were countless other clergy who showed up in Ferguson, Baltimore, and other places around the country to quietly take their place in this twenty-first-century civil rights movement. Some took up roles on the sidelines of protests as human rights observers. Others wore clerical collars or clothing to identify themselves as chaplains ready to pray with protestors and police. Still others staffed emergency stations where they distributed water and carried milk to relieve the burning eyes of protestors at whom police fired tear gas cannisters.

By and large, though, the overwhelming majority of U.S. clergy, including many African American clergy, has deliberately failed to engage the Black Lives Matter movement. At worst, they have critiqued and undermined the movement; at best, they have been silent. Both stances are costing the church deeply. Several news stories have documented that there is a small yet significant exodus of African American Christians from institutional churches that may be directly connected to how those churches have handled, or mishandled, state-sanctioned anti-Black violence and the resulting protests. *New York Times* reporter Campbell Robertson began to recognize this as he began investigating why African Americans were leaving predominantly White churches. Robertson noted that his conversations with people across different parts of the country revealed that their disenchantment with the church shared remarkably similar timelines—beginning with the acquittal of George Zimmerman for the murder of Trayvon Martin in 2013, punctuated with the deaths of Eric Garner and Michael Brown in 2014, and solidifying with the overwhelming White Protestant support for Donald Trump's election to the presidency in 2016. While much of the media attention has focused upon African Americans in evangelical or White mainline congregations, the impact is also being felt in many historically Black churches. In her ethnographic study of the spiritual lives of young African Americans, Almeda Wright notes that African American youth and young adults engaged in social activism and community work "far too often . . . do not see or feel space for their outcries within Christian contexts."[1] Meanwhile, in almost any gathering of African American churchfolk, the question arises, how can we get and keep young people engaged in our congregations? What Howard Thurman wrote in *Jesus and the Disinherited* remains just as relevant today as it was in the 1940s:

> To those who need profound succor and strength to enable them
> to live in the present with dignity and creativity, Christianity often
> has been sterile and of little avail. The conventional Christian word
> is muffled, confused, and vague. Too often the price exacted by
> society for security and respectability is that the Christian movement in its formal expression must be on the side of the strong
> against the weak.[2]

To what avail is the twenty-first-century church in the midst of the onslaught of state-sanctioned violence against Black lives, the resurgence of

1. Wright, *Spiritual Lives of Young African Americans*, 155.
2. Thurman, *Jesus and the Disinherited*, 11.

White nationalism, and the election of a White supremacist president on a tidal wave of evangelical Christian support? This, I believe, is the question that Thurman would pose to us today.

This book, *Spiritual Care in an Age of #BlackLivesMatter*, is an attempt to respond to the question within the framework of pastoral theology and pastoral care. The authors in this volume weave together critical pastoral theological scholarship and cultural studies with their quotidian experiences as pastors, chaplains, activists, and organizers to advance the conversation about how and why African American congregations and faith leaders must grapple with the reality that #BlackLivesMatter is the defining issue of spiritual care for African Americans in the twenty-first century. In these pages, they help us to understand how the deaths of Michael Brown, Eric Garner, and Sandra Bland—and the state's failure to hold their killers accountable—impact spiritual care issues that arise in communities on a daily basis. They help us to understand how racism within the criminal justice system leads to conflicted loyalties for African American victims of domestic violence and impedes pastoral caregivers from prioritizing victim safety and perpetrator accountability. Further, these authors help us to critically discern the tangled relationships between mental illness, drug addiction, HIV/AIDS, and racialized police violence. Ultimately, they prompt us to interrogate our own beliefs about whether all Black lives do indeed matter.

The essays in this volume challenge us to rethink how we interpret Scripture, implore us to stop using ideologies of shame that render some Black bodies less deserving of dignity and protection than others, and inspire us to explore tools such as mindfulness in our search to build a world without violence. These writers urge us to collaborate with mental health professionals to attend to the psychological needs of community members who otherwise may be failed by the system, and they urge us to consider how even the language of "nonviolent direct action" can be complicit in churches' refusal to engage #BlackLivesMatter activists and movements. Taken together the chapters in this book help us to see that while the roles of churches and clergy in the modern Black Life movement are not identical to those of the past, to abstain from this movement would be to neglect our "duty" (as Assata Shakur might say)[3]—even to fail in our Christian mission to uphold the needs of "the least of these" (Matt 25:40) and to call the powerful to repentance.

3 See Shakur, *Assata*, 52.

Preface

Why This? Why Now?

Danielle J. Buhuro

Wednesday, November 9, 2016. This is the day that changed America. A Republican business mogul and reality television host who once proclaimed that if women didn't accept the intimate advancements of men, then men were eligible to simply grab these women by a particularly sensitive extremity below their stomachs, snatched the electoral collegiate vote from former secretary of state and Democratic front-runner Hillary Clinton. Some progressive, liberal women struggled to explain to their daughters what happened the day before, Election Day 2016, while African Americans feared that forward-thinking legislation by the first African American president, Barack Obama, number 44, would be reversed and/or thwarted.

Since taking control of the Oval Office, Trump has worked tirelessly on reversing Obama's progressive policies and pushing immigration legislation backwards, desiring to create a wall between the United States and Mexico, which, by some accounts, doesn't necessarily keep non-Americans out but inherently traps Americans in—in an insular racism, sexism, patriarchy, and heterosexism.

Trump has shown that he doesn't care about poor people, instituting policies to give overwhelmingly high tax breaks to the wealthy. Trump has shown that he doesn't care about the environment, putting research and policy restrictions on the Environmental Protection Agency and the Centers for Disease Control. Trump has shown that he doesn't care about college students, cutting government-funded tuition assistance and financial aid to many vulnerable students. Trump has shown that he doesn't care about progressive, liberal justice, nominating a Supreme Court justice with a horrid history of dogmatic conservatism. Trump has shown that he doesn't care about America's image in the eyes of its global counterparts, being the only leader of an industrialized nation to walk away from the Paris Agreement to combat climate change.

If his unpleasant policies weren't enough, he's brought scandal to the White House with rumors of collusion with Russia, mistresses whom he's paid to remain silent, a wife who never looks happy, staff members whose employment is a revolving door, and a Twitter account that's used daily to spew racism, heterosexism, and hate.

Is this the way to make America great again?

Since taking office, Trump's most volatile damage has been invigorating white supremacy. The KKK has come out the woodwork to play, front and center. Racism is no longer America's dirty little secret hiding in the shadows. Racism is taking the main stage, sitting at the head of America's dinner table, dictating who's welcome to sit at the table and who's welcome to eat. Trump's election slogan "Make America Great Again" has been nothing short of a coded invitation shouted through a bullhorn to ignite Jim Crow, Willie Lynch and every descendant of White Christian slave masters.

Message received.

Rates of police brutality against African Americans continue to rise with lack of justice for victims, making it impossible for me to provide an up-to-date list of those names because a new name keeps getting added.

Where is the hope?

This vital resource guide is unique because it incorporates the basic understandings of spiritual care with the current social, emotional, existential, and spiritual needs of African Americans simply surviving in Trump's violent America. It's one-of-a-kind because it offers specific spiritual care strategies and interventions for African Americans dealing with particular physical, social, and emotional health challenges in the midst of rising statistics of racism, sexism, classism, and homophobia leading to violence in the United States.

Intended for anyone in academia or the helping professions, this comprehensive work is beneficial for those who seek to provide spiritual care to African American hospital patients, counseling clients, churchgoers, military veterans, and returning citizens. The contributors to this anthology are experts in their respective fields who offer a new, refreshing, and energizing perspective on important issues impacting African Americans.

It is my hope that one reads this book and becomes convicted.

It is my prayer that the spirit of Yahweh, Buddha, Allah, and Jesus Christ compel you to justice.

It is my conviction that encourages you to love with an unspeakable joy until you take your final breath.

Read in conviction. Act in power.

Ashe!

Contributors

Liz S. Alexander (MA, MSW) is the founder of the She Dreams of Freedom Consulting Group and a member of the LGBTQI/GNC Juvenile Justice Workgroup of the Administration of Children's Services of New York City. She is also a member of the Women and Girls Committee of the American Probation and Parole Association.

Afri A. Atiba (DMin) is an Adjunct Professor at Triton College and a faculty member of the OMNIA Institute for Contextual Leadership in Chicago.

Delois Brown-Daniels (DMin) is a Clinical Pastoral Education Certified Educator and served as Vice President for Mission and Spiritual Care at Advocate Illinois Masonic Medical Center.

Danielle Buhuro (DMin) is a Certified Educator/CPE Supervisor in the Association of Clinical Pastoral Education at Advocate-Aurora South Suburban and Trinity Hospitals. She also serves as an adjunct faculty member at McCormick Theological Seminary.

Lee H. Butler Jr. (PhD) is Distinguished Service Professor of Theology & Psychology at Chicago Theological Seminary.

Amber Coates is Coordinator for Client Services at Volunteers of America Illinois (Chicago) and Associate Pastor at First Baptist Church of University Park.

Michael Crumpler (MDiv) is Manager of LGBTQ and Intercultural Programs at the Unitarian Universalist Association.

Sharon Ellis Davis (PhD, DMin) is an Affiliate Professor at McCormick Theological Seminary in Chicago and a Senior Mentor at United Theological Seminary in Dayton, Ohio.

Julian DeShazier (MDiv) is an Emmy Award-winning hip-hop artist and is a member of the adjunct faculties at McCormick Theological Seminary and the University of Chicago and serves as Senior Pastor of University Church in Chicago.

Derrick Floyd (MEd) is Principal of RISE Academy High School in Tyler, Texas.

Ardella Gibson (MA) is a Certified Educator/CPE Supervisor in the Association of Clinical Pastoral Education at Mercyhealth in Rockford, Illinois.

Mariela Gonzalez (MHS) is a Chaplain Resident at Advocate Trinity Hospital in Chicago.

Jamie D. Hawley (MDiv) is a Chaplain at the University of Chicago, a college counselor for KIPP Chicago, and Senior Pastor at Lincoln Memorial United Church of Christ in Chicago.

Charlene Hill (MDiv, MSW) is a Licensed Psychotherapist and Senior Pastor at the United Church of Hyde Park in Chicago.

Karen Hutt (MDiv) is a Certified Educator/CPE Supervisor in the Association of Clinical Pastoral Education and is Director of Student Experiences at United Theological Seminary of the Twin Cities.

Rochelle Johnson (MDiv, MSW), a doctoral candidate, is a Licensed Clinical Social Worker at Intertwined, LLC.

Heather C. Lofton (PhD) is a clinical staff therapist in the Family Institute at Northwestern University.

Micheal Smith (DMin) is a Chaplain Fellow at Bishop Anderson House and at the John H. Stroger, Jr. Hospital of Cook County.

Marsha Thomas (MDiv) is a mindfulness instructor, and peace coach, and Founder of SuperKids for Peace.

Terrance Thomas (MDiv) is a Clinical Pastoral Education Supervisory Education Student at Advocate South Suburban and Trinity Hospitals, and is Pastor of Unity Temple AME Church in Chicago.

Chanequa Walker-Barnes (PhD) is Associate Professor of Pastoral Care and Counseling at Mercer University.

Karen Walker-McClure (DMin) is the Presiding Elder of the Chicago District of the Christian Methodist Episcopal Church, and Pastor of Murchison-Isom CME Church in Chicago.

Damon A. Williams is Codirector of the #LetUsBreathe Collective and Cochair of the BYP 100 Chicago chapter.

Joseph Yao-Kotay (EdD) is a Certified Educator/CPE Supervisor in the Association of Clinical Pastoral Education at OSF Healthcare Saint Francis Medical Center in Peoria, Illinois.

Introduction

Lee H. Butler Jr.

Life is always defined by experience, and new encounters are regularly interpreted by events from the past. Sometimes the new events articulate new living conditions, and sometimes they expose attitudes within society that had been previously hidden. Either way, some events can be identified as monumental and are experienced as defining moments in history. By way of an example, when Barack Obama became the forty-fourth president of the United States of America, it was monumental and a defining moment in history! His years in the White House not only sought to legislatively articulate a new way of living, but they revealed racial attitudes within America that many thought had been overcome.

April 4, 1968, was a monumental and defining moment in history. On that day, there was another "shot heard around the world," a shot not unlike the Revolutionary War's first shot on April 19, 1775, in Lexington and Concord. April 4, 2018, called our attention to that defining moment in American history as it marked the fiftieth anniversary of the assassination of the Reverend Dr. Martin Luther King, Jr.

In March 2018, I traveled to Memphis, Tennessee, the city where Dr. King breathed his last breath. The flags hanging from streetlight posts made it clear that Memphis was commemorating the fiftieth anniversary of King's assassination. In days gone by, Memphis was not unique as an American city divided against itself. During the 1960s, Memphis was emblematic of the realities of America. This was the era when American violence was photographed and televised for the world to see. As I moved about the city and reflected on the Memphis protest that declared, "I Am a Man," I had an odd feeling as I viewed the signage declaring, I am Memphis. Other signs asked the question, where do we go from here? For it was in Memphis, at the speed of sound, that violence sought to silence nonviolence and the declaration that Negro lives matter.

As a city that sits on the Mississippi River, Memphis conjured for me during my visit a variety of thoughts and images. Reflecting on the life and death of Dr. King while viewing the Mississippi, I was drawn to Psalm 137. Like those who sat and wept by the rivers of Babylon, in Memphis African Americans moaned with the sorrow songs of our souls that somebody called the Blues. A cord was struck in Memphis by an assassin's bullet that produced a blues song in the key of rage. At that moment, the rageful lament of the psalmist who exclaimed, "Happy shall they be who pay you back what you have done to us! Happy shall they be who take your little ones and dash them against the rock!" (Ps 137:8b–9) became a prophetic statement within the United States of America. That shot in Memphis ignited rioting in over one hundred cities across America, including Washington DC. Hope dashed. People clashed. Buildings burned. Blood flowed. The Dreamer was killed, and the dream became a nightmare for everyone. There was no peace in our waking hours and no comfort in our sleep. Able to neither stay awake nor go to sleep, we found our days filled with lament and our nights consumed by torment. Reflections on "why we can't wait" became more poignant; and the question, "where do we go from here?" became more problematic.

The year before King was assassinated, he wrote *Where Do We Go from Here: Chaos or Community?* The book was a critical examination of what America had gone through, and the nation's prospects for the future in light of the civil rights, human rights movement. The American crisis that resulted from that fatal shot from an assassin's weapon did not create the chaotic American dilemma; rather the killer merely exposed the chaos and the ongoing American dilemma.

What is America's nature that regarded Black bodies as meat for dogs, trophies for rapists, "strange fruit" for gluttons, flames for hoses, conquests for the lustful, and property for exploitation? To America, the sacredness of Black bodies was sacrilege. Within America, Black bodies were identified as the problem to be dealt with. As African Americans struggled to be citizens of faith and faithful citizens, there was no clear answer on where we could go. At the defining moment of the assassination, the voice of the 137th psalm resonated with the Black experience in America: "How can we sing the LORD's song in [such] a strange land?" (Ps 137:4). Because the spirit of Black America was living in terror while exploding with rage, the Lord's song became the spirituals and the blues. These genres are two modes of storytelling in one dark body's experience with violence in America. They declared African American spiritual and prophetic needs for justice and peace within America.

The Problem

Black America has sought to address the continuing American dilemma by embracing King's beloved community with an emphasis upon an ideology of integration. With an evangelical spirit of Christian piety, Black Americans have been guided by the hope of full citizenship through a vision of America being "one nation, under God, indivisible, with liberty and justice for all," regardless of race, color, or creed. Unfortunately, America's approaches to integration have maintained Black bodies as the problem in America. When African Americans are seen as the problem, African Americans are identified as the ones who must change, who must repent, who must forgive, even when there is no confession of wrongdoing by their perpetrator. We witnessed this after the massacre of the Charleston Nine in 2015. African American Christians offered forgiveness to Dylann Roof even though he had not confessed wrongdoing or repented of his crime. Within the system of Black survival, forgiveness has been part of our spiritual discipline: to forgive, regardless.

The Christian Scriptures declare: "*If* you confess with your mouth that Jesus is Lord and believe in your heart that God raised him from the dead, you will be saved. For one believes with the heart and so is justified, and one confesses with the mouth and so is saved" (Rom 10:9–10). Without confession and repentance, there is no forgiveness. With a spirit of nonviolence, Black Church theology has come to believe that forgiveness is all about God's grace and has simultaneously ignored the need to hear confession when we have been offended.

This attitude of forgiveness without confession has led some to believe that some behaviors require no confession. We have accepted the attitude of King David: "Against you, and you alone, have I sinned; / I have done what is evil in your sight" (Ps 51:4, NLT). David did not consider that he had offended Uriah and Bathsheba, nor did he regard the fact that he placed a contract on Uriah to cover his wrongdoings. Thomas Jefferson, on the other hand, was very aware of the major offenses committed by white Americans against Africans in America. Nevertheless, rather than seeking reconciliation and establishing a new community that regarded Africans as created equal with Europeans, he concluded that Africans were the problem, and it was better to send Africans back to Africa for the sake of peace.

When African Americans are seen as the problem, African Americans are compelled to conform to an image of humanity that erases Black skin. When the color of sin is the color of one's skin, it should come as no surprise that many Black evangelical Christians sing numerous songs about Jesus washing Black bodies whiter than snow. This is another indication of the chaos that governs our existence and the way the problem of America has been understood to be a Black problem.

African Spirituality

Caring for the spiritual needs of African Americans requires attentiveness to the conditions that fostered African American culture and community. African American religion and culture were born in the midst of chaos and have continued to fight with the steady beat of Black radicalism. The blood of slaughtered Black bodies has marked a path from capture on the continent of Africa through the traumas of the Middle Passage to enduring the indignities to Black humanity in America. Black bodies always being surrounded by White supremacy, like a wheel of resistance in the middle of a wheel of hatred, points to the necessity of pronouncing that #BlackLivesMatter.

#BlackLivesMatter is the reframing of King's concerns regarding chaos or community. Nevertheless, spiritual care in this present age should not ignore our hope in ages past. Truly caring for Black bodies and souls means that Black traumas cannot be viewed in isolation. African American spirituality promoted our survival through an insistence that we maintain our self-understanding as whole and holy human beings. Our spirituality maintained the unity of blood and nonblood relations, public and private life, physical and spirit world, church and community. I am because we are, and because we are, I am.

American culture socializes its citizens to think about relationships in dichotomies and polarities; i.e., good or bad, right or wrong, woman or man. Being governed by the oppositional views of "us against them" maintains chaos by always fighting to prove differences. Because Americans regularly think of relationships as a process of reconciling differences, when differences cannot be reconciled, the different ones tend to be defined as "less than" and labeled the problem for extermination. If our spiritual care practices refuse to address the inclination toward extermination within American culture, then Black alienation and spiritual homelessness will increase. When an image of Black life that was intended to destroy African culture guides our ministries of caring for the spiritual lives of African Americans, those care ministries become destructive and self-destructive by reframing #BlackLivesMatter into #AllLivesMatter.

The Problem of Projection

When African Americans are seen as the problem, the focus of the problem is not American citizenship. The problem is always associated with what it means to be human; and humanity is always associated with what it means to be in relationship with God. This problem of humanity is the underlying presupposition of racism. Racism is always a question of human origins created by the supremacist who wants to see himself or herself as God.

There is a psychological interpretation of racism that concludes racism is a projection. That is, racism is the inability of the racist to accept the negativity she or he holds with regard to his or her own personhood. Unable to see themselves as the problem, they project the negativity onto an-other, making an-other the problem that can subsequently be exterminated. It is like someone being asked a question about the alt-right, and rather than acknowledging the alt-right within himself as the problem, he counters with a deflection that is a projection question: what about the alt-left? The alt-right is the formal name for a specific orientation and organization. There is no group that identifies itself as the alt-left.

Spiritual care of African Americans must help them to cease from seeing themselves as the American problem. To be released from seeing themselves as the problem in America releases African Americans from the burden of finding the solution to this ongoing American dilemma. When we are able to accept that the problem is not us or ours, but those and theirs who act against us, we experience the freedom we have fought for and died to obtain. At that moment, African Americans will be able to sing with conviction, "Out of a gloomy past / till now we stand at last / where the bright gleam of our bright star is cast."

Neo-Reconstruction

As America continues to live in the transitional wake of 44 to 45, we metaphorically find ourselves on the balcony of the Lorraine Motel in Memphis. We are standing at a painful and pivotal moment in history where "the principalities and powers and spiritual wickedness in high places" that conspired to move James Earl Ray to fire that fateful shot are once again conspiring. Whereas there is nothing new under the sun, America is re-orienting itself through activities we might identify as Neo-Reconstruction through misinformation and miseducation.

Since 2015, America has been living in an era of Neo-Reconstruction, that is, an era of Deconstructionist violence designed to return America to a mythical past greatness. The dynamics of this contemporary moment and movement are marked by the violent aggression that seeks to return us to an imagined golden age of freedom and prosperity. The South will rise again by "making America great again." Neo-Reconstruction thrives on "revisionist history" and what are today called "alternative facts." Where neo-Reconstructionists do not like the story being told, they declare "fake news" and rewrite the story to meet their needs. The pain of loss, the feeling of being taken advantage of, the frustration from job insecurity, the fear of losing a privileged place in society has resulted in violent outbursts to attack Black bodies as the source of the problem.

Book Overview

To address the care needs of African Americans, both spiritual and prophetic, focused attention must be given to the ways African Americans experience the national assault on Black bodies. In the same way that there are multiple medical challenges more likely to end the lives of African Americans (like various forms of cancer), there are psychosocial traumas that destroy Black lives at epidemic rates. A spiritual care that affirms that #BlackLivesMatter attends to the ways that African Americans have introjected and internalized the problems of America. Caring for the spiritual and prophetic needs of African Americans is to attend to the ways African Americans have turned aggression and rage inward, resulting in domestic violence in the forms of intimate partner abuse, child abuse, and heritage abuse. A new paradigm needs to be developed that reinterprets Black homicide by Black bodies as sometimes being an act of suicide resulting from the generations of being a problem in America. New paradigms need to be developed that reinterpret substance abuse and addiction, which are bodily self-destruction, as being no different from the destruction of property as another way of terminating the physical world.

This book, therefore, has been structured into four thematic sections of caring for Black Lives. Part 1 focuses on caring for victims of violence and the work of social justice to end the violence that consumes Black life. Part 2 focuses on caring for our bodies and the more existential realities that assault our souls. Part 3 focuses on caring for marriages and families beyond gender normativity. And finally, part 4 focuses on caring for Black lives within systems of institutional healthcare where we are often the most vulnerable. These four sections encourage a care that breaks new ground and advocates for life to break in to regenerate African Americans in a violent America through the rallying call that #BlackLivesMatter!

PART 1

Caring for the Victims of Violence
and Social Justice Activism

1

From Viral to Voyeuristic

When Police Brutality Videos Turn into Black Death Tourism; Self Care for Black Trauma

DANIELLE J. BUHURO

Get away [garbled] . . . for what? Every time you see me, you want
to mess with me. I'm tired of it. It stops today. Why would you . . . ?
Everyone standing here will tell you I didn't do nothing. I did not sell
nothing. Because every time you see me, you want to harass me. You
want to stop me (garbled) Selling cigarettes. I'm minding my business,
officer, I'm minding my business. Please just leave me alone. I told you
the last time, please just leave me alone. please please, don't touch me.
Do not touch me . . .

    I can't breathe. I can't breathe. I can't breathe. I can't breathe. I can't
breathe. I can't breathe. I can't breathe. I can't breathe," he said, as officers
restrained him.[1]

These were the last words of Eric Garner, an obese African American
middle-aged male suffering from asthma and cardiovascular disease, on
July 17, 2014, in Staten Island, New York City, after a New York City Police

1. Capelouto, "Eric Garner."

3

Department (NYPD) officer, Daniel Pantaleo, put him in an NYPD policy-banned choke hold for between fifteen and twenty seconds while attempting to arrest him under suspicion that he was illegally selling individual cigarettes.[1] When Officer Pantaleo tried to pull Garner's wrist behind his back, Garner pulled his arms away. Pantaleo then put his arm around Garner's neck and thrust him to the ground. After Pantaleo removed his arm from Garner's neck, he pushed the side of Garner's face into the ground while four officers moved to restrain Garner, who repeated, "I can't breathe" several times while lying face down on pavement.[2] Moments later Garner lost consciousness, and subsequently died.

The New York City medical examiner's office report stated that Garner's primary cause of death was "compression of neck (choke hold), compression of chest and prone positioning during physical restraint by police."[3] Eric Garner's name joins an unfortunately long list of other noted names: Sandra Bland, Tamir Rice, Sean Bell, Amadou Diallo, Alton Sterling, Philando Castile, and Mike Brown—just to name few—who were killed by police officers' excessive use of force, making the popular hashtag #BlackLivesMatter a trending focus on Twitter and other social media outlets.

Initially, the #BlackLivesMatter hashtag sparked popularity following the George Zimmerman not-guilty verdict in which a neighborhood patrolman Zimmerman stalked an unarmed African American teenage boy, Trayvon Martin, in a gated community complex when Martin was simply returning home from walking to a convenience store to purchase an Arizona Ice Tea and a bag of Skittles. After the verdict was announced, three young African American women who supported the murdered Trayvon Martin—Alicia Garza, Patrisse Cullors, and Opal Tometi—took to Twitter in protest, voicing their anger and frustration, and concluding their tweets with the hashtag #BlackLivesMatter. The hashtag picked up notoriety and was then used by Martin supporters nationwide. Garza, Cullors, and Tometi then went further and turned the hashtag into "a Black-centered political will and movement building project."[4]

Their project progressed in 2014, when unarmed African American teenager Michael Brown was murdered by Ferguson police officer Darren Wilson in Ferguson, Missouri, causing outrage and protest primarily from African American community members. In response, law enforcement

2. Schram et al., "NYPD Chokehold Death."

3. Sanchez, "Choke Hold by Cop Killed NY Man."

4. "Herstory," para. 1.

ignited tear gas and pepper spray on protestors during nighttime hours. Darnell Moore and Cullors organized the "Black Life Matters Ride," a national fifteen-hour ride during the 2014 Labor Day weekend. Organizers directed riders to travel to protest areas in order to support African Americans in their demonstration efforts. The ride's results were successful: roughly six hundred people gathered to support protestors in Ferguson and to work to change policy across the nation in depressed communities of color.[5]

As law enforcement continued using tear gas, pepper spray, and other forms of brutality to halt protestors, #BlackLivesMatter community organizers and protestors turned to social media as a resource to shine light for the nation and world to see on the happenings of Ferguson. Videos began circulating online on Facebook and Twitter showing protestors being tear gassed and pepper sprayed. Just as the media were pivotal in showcasing police brutality against protestors during the civil rights movement, new social media was also helpful in highlighting police brutality against Ferguson protestors.[6]

Social media has also been helpful in the Eric Garner case, specifically because the actual video of Officer Pantaleo forcing Garner into a choke hold has been viewed and shared widely to date around the world.[7] Viewers actually witness his last moments of life and hear the last words Garner ever spoke.

The Garner video is similar to two other police brutality videos widely shared online in which the victims' last moments of life are recorded. According to PBS, "When video of the Baton Rouge shooting death of Alton Sterling first surfaced on July 5, [2016] social media networks became immediately populated with Sterling's final moments. The following day, the shooting death of Philando Castile was streamed live by his girlfriend on Facebook. The video, which shows Castile gasping for air after being shot four times by a Minnesota police officer, has since been shared on Facebook more than 5 million times."[8] On September 16, 2016, video circulated online of forty-year-old African American Terence Crutcher, who was shot and killed by White police officer Betty Jo Shelby in Tulsa, Oklahoma, as he

---

5. Ibid., para. 6.

6. Ibid.

7. Feuer and Apuzzo, "With Prosecutors at Odds."

8. Downs, "When Black Death Goes Viral."

stood unarmed in the middle of a street trying to repair and seek assistance with his stalled truck.

While uploading and sharing police brutality videos and #BlackLives-Matter hashtags have raised awareness of racism and police brutality in America, according to Monnica Williams, clinical psychologist and director of the Center for Mental Health Disparities at the University of Louisville, graphic videos (which she calls vicarious trauma) combined with lived experiences of racism, can create severe psychological problems reminiscent of posttraumatic stress disorder.[9] According to a 2012 study that surveyed thousands of African Americans, Hispanics, and Asian Americans, "blacks who perceived discrimination the most, were more likely to report symptoms of PTSD. Although African Americans have a lower risk for many anxiety disorders, the study reported a PTSD prevalence rate of 9.1 percent in Blacks, compared to 6.8 percent in Whites, 5.9 percent in Hispanics, and 1.8 percent in Asians."[10]

According to Williams, "Social media and viral videos can worsen the effects. During the week of Sterling's and Castile's deaths, a scroll through timelines of black social media users could uncover subtle expressions of mental and psychological anguish, from pleas for others not the share these videos, to declarations of a social media hiatus. These expressions of anger, sadness and grief can hint at something much more serious."[11]

"It's upsetting and stressful for people of color to see these events unfolding," she says. "It can lead to depression, substance abuse and, in some cases, psychosis. Very often, it can contribute to health problems that are already common among African-Americans, such as high blood pressure."[12]

As a result of the "weathering effect," which is what scientists call the result of cumulative stress associated with confronting racism on a daily basis, "African Americans [regardless of income] have disproportionately higher levels of blood pressure and more instances of chronic disease and earlier deaths than whites."[13]

April Reign, a former attorney and now managing editor for the website *Broadway Black*, which reports on African Americans in the performing arts, adds, "White people used to have picnics at hangings and

9. Ibid.

10. Jackson, "Trauma of Police Brutality."

11. Downs, "When Black Death Goes Viral."

12. Ibid.

13. Ibid.

at lynchings, bringing their children to watch black bodies suffer and die. We are not far removed from that, it's just being played out through technology now. And it hurts."[14]

A social psychology expert and president of the Center for Policing Equity, Phillip Atiba Goff, adds, "The perception that the perpetrators of violence face no consequences for their actions can transform that trauma into terror."[15]

According to Goff, "If you're conditioned to a trauma, and that trauma occurs and recurs in a context where it feels you have no control over it, and it's being done by powerful people for whom there are no consequences—that's why I'm saying we move from trauma to terror."[16]

"That feeling of helplessness and hopelessness can undercut efforts to end police brutality against black people," said Susan Moeller, director of the University of Maryland's International Center for Media and the Public Agenda. "Because the videos are so horrifying, some people try to shut them out and turn away—which makes those individuals less likely to pursue political action aimed at reform."[17]

There are some steps African Americans can take to employ self-care and limit stress in the midst of Black trauma. First, don't be afraid to log off social media once or twice a week. Refraining from social media gives persons the ability to rest and reinvent themselves, to build up one's defense barriers or walls again. Refraining from social media gives persons the opportunity to decrease their anxiety and worry that the overuse of technology can sometimes create. Instead of being online every day, take some time to engage in pleasant mood activities offline such as gardening, exercising, going to the spa, adopting a pet, eating a healthy meal, talking with friends (refraining from controversial topics), observing nature, camping, praying, and meditating.

Second, African Americans can refrain from continuously commenting in social media discussion groups and controversial conversations about police brutality. Don't get baited by others' Facebook statuses. Refrain from replying to tweets. Resist the urge to be triggered by online chats. Incorporate personal and professional strategies to stop your triggers from arising.

14. Williams and Mazzie, "Tackle Problems of Policing, Racism."
15. Ibid.
16. Adetiba and Almendrala, "Watching Videos of Police Brutality."
17. Ibid.

Third, sometimes resist the urge to press play on police brutality videos that may come up in your newsfeed. Turn off video auto-play in your Facebook settings. Sometimes refrain from sharing police brutality videos that others may share on your timeline. You may want to consider updating your settings so that others can't post on your timeline.

Subsequently, affirm your individual and collective gifts, skills, and talents. Spend time journaling about what your individual strengths and abilities are. Take a moment to reflect on and post on Facebook or tweet the gifts of your culture, ethnicity, and traditions. Persons sometimes allow their victimization to cloud their perception of their identity, ignoring their positive attributes. Reflecting on your positive attributes and remembering the tenacity of your cultural ancestors and elders will impact your mood and emotions, igniting peace and joy even in the midst of pain. Bring into your remembrance the mountains your elders climbed over, and find courage in their achievements.

2

If They're Black, Call 911 First

*Addressing Some White Persons' Biased Illogical
Paranoia and "Personal Racism Valet" Use of Police*

DANIELLE J. BUHURO AND JAMIE D. HAWLEY

Lolade Siyonbola is an African American graduate student in African studies at Yale. One evening during her spring courses she fell asleep while working in her dormitory common area. A European American woman who lived in the dorm contacted campus police, reporting Siyonbola for illegally being in the common area.

Sleeping in a dormitory while Black.

Three Black teenagers decided to visit a Nordstrom Rack store in suburban Saint Louis in search of accessories for their prom night when they were followed by store employees who contacted the police to search the teens' purchased items outside.

Shopping while Black.

Three Black people were checking out of an Airbnb home in Rialto, California, in April 2018 when they were approached by police, along with a police helicopter flying overhead, after a neighbor alerted law enforcement that the three renters were burglars.

Renting an Airbnb while Black.

Rashon Nelson and Donte Robinson, both African Americans, were waiting for another man for a business meeting at a Starbucks in downtown

Philadelphia in April 2018. An employee asked the two men to leave the coffee shop. When they refused, the police were called.

Sitting in Starbucks while Black.

What is the internal mechanism that tells some European Americans to contact law enforcement and report African Americans who are simply engaging in daily, nonthreatening life activities?

Why do some European Americans use law enforcement as commodified racist weapons against African Americans?

What is the psychological impact on African Americans who are constantly terrorized by European American harassment via law enforcement?

When Threats Occur

What does *threat* mean?

Threat is a feeling that a person experiences when he or she believes that another person is likely to inflict pain, injury, damage or danger to his or her survival.[1] The controversial word in this definition is *feeling*. What one perceives as a threat is based primarily on that person's emotional state and less about the actual actions of the other person who is perceived as the oppressor.

How does this happen? According to Dr. Rick Hanson, a psychologist at the the Greater Good Science Center at the University of California, Berkeley, "The alarm bell of your brain—the amygdala . . . uses about two-thirds of its neurons to look for bad news: it's primed to go negative. Once it sounds the alarm, negative events and experiences get quickly stored in memory—in contrast to positive events and experiences, which usually need to be held in awareness for a dozen or more seconds to transfer from short-term memory buffers to long-term storage."[2] Thus, in other words, people tend to relate to others, particularly to those who are different, with distrust and pessimism, believing others will take advantage of them.

These writers assert that a threatened feeling can be reality or imaginary. The feeling of impending threats can be based on unbiased social historical data. For example, some older African Americans who report being afraid of European Americans experience these feelings based on the period of African enslavement in the United States from 1619 to 1865. At the same time, the feeling of impending threats can also be based on biased,

1. Wormwood, "How Feelings Guide."
2. Hanson, "What Makes You Feel Threatened?"

illogical paranoia. For example, when a European American police officer named Darren Wilson in Ferguson, Missouri, was asked why he shot an unarmed African American teen named Micheal Brown, Wilson replied, "It looked like a demon."[3] Aside from the fact that Wilson defined a human being using the pronoun *it*, Wilson's response was based on biased, illogical paranoia. There is no unbiased social historical data that suggests that African American boys are demons.

Another example can be found in the testimony given by European American male Dylan Roof, who entered a church Bible study one evening in South Carolina and killed nine innocent African Americans. When asked why he committed this act of domestic terrorism, Roof informed law enforcement that something had to be done to stop African American males from continuously raping European American women on a daily basis throughout the country. Again, Roof's response was not based on unbiased social historical data.

How does one began to address some European Americans' biased, illogical paranoia?

Is it the responsibility of African Americans to be the *Olivia Pope* who "fixes" White folks' fear?

Reflecting on how some European Americans rely on the police must start with how African Americans experience law enforcement versus how European Americans experience law enforcement. According to Vesla Mae Weaver, the Bloomberg Distinguished Associate Professor of Political Science and Sociology at Johns Hopkins University, "Let's start by discussing what happens when black Americans call on the police for protection. First, police take longer to come to their communities—and may not come at all. In Chicago, for example, one study found that the average time to arrival for calls to police in nonwhite neighborhoods was twice as long as in predominantly white neighborhoods. One woman told me, after waiting for the police to arrive as a 15-year-old girl in her neighborhood lay dying: 'They don't come fast. They give you time to die.'"[4]

Weaver goes on to assert that "nonwhite people who try to enlist law enforcement for help are more likely than whites to themselves come under suspicion. These voluntary callers may find themselves getting searched, detained, or removed from the premises . . . Things can, as one of our research subjects put it, 'go left' very quickly. Black Americans are more likely to be seen as defiant if they ask questions of the police, are reluctant

3. Wormwood, "How Feelings Guide."
4. Weaver, "Why White People Keep Calling the Cops."

to furnish their identification, or ask the police to leave. Thus, calling the police if you are black can often be useless and slow, and at worst is outright dangerous."[5] However, most European Americans experience law enforcement as "helpful, benevolent, fair, and efficient problem solvers."[6]

Incidents of some European Americans calling the police to report African Americans doing nothing but normal daily activities is not a new phenomenon. According to Jason Johnson, professor of politics and journalism at Morgan State University, "I think this has always been happening. What's been different is that over the last couple years there has been a larger number of White Americans who are empathetic and sympathetic to this kind of harassment. And therefore, mainstream press outlets are actually covering it because there's an audience that wants to know now."[7] Johnson goes on to say that the ultimate problem is some White people see the police as their "personal racism valets"—meaning just as persons have their cars taken away through a valet process at an upscale restaurant or hotel, for example, likewise some White persons can have black people escorted away, out of sight, like an inanimate object such as a car.[8]

According to Professor Weaver, "American legal history is replete with evidence of white people saying black people committed a crime (what the legal scholar Katheryn Russell-Brown terms "racial hoaxes") to distract police attention from their own criminal activity, to maintain control of White space, to retaliate against Black people for violating unspoken racial codes—or simply because they can. These cases are quite common: Russell-Brown documented sixty-seven such cases nationally just in the years between 1987 and 1996."[9]

Furthermore, "such cases are so common, in fact, that one state, New Jersey, proposed legislation to apply a criminal penalty to someone who 'knowingly provides false information to a law enforcement officer with purpose to implicate another because of race.' (The law never passed.) Many remember the case of Susan Smith, who murdered her two children but sparked a manhunt for 'a young black male.' And seared in our nation's racial collective memory is the Scottsboro case, where nine black boys were sentenced to death for the fabricated rape of two white women."[10]

5. Ibid.
6. Ibid.
7. Johnson, interview.
8. Ibid.
9. Weaver, "Why White People Keep Calling the Cops."
10. Ibid.

The irony is that while some European American adults find comfort in calling the police on innocent African Americans engaging in day-to-day activities, mass-casualty school shootings facilitated by racist, murderous, hate-inspired European American teenage boys and young men continue unabated in the United States. As of May 2018, forty school shootings have taken place in the United States.[11] Where is the outrage for these incidents from European Americans—from the same European Americans who place bogus calls to police on innocent African Americans simply living life?

According to Mike Males, a senior researcher for the Center on Juvenile and Criminal Justice in San Francisco, "White people should be more afraid of other whites than they are of people of color."[12] Males explains, after examining statistics generated by the Centers for Disease Control, that "rates of homicides, gun killings and illicit-drug fatalities are highest in counties where nine in [ten] residents are white, and where President Trump won in the 2016 election."[13] Similarly, "the white Americans who are safest from such deaths are those who live in racially diverse areas such as Los Angeles, New York and Chicago, where two-thirds of residents are nonwhite, where millions of immigrants live, and where voters favored Hillary Clinton in 2016."[14]

Males asserts that "whites are so much safer where there are fewer whites and Republicans, in fact, that it raises the question of what exactly underlies this strong correlation between white safety and voting patterns"; contrary to popular belief, "white Americans enjoyed the largest real income and employment gains of any race during President Obama's administration, particularly in Rust Belt states, where federal economic stimulus was strongest."[15]

Charity Starts at Home

Liberal European Americans must challenge their own. First, these writers suggest that it is the responsibility of progressive European Americans to challenge their own cousins, aunts, uncles, mothers, fathers, sisters, and

---

11. Jeffrey, "School Shootings in U.S."
12. Males, "White People Should Be More Afraid."
13. Ibid.
14. Ibid.
15. Ibid.

brothers who wrestle with biased, illogical paranoia. For quite some time now, liberals have been very comfortable consuming themselves with ministry to those on the margins. This ministry is easy compared to the harder, more treacherous task of confronting the pharaohs that resemble one's own makeup, identity, and bloodline. This is why several liberal European Americans rush to do ministry in Third World countries rather than to confront the history and current state of racism in the United States.

Second, some European Americans must ask themselves the why question. Why would one feel threatened after observing a Black female student sleeping in a dormitory common area? Is this feeling based on emotional reasoning or cognitive reasoning? If this feeling is based on emotional reasoning, how does one resist those feelings?

Jason Johnson adds, "What needs to happen is people who make malicious prosecution calls on black people need to be fined. Look. If I pull a fire alarm at a school, and the fire truck has to show up, and it's no fire, I'm going to get a ticket. I'm probably going to have to go to court about it. If you call the police saying, I see a group of black people, and they're jumping up and down and screaming—I don't know if it's Howard's graduation or a riot—and the police show up and say it's Howard's graduation, then that person needs to be ticketed. And I think if people started suffering consequences for this kind of behavior, you would see a drop in these kinds of phone calls."[16]

Last but not least, some European Americans must grapple with mission. What purpose does one serve by contacting the police and reporting African Americans engaging in daily life activities? Some would argue that the mission of some European Americans is to instill control and dominance, and this is why 911 calls reporting nonthreatening African Americans are on the rise. The calls are motivated instinctively by a desire to remind African Americans that they are forever in a system that sees them as less than human, undeserving of equal rights, and never fully liberated. These ideologies last existed during the period of African enslavement in the United States. Maybe the mission of some European Americans is to go back to that time period. Or maybe we never really left.

16. Ibid.

3

Brown Lives Matter

The Demonization of Immigrants, Refugees, and Asylum Seekers Is Not New

M ARIELA J ANELLE G ONZALEZ

The demonization of immigrants, refugees, and asylum seekers is not new. As early as 1775 Benjamin Franklin wrote warnings of German immigrants. Whatever group is already present can succumb to nativism and become suspicious of outsiders. In the 1800s propaganda spread against Irish, German, and Chinese immigrants.[1] Later, in the 1940s, President Franklin D. Roosevelt ordered the internment of Japanese Americans.

In *Korematsu v. the U.S.*, the Supreme Court in a 6–3 ruling upheld the constitutionality of the government to hold its citizens in internment. Justice Robert Jackson provided a dissent, however, pointing out the behavior of Korematsu was not usually criminal. "'Korematsu . . . has been convicted of an act not commonly thought a crime. It consists merely of being present in the state whereof he is a citizen, near the place where he was born, and where all his life he has lived.' The nation's wartime security concerns, he contended, were not adequate to strip Korematsu and the other internees of

1. Hernandez, "Brief History of Anti-immigrant Propaganda."

their constitutionally protected civil rights."[2] The reasoning of this dissent is pertinent to the current conditions because seeking asylum at an entry point is also not criminal; however, the current policy is to block asylum seekers because of an irrational fear that noncitizens of the United States pose threats to U.S. citizens. A legal team reopened the *Korematsu* case in 1983. "They showed that the government's legal team had intentionally suppressed or destroyed evidence from government intelligence agencies reporting that Japanese Americans posed no military threat to the U.S."[3] The justification for interning present-day immigrants or noncitizens ignores statistics that show that the likelihood is low that immigrants or noncitizens will threaten U.S. citizens.[4]

Also, the demand during the 1940s that Japanese Americans prove themselves certified loyal is echoed in the insistence today on a certain reaction to the U.S. flag and the national anthem. The vilification of athletes for taking a knee in order to draw attention to police brutality and other unjust actions by law enforcement is the product of a regime with authoritarian tendencies.

The U.S. Immigration and Customs Enforcement (ICE) began in 2003 in conjunction with the Homeland Security Act. By its founding in connection with antiterrorism, ICE conflated immigration with threats to security and with criminality. In 2003 the perpetual War on Terror was young, and many politicians, and some news outlets spread a narrative of fear of brown-skinned immigrants, particularly persons of the Muslim faith. Due to this fear, ICE gained more control at borders and entry points. "ICE was granted a unique combination of civil and criminal authorities."[5] Through the past fifteen years the agency expanded, ramping up its focus on the southwest border. The so-called threat need not be terrorism to be an ICE issue. Any safety issue that can be pinned on those outside the U.S. could succumb to ICE's expanding power. To be emphatic, ICE does not exist to provide care and compassion for refugees and asylum seeking neighbors; nevertheless, care and compassion is the humanitarian response that persons fleeing from war, crime, and abuse need. In its very foundation ICE perpetuates the fear of brown-skinned Muslim immigrants, and this relates

2. "Facts and Case Summary—*Korematsu v. U.S.*"
3. Ibid.
4. Horsley, "Fact Check: Trump Illegal Immigration, and Crime."
5. "Facts and Case Summary—*Korematsu v. U.S.*"

to fear of brown-skinned Mexican, Central American, and South American immigrants because of White fragility.

During the Obama administration, unaccompanied minors were detained, and families were detained together. Many were asylum seekers, fleeing turmoil in Central America. In 2015 the Flores Settlement was reviewed for its application in the care of immigrant detainees. There was some improvement due to legal aid and human rights advocacy, and because the volume of immigrants took a downward trend. Also during his administration, President Obama advocated for the Dream Act, finding a path to citizenship, eventually signing the order to establish Deferred Action for Childhood Arrivals. With ICE still in play, we can't say mistreatment completely went away. Racism is woven in the fabric of enforcement agencies like ICE (and the police).

Throughout this nation's history there have been waves of nationalism. This relates to whiteness because white supremacy is in the foundation of who is a citizen. The Naturalization Act of 1790 allowed citizenship for free White people who had lived in the country for two years. With the emancipation proclamation, African Americans were granted citizenship. Quickly, White supremacist groups made efforts to roll back the rights of Black folk. In 1924 the first immigration quota laws were put in place, favoring persons from northern and western Europe. Asian, Latinx and Hispanic, and Indigenous people were also systematically shut out of citizenship and its rights, including land ownership, and participation in the justice system— e.g., giving testimony, serving on a jury, or having a jury of peers.[6] While there have been some strides forward in rights for people of color, the current administration essentially promises to make things worse.

On the campaign trail, now president Donald Trump said that people from Mexico were bringing crime and drugs, and that they were rapists.[7] He also called for a complete shutdown on immigration from majority Muslim-faith nations. Not only has Trump been worried about non-U.S. Muslims, but he has mentioned surveillance of mosques within U.S. borders, stating in an interview, "'You have to deal with the mosques, whether we like it or not. I mean, you know, these attacks aren't coming out of—they're not done by Swedish people.'"[8] This leads me to suspect that President Trump believes that White people are better than people of color. Trump supporters have

6. Smith et al., dirs., *Race*.
7. Phillips, "'They're Rapists.'"
8. Solis, "Six anti-Muslim Comments."

literally said as much. (Trump gained traction in politics by lending his voice to the birther movement, which is the racially motivated questioning of President Barack Obama's legitimacy as a U.S. citizen.) In January 2018 in a bipartisan meeting, President Trump referred to African nations, Haiti, and El Salvador with a crass epithet. A source who attended that meeting reported, "When the group came to discussing immigration from Africa, Trump asked why America would want immigrants from 'all these shithole countries' and that the U.S. should have more people coming in from places like Norway."[9] It is not a leap to deduce that according to President Trump, White people from places like Norway and Sweden are welcome, but Black and Brown people are meant to be shut out. Black and Brown people are deemed nefarious outsiders, or to quote President Trump, "bad hombres."

Recently, children—including toddlers—were separated from parents who are entering the country. "Under the zero-tolerance policy, cases that had been handled administratively in immigration court were now prosecuted as misdemeanors or felonies in federal court. Migrants were charged with crossing the border illegally and separated from their children, who were placed in shelters."[10] According to a former caseworker at a Tuscon shelter, their facility and staff are not equipped to handle the influx of youths. This is in part because of the volume of persons now requiring care. Furthermore, spaces were designed for transient care but are forced to operate long-term. Caseworkers may not be educated and experienced in type of care needed after the trauma of forced family separation.[11] Due to lack of capacity and the desire to control a population—which the rhetoric characterized as dangerous, dehumanized "illegals"—the conditions meeting immigrant youths are prison-like rather than a compassionate refuge. In mid-June 2018, President Trump signed an executive order to cease family separations.[12] However, there is no clear plan to reunite families, the harsh stance on immigration continues, and there is potential to detain families indefinitely.

Underlying and purposeful systemic racism contribute to this justice issue. A police officer views a Black man with a cell phone as a criminal with a weapon because the officer has implicit bias against the man's Black skin tone. Similarly, Brown-skinned people are viewed as threats to White

9. Vitali, et al. "Trump Referred to Haiti and African Nations."

10. Hennesy-Fiske, "'Prison-Like' Migrant Youth Shelter."

11. Ibid.

12. Shear et al,. "Trump Retreats on Separating Families."

America's homeland. The prejudice toward Brown folks occurs at the same time as anti-Blackness racism by emboldened White supremacists. In the age of declaring Black Lives Matter, we can gain momentum by breaking down White supremacy at the points that it also attacks Brown brothers and sisters. The Reverend Dr. Martin Luther King Jr. spoke about resisting oppression in its multiple forms in his speech "Beyond Vietnam." He drew criticism for taking focus away from the civil rights of Black people. Still, Rev. Dr. King recognized we are called to compassion wherever it is needed. He saw his task not in gaining only certain rights for some people, but he envisioned complete liberation:

> Beyond the calling of race or nation or creed is this vocation of sonship and brotherhood. Because I believe that the Father is deeply concerned, especially for His suffering and helpless and outcast children, I come tonight to speak for them. This I believe to be the privilege and the burden of all of us who deem ourselves bound by allegiances and loyalties which are broader and deeper than nationalism and which go beyond our nation's self-defined goals and positions. We are called to speak for the weak, for the voiceless, for the victims of our nation, for those it calls "enemy," for no document from human hands can make these humans any less our brothers.[13]

Here is our opportunity for spiritual care. Faith leaders can respond on three levels. These levels are adapted from human resource practice, and are matched with a spiritual care element inspired by the Christian faith tradition. These levels of response are *macro* or *prophetic*, *mid* or *apostolic*, and *micro* or *pastoral*. In this way spiritual care extends from systemic change to group dynamics management to direct care for individuals and back again. The macro/prophetic tasks include demonstrating, advocating, educating, and lobbying. The mid/apostolic tasks include analyzing, making policies, managing solutions at the local level, and anticipating problems and successes. The micro/pastoral tasks include rescuing, caring, teaching, empowering, and making and fulfilling referrals. Let's unpack each area.

The prophetic care is that of social justice. The goal is to call out oppression, and at the same time to call in the people to break free from the oppressive system. This occurs at least through the above-mentioned tasks. Demonstrating may take the form of marches and rallies, or raising public demand through media. The point is to draw attention to one's cause.

---

13. King, "Beyond Vietnam."

Prophetic voices speak to how the world is, and how the world could be. Advocating on the macro level is the attempt to give voice to a group of people. An advocate might effectively kick a door in, and then step aside, all the while saying, look and listen to the people that the powers that be have deemed lesser. Or an advocate might start with stepping aside, pushing back the loudmouths and liars with themself. (Listen to Black women. They create justice movements, like #Black Lives Matter and #MeToo.) Educating is introducing knowledge and awareness. This might be through well-researched writing or may mean marginalized perspectives come to the forefront. Lobbying combines and utilizes strengths and resources to influence. Boycotting is also an option, and I'm starting to think of it as reverse lobbying.

When Attorney General Jeff Sessions reasoned for separating families using a New Testament scripture that called for law abiding, Christian faith leaders responded with more astute homiletics. They pointed out that in the gospels Jesus said, when we don't welcome the stranger we do not welcome him. Many churches denounced Sessions's statements and the Trump immigration policy. Rev. John Dorhauer, United Church of Christ president, called out the injustice and called on constituents to take action with these words, "As a faith leader, I say without equivocation there is nothing remotely humane in this policy. It is beyond sinful—it is evil. I call on all leaders of our church to contact their representatives. Ask them not to abdicate their responsibility. Tell them not to fund this atrocity. Tell them to use their power, their voice, and your vote to repeal this morally repugnant policy."[14]

Apostolic care is again concerned with social justice, this time with affinity for groups and relationships. The analyzing on this level might involve noticing trauma symptoms in children who are forcibly separated from their families. One may further analyze how migrant families as a whole have dealt with violence and turmoil along their entire journey. There's also room for social-historical analysis, like questioning what political parties, laws, and other events contribute to the way things are today. The mid-level justice worker wants to implement concrete steps between the monumental call for justice and a person's experienced freedom. They are answering what policies can bring change, and what will be the interconnected reactions. Apostles think of systems like bodies, and can break down how each group plays its part in a system. They will be able to identify

14. Larkman, "UCC Leaders."

the gifts, talents, and skills as well as growing edges. Then the goal is to coach or manage the body to solve its problems and function.

The American Civil Liberties Union, or ACLU, practices practical activism. The ACLU reviews cases of small groups or individuals, attending to how these cases impact greater justice issues. They fact-check statements made by the Trump administration, like the claim that Trump's immigration policy is enforcing a law that Democrats are responsible for.[15] The ACLU compares the content of the Flores Settlement (which sets conditions for under what circumstances and for how long the U.S. government can detain immigrant children) with politicians' claims.[16] They look to implement solutions like class action lawsuits. In such lawsuits, they consider a myriad of family situations and worked toward the best outcome for their clients. In its statement, we see how the ACLU focuses on interconnected groups. "The ACLU is actively working in the courts, in Congress and in communities to stop this once and for all."[17]

Pastoral care includes justice with a shift in focus toward healing. This might start with getting an individual or family to a safe space, essentially rescuing them. Caring includes pastoral interventions such support, reassurance, and addressing violations. The microlevel approach of teaching emphasizes lessons for the individual or for a close-knit group, while also keeping the context in mind. The point is to teach, on the microlevel, the prophetic lessons from the whole system: like, what is the meaning of this injustice to you personally? Resources are assessed, and the pastor empowers a path forward that draws from those strengths. The pastoral helper sees the details on the individual or personal level. The helper designs a specific approach to meet the need or needs, which might involve experts from other fields. The pastoral helper will make referrals to other direct care providers, and ministry becomes interdisciplinary work. Referrals that involve other experts expand the resources for the person in need.

Micropractice or pastoral work is done by direct care providers, like social workers, mental health aides, lawyers, and the like. There are possibilities for many individuals to directly show care. Senator Dick Durbin, from Illinois, got an idea from his granddaughter—to deliver notes of

15. Cheng, "Fact-Checking Family Separation." Trump's claim that Democrats are to blame for the family separation policy was issued by tweet. The ACLU article links a tweet from @realDonaldTrump at 4:58 a.m. on June 5, 2018, via Twitter.com/.

16. Elkin and Smith, "What Is the Flores Settlement?"

17. American Civil Liberties Union (ACLU), "Fuel the Fight."

encouragement to children in shelters.[18] With these acts of kindness, kids can know they are facing the difficulty of the detainment with love and support from a community.

Through my Latinx heritage I feel connected to this community of Brown folks. Still, I have not lived the Latinx and Hispanic or immigrant experience. I am Puerto Rican, so my family lives with the help and harm of coming from a U.S. colony. (The economic policies and slow recovery after the 2017 hurricanes feels telling of our determined worth as Americans.) It is possible that my Hispanic last name will have me dropped from the voter registration rolls. This has happened to others. I worry that at some point there will be a policy mandating that anyone with Latinx heritage is danger-ous and should be displaced. Even so, so many of us are already impacted and will be affected if the oppression continues.

I am European American on my mother's side. Sometimes it is easy to blend into Whiteness when I'm tired of being exoticized, tokenized, or excluded. But in times of injustice I put aside that tired feeling. I know my ancestry includes colonization and slaughter, on the giving and receiving ends. And I wrestle with that identity in myself. So, I research history and current events. Then I think about how to be on the side of justice with the divine, and how to engage the world prophetically, apostolically, and pastorally.

18. NBC-5 Chicago News, "Chicago Senator, Kids Make Cards."

4

When the Movement Gives Back

Julian DeShazier and Damon A. Williams

It may well be that we will have to repent in this generation. Not merely
for the vitriolic words and the violent actions of the bad people, but for
the appalling silence and indifference of the good people who sit around
and say, "Wait on time."

—MARTIN LUTHER KING JR.

"Stay Woke" is a powerful image. Constantly alert. Eyes open. Paying attention. Ready to respond.

Powerful and poetic—*ironic*, perhaps—in that "Stay Woke" echoes the
charge laced throughout biblical texts (Matt 24:42–43; Mark 13:23, 33—"Be
alert! You never know when the day will come"; 1 Thess 5:6—"Let us not
fall asleep like others do . . . *keep awake* and be sober"; Rev 16:15—"Blessed
is the one who is *awake* and clothed"; among many other examples), yet the
phrase was born not in the church but from within #BlackLivesMatter, a
campaign that is decidedly and intentionally—that is, *strategically*—distant
from the traditional, faith-based activism of twentieth-century movements.
That the worlds of church (not a monolith) and activist (not a monolith)
are so often moving in different orbits yet are bound by such compelling
language is a beautiful irony.

It is necessary to say a third (perhaps obvious) thing about "Stay Woke": it is exhausting. In the most literal sense: picture the famous scene of young Alex DeLarge in the film *A Clockwork Orange*, his eyes pried open and being forced to watch images of pain and suffering on a timeless loop, as punishment for his youthful enthusiasm gone too far. Our body hurts *for* him. Now imagine staying awake for even thirty-six straight hours (!), the weight of one's face, the sag of the entire body, and the *damp* feeling that fatigue introduces to the body. "Woke" is a visceral, physical reality.

And return to this call—no, *mandate*—to perpetual ("STAY") awareness and readiness ("WOKE"). The Activist-as-Composer is so prepared to respond to the *discordia* of injustice that one never manages to create a rhythm for oneself: the talented composer never gets to craft from a clean tablature but must always correct the cacophony of abusive power. Activist is by definition a pattern of reactivity, of shaping the world through negative definitions—"This thing they have done is *NOT* the way the world should be"—and it is wearisome.

Burnout is *real* within the activist community. So much so, that those thinking about the health of activists ("advocates for advocates") have begun to talk about something called "sustainable activism": an approach that calls for the long-term health of both the cause but most importantly, the advocate. Think of it this way: if a boxer receives built-in rest between three-minute rounds of boxing, then why not the freedom fighter?

And for these periods of self-care—of receiving therapy, of reflecting on action, of rest—it is commendable that people of faith outside the leadership of this iteration of "the movement"—people from churches called clergy and chaplains and laypeople—would want to offer respite, to offer a connection beyond language, and this entire book illustrates the excitement around this possibility.

Let us go one step further than commendable, however: churches are more suited than any other civic institution to offer spiritual care to the weary activists of this world. The very first churches were curated as safe spaces for the afflicted and oppressed throughout the Roman Empire: as much as they were *sacred spaces* they were *social locations* for community and healing and inspiration. Church began as an ethos and grew into an institution simply by being so effective at conveying a worldview that it had to move into a separate building to give a few gracious hosts their living rooms back.

The church and activist worlds were separated as a circumstance of history; this separation was reinforced by questionable decisions by an organized and empowered Christianity—and now it feels appropriate to ask *whether* and *how* a few justice-minded faithfolk can make amends and offer care to activists in these times.

They have more in common than we tend to articulate. For example: clergy know about burnout, too. The lives of pastors and chaplains are, too, constantly undone by tragedy that requires an immediate response. So too are the rhythms of pastoral life hard to ascertain. It is a life in jazz: constant improvisation. And many spiritual caregivers burn out quickly, or their loving relationships do, or their healthy practices do.

However, the stats floating around the internet about pastors leaving ministry in record numbers are suspect. Seminary enrollment seems to decline at about 1 percent a year, on par with other degree programs, and ten new seminaries have been accredited by Association of Theological Schools (the primary accrediting body) since 2010. Nothing seems to indicate a shortage of pastors; it is probably more accurate to describe a shortage of jobs available.

These beautiful ironies and the possibilities therein form the preamble to our primary goal in this chapter: to allow two passionate, vulnerable and curious practitioners in their respective fields—a pastor and an organizer, both in Chicago, both practicing in the heart of an active movement for black life, and both hopeful and cautious about the potential for partnership—to examine the question of the church's current capacity to offer spiritual care to the Black Lives Matter movement. It is also our hope to describe, from within both church and activist contexts what can be done to expand the church's capacity.

What we believe is this: while the church has much to offer toward the spiritual health and regeneration of activists, this potential will not be realized in its fullness until the church takes a few lessons from the activists and re-forms itself in some vital ways. Inasmuch as the church can offer healing, aspects of the movement can heal the church. The healing we seek is *reciprocal*.

Why Is Capacity a Question?

Every care relationship, whether spiritual (e.g., serving as someone's pastor) or otherwise (e.g., serving as someone's doctor or lawyer) begins and ends with trust. A person with a broken foot depends upon a skilled practitioner to properly diagnose and treat that injury. *Primum non nocere*, or nonmaleficence ("Do no harm") is the fundamental reminder to every medical student, and our basic trust in the efficacy of their training under this practice fuels the healthcare industry. (Whether it can be called healthcare or not, is a different debate.) We want our doctors to follow protocol, to not guess about what may be wrong but to use their years of training and knowledge. And above all, we want our doctors to be healthy themselves. Anything less feels like a breach of trust.

The same is true with people and their pastors. No one seeking forgiveness or clarity on the most intimate of issues wants to see their pastor engaged in unethical behavior or teaching outside of the tradition or straying from the teachings of the Bible in their own lives. Any of these would constitute malpractice—a breach of trust—and would be grounds for ending a relationship.

This is the predicament of the Christian church right now as it pertains to the Black Life movement. As younger activists have mobilized against capitalism and militarism and diabolical racism, and have rallied the voices and leadership of society's most marginalized—Black, Women, Trans, Queer—they have also noticed that one of society's most impactful institutions, the church, has failed to do these things. Again, "church" is not a monolith, but, on the whole, the leadership and ethos of this iteration of the movement has not aligned with most church structures and visions. The quote at the beginning of this chapter then becomes even more elucidatory: it was the Reverend Dr. Martin Luther King Jr.—a pastor himself—who raised this indictment against his "fellow clergymen" and called for a new order of operations inside religious institutions.[1] (The subsequent mythologization of King, and its consequences, is a concern we will address momentarily.)

The church's participation in capitalism—and silence around militarism and racism—calls into question its capacity to offer spiritual care. Although most congregations remain a location for much-needed charity, it is no longer the case that the most vulnerable can feel most safe inside a sanctuary. The public has cried, "Malpractice!" and the breach of trust is felt in the activists' reluctance to call upon pastors to speak or offer spiritual care when being woke is most tiring.

There is a Black Life movement that is leading the cause of wellness for teens, LGBTQ people, women, the poor and working class, students—and

1. See King, "Letter from Birmingham City Jail."

most of their organizers are not on the front lines wearing collars or citing scriptures. Something has been broken in the language and practice of the church, which is the literal way of saying what the apostle Paul said in his first letter to the Corinthians: "Many have fallen asleep" (1 Cor 11:30).

Church Confronting Itself

On April 4, 2018—the fiftieth anniversary of the assassination of MLK—the National Council of Churches convened spiritual leaders from across the globe to Washington DC's National Mall for a rally to end racism. Seems typical enough: *Racism exists; let's yell at it.* But something was different about this rally. All the speakers asked to wax poetic and prophetic about the legacy of King were invited to do so under one prompt, one condition: *talk about your own complicity* in these pervasive systems of oppression and dehumanization. This was no mere idol worship.

What resulted was a refreshing series of confessionals and minisermons pointed not at the White House but at church practice, indicting everything from lack of imagination from church leaders and a dearth of community partnerships to outright cowardice. The event remained primarily symbolic—that is, after all, the prima facie purpose of rallies—but the tone was significant in that denominational leaders were finally showing a willingness to live out Matthew 7 and deal with the plank in their own eye before calling out the speck in others'.

To do this work—of offering care to people broken by injustice—beyond the rally experience will require two shifts that may change what it means to be church in this day and age: a shift in language and a shift in leadership. Lessons, questions, and tools from the movement will guide the way.

Shifting Language

The legacy of twentieth-century social movements includes a deep relationship with the church. The Black Church in particular—the institution congregated primarily by African Americans and espousing the values and freedom of Black Americans—has been a haven and resting place for those involved in the struggle for justice. The examples are too many to cite, but due credit belongs to Sixteenth Street Baptist Church in Birmingham, Alabama; Olivet Baptist Church in Chicago, Illinois; Ebenezer Baptist Church in Atlanta, Georgia; First Baptist Church in Montgomery, Alabama; and several other locations—not all of them Baptist—which opened their doors to the people and made space for the movement as it was being born.

These congregations were more than mere "meeting houses." As E. Franklin Frazier describes in *The Negro Church in America*, "Negroes were captured and enslaved and inducted into the plantation regime [which] tended to loosen all social bonds among them and to destroy the traditional basis of social cohesion," and Black churches served as a distinct institutional presence to counter this. While colored people were being torn apart by poverty and racism, the Black Church was a trusted holding place where grief and hope and *social cohesion* were held as the highest values; the sanctuary was an unassailable, safe place.

We must not underestimate the role of language in creating this safety. After all, church was a space where, if your boss had been cruel or you had been dehumanized up and down the block all week, on Sunday you were certain to hear that you are a beloved child of God. If you had to keep your mouth shut about ills perpetrated against you in order to protect your family, it was in *church* where you could sing the beautiful lament of "Come Sunday": *"Lord, dear Lord above, / God Almighty, God of Love, / Please look down and see my people through."* Or you could simply *moan* with, as Paul says in Romans, "sighs too deep for words." The point is, it mattered that what you were hearing and were able to say inside of church was different from what you heard and how you could speak outside of church. It was a holy language, set apart from the rhythm of everyday life, which allowed for the type of cohesion that gives birth to movements.

The church did not invite the movement through its doors: through its language of affirmation and challenge, the church became an incubator for a movement that was still figuring itself out and constantly reeling as it moved to respond to every tragedy. We can say the same thing about the Black Lives Matter movement today.

The difference is, many Black churches are espousing a capitalist gospel of prosperity, which not only flows downstream along with cultural trends but also supports the machinations of an exploitative model of economic growth tied into one's faith.

If people are wondering why the activists are not calling on the church, the answer is obvious: many churches are speaking the radical opposite from the values espoused by the movement.

The intention is not to call out pastors but for all potential spiritual caregivers to ask: *Does the gospel we preach and live protect the most vulnerable in our communities, or does it medicate them and further empower oppressive practices?*

When activist collectives perceive the church empowering oppressive practices, the church will not be able to offer the kind of spiritual care that activists most need.

Nonviolent vs. Antiviolent

Blink two times if you've ever used the phrase "nonviolent direct action" to describe your work. It is an important phrase and strategy, and has had such affect and effect that every direct action campaign, even the ones that use violence as a strategy, must respond to nonviolence as the organizing status quo.

But there's a problem with that word: *nonviolence.*

The legacy of violence perpetuated against Black communities is astounding, and it has existed for as long as Black people have been in America. It is so pervasive that violence is almost seen as pathological in Black realities. To counter this, activists around the beginning of the twentieth century began using the term *nonviolence* as a way to describe a response to injustice (and outright violence) that did not beget more violence. Its roots come from the practice of *ahimsa*, one of the core principles of Buddhism and Hinduism, which commands respect for all life as a logical extension of self-respect and self-love.

The problem is that these understandings of *nonviolence* are often too simplistic and rarely offer up a definition of *violence* beyond "hurting the body of another person."[2]

The World Health Organization defines violence as "the intentional use of physical force or power threatened or actual, against oneself, another person, or against a group or community, which either results in or has a high likelihood of resulting in injury, death, psychological harm, maldevelopment, or deprivation."[3] Because *force* and *power* are of themselves neutral, it is important to look at the word *intentional*: the use of force or power with the intent to harm.

2. "What is violence?" (Google Dictionary search): https://tinyurl.com/y2gcr6uk/.

3. Krug et al., eds., *World Report on Violence and Health*, 5.

With this expanded and perhaps enlightened definition, we see now that violence is not just gang conflict, urban uprising, and public shooting. It is also war, and the perpetual investment in a war economy. It is policing: the taking of Black life and the protocols and paradigms that ground a militarized police force are both forms of violence.

Less obviously, it is resource development, school closings, service reduction, and punitive restrictions. Food deserts (the absence of healthy food) and toxic swamps (the pervasive presence of unhealthy food) are violent. The unregulated, polluted air of a factory, which poorer citizens then must breathe on a daily basis, is violent. Foreclosures are violence. Our nation's highway construction was violence. Corporate and government austerity is violence.

Violence is a powerful force, and the lessons of physics teach us that the status quo of violence and subjugation will go unmoved unless acted upon by a force (Newton's First Law); that the change in momentum is proportional to the force causing it (Newton's Second Law); and that for every action, there is an equal and opposite reaction (Newton's Third Law). In other words, nonviolence rarely stops a violent act. There must be a *violence against violence*, which some are wanting to call nonviolence, but the framing of this issue matters. It is possible to be nonviolent and operate congruent and alongside violent contexts. In fact, this is one of the primary critiques of faith communities by the activist collectives: congregations talk against violence and stand right alongside it, peaceful yet abiding. Using too narrow a definition of violence, churches can rally against police shootings and ask nothing about the militarized, detached ethos of policing in general.

What Is Needed Is Antiviolence

The position of nonviolence is similar to the insignificance of a White person arguing they are nonracist or "not a racist" while benefitting from oppressive systems. There's an element of ridiculousness for an American to claim nonviolence while goods we consume are produced by slaves, while the natural resources required for our production are extracted in ways that destabilize ecosystems and nations, and while our global political dominance is maintained by our collective investment into militarism and weaponry at a rate the world has never seen.

Antiviolence is intentional action to reduce and prevent harm, provide benefit, and protect from violence. It is active and not passive. Antiviolence leaves room for vocal and forceful accountability when violence inevitably occurs (whereas the false violent/nonviolent dichotomy reinforces dominant power and propels violence because it provides no avenue to adequately address how harm occurs). The position of nonviolence is often offered from privilege because the risk and direct consequence of nonviolence have been redistributed to populations with less access to sustaining environments. You can be nonviolent behind the gate while carnage ensues on the other side of the fence; antiviolence, however, can be owned and practiced by all.

The church has used the principle of nonviolence as a way of avoiding engagement with #BlackLivesMatter activists, citing their aggression and use of force as undeveloped, immature, and brash. But this use of force falls squarely within our definition of *antiviolence*, which is the resistance of violent people, institutions, and processes (whereas *nonviolent* keeps the focus on people, emphasizing the types of response by those being harmed). To be antiviolent is to demand accountability wherever violence exists: it is the ethical commitment to harm no person, mixed with the existential commitment to stop one's own or another person's harm.

To address individual financial struggles within an antiviolent framework is to provide more than prayer and budgeting strategies; it is also to connect to the accessibility of local resources relative to exploitive imbalance and provide avenue to hold accountable entities that exert or benefit from causing financial harm. It is to do all of these things, and more yet to be imagined, with the goal of empowering people and reshaping conditions that yield unjust outcomes.

To address an illness like diabetes from an antiviolent framework is more than to pray for healing and to resource to treatment and therapy; it is to connect personal illness to local access to nutrition, and to build outlets to address global food production in conjunction with our medical and pharmaceutical industries within the context of an inadequate health-care system.

Here is another question that churches should ask: *Do we speak "nonviolence" in too narrow a fashion, and do we understand the depth of violence happening in our immediate vicinity?*

The answer to this question may expose a too-narrow definition of *violence*—one focused solely on guns while ignoring the displacement and divestment that throws disinherited peoples into competition with each other over (what we are told are) scarce resources: the violence that causes violence must also be our concern. Without this full understanding of violence, which grounds the Black Life movement, churches will seem at best ignorant and at worst participatory in systems of subjugation.

A good homework assignment for any potential caregiver (after answering the question above) is to locate the organizations inside their community that are talking about violence in a more expansive way. You don't have to become allies, but invite them to teach your congregation about violence and what it means to be antiviolent. The resulting relationship becomes the foundation for a multitude of care possibilities. Establishing trust is not about knowing everything, or presenting expertise that can teach the activists; sometimes it is simply being willing to learn, and being vulnerable enough to ask.

In this understanding of care, which includes expressing concern, easing anxiety, and reducing suffering; this work connects to the personal by showing a willingness and capacity to connect to the local and global. Churches have to *present* as engaged and informed, and these subtle shifts in language (creating space for social cohesion, and reimagining/engaging violence more directly)—represent much larger shifts in what it means to be church, and what it means to be part of this ongoing movement in a meaningful and less marginal way. To provide care is to create or shape space as well as to provide training for people to collectively take on the task of eradicating the harm they experience through structural processes.

Until this shift is made—from avoiding violence to using power to engage it honestly—a mutual partnership between the church and the movement will be virtually impossible.

Shifting Leadership

Churches have simple leadership models, linear and horizontal, where power flows from one direction to another. Simple in design if not always in execution, these structures emerge from a particular myth about the prophet and priest that is grounded in ancient tradition and sacred text. The myth goes like this: a person (come on, a *man*) or a group of persons, if we are to consider the tribe of Levi (the Levites) is set apart and holy before God, shrouded in a sort of divine mystery, and given the consent to decree, with almost no room for debate. Even when the Protestant Reformation chips away at that mystery and declares "the priesthood of ALL believers," there is still a fairly concrete understanding that the body must have *a* head (singular)—one leader upon whose shoulders the government will stand (paraphrasing Isa 9). This person is a HERO.

Despite history incontrovertibly proving the instability of such a paradigm, the individual hero-as-figurehead representing the masses is a norm of lasting consequence far beyond Christianity. Social justice movements, many of which either began in churches or use a moral-theological framework to ground their being—or both—also find themselves grounded in some hero archetype.

Take Martin Luther King Jr., for example. His success in leading the Southern Christian Leadership Conference (SCLC), one of many organizations active during that time, and his success in coordinating campaigns in Montgomery and Selma, part of a vast network of campaigns, has resulted in his being taught to every child as being *the* leader of the civil rights movement. The way his legacy has been projected onto Barack Obama made one man solely responsible for the destiny of millions in 2008 (although this type of hero-dependency had been foisted upon the United States presidency hundreds of years earlier). Following the struggle for the MLK holiday—first recognized nationally in 1986—gave the man born Michael King an almost mythic status. He was, for Black people everywhere, far larger than a sociopolitical change agent who confronted racism directly: he was what a leader is. The civil rights movement is how you do a movement. And a common question now asked of today's Black Life movement is, who's the leader?

Making MLK or Michael Jordan or Michael Jackson, or even Bugs Bunny or Batman, the prototype of a leader is wrong for a few obvious reasons. First, many women have led throughout history and continue to lead from the invisible trenches. Second, these leadership models fueled a masculinist hierarchy driven by selfish competitiveness ("there can only be one of us in charge"), turning potential partners into fierce rivals. Third, these models assume one potential source of wisdom and goodness and fail to make room for the collaborators, the songwriters, the Scottie Pippens, or the Robins that make their leadership possible. If the violence we defined earlier has the result of tearing apart the sense of and opportunity for developing a community ethos, then we can easily make the next leap and say that these leadership-by-hero models are inherently violent.

Even when it is a woman taking the role of a man as leader-hero, this remains true. It is like a White person who is not racist because they "have many Black friends" (that is, their White friend slots have simply been swapped out for Black ones). The debate around appropriate representation and identity politics aside, the system remains soundly intact.

This is not to say that churches shouldn't have pastors. As full-time (if not always paid full-time) caregivers and resident theologians, pastors and chaplains serve in distinct and important roles inside the formation of faith communities. But the myth of the messiah (*myth* is not pejorative here)—that action and wisdom flow from the one to the masses—is linear.

What Is Needed Is Circular Leadership

Circular power formations delineate from Afro-indigenous traditions and the diaspora. Despite the framing of the movie *Black Panther*, which employs linear hero myths to fit a comic universe, the spaces to which today's activists are accountable deploy *rounded* processes, to design a less comic and truly *non*violent Afro-futuristic world. They/We gather, heal, confront, share, learn, and—most significantly—decide in a circle.

Sometimes this takes on the literal vision of a circle of leaders gathered in a room, but more significantly, circular power is defined by the ethos of a circle.

Instead of power on top (hierarchy) or on the bottom (congregationalism), it is in the center, and all points of perimeter (locations of power, "leaders") are equidistant to the center. Circular leadership is inclusive and participatory, intended to distribute power in an accessible and efficient manner. Some local chapters of #BlackLivesMatter may name a president, but this is almost always an artificial designation used to create accessibility for institutions that want to engage but find it hard to approach this model.

Let us reconsider the palpable tension, called *irony* earlier in the chapter, in the relationship between church folk and activist folk: the Black Church—which gave birth to the civil rights iteration of this movement in the early twentieth century—is having great difficulty with this circular model of power. It is too unrestrained, too nebulous. Meanwhile, the activist collectives—Black Youth Project (BYP100), Let Us Breathe, and Assatta's Daughters, among at least twenty others in Chicago alone—are having great difficulty abiding in traditional, male-centered, heteronormative models of power that have kept access to the throne from those that don't fit in these categories of acceptance. In the circular model, there is no throne. The head of the Black Life movement is plural, and potential leaders are challenged not to think of the public implications of their private revelations, as if they are coming from out of space and time, but are challenged to operate *in space* while intersecting within the space and experiences of others, within the space of violence and privilege. Leading in the new, circular model requires a sensitivity to space, and to how much space men in particular are taught to occupy without apology. It requires dealing with the insecurity that naturally comes with having space and power taken from you; it is given freely in behalf of the circle's health. It requires trust: this is what we've been talking about all along.

This iteration of the movement is younger, more affirming of sexuality, less restrictive of gender, and decidedly more womanist in tone. For some churches and potential caregivers, it will appear painfully chaotic. But pastors and other clergy ought suspend judgment.

Instead, a question to ask is, *do our leadership structures make room for voices and faces that are rarely seen in more traditional settings, or do we reinforce the lifting up of "heroes"?*

A good homework assignment for any potential caregiver would be to invite one of the groups, leaders, or collectives that you are hoping to provide care for to one of your upcoming board, session, or council meetings. Invite them to observe and provide feedback on the flow of leadership and whether those most affected by injustice and violence might feel comfortable in that space. The lessons from this, if they can be received nondefensively, will go a long way toward establishing a loving relationship of mutual care.

Next Steps

If the Black Lives Matter movement is about confronting systems that oppress, this must now necessarily include the Christian church. If there is any hope for ministers to provide genuine spiritual care toward the wholeness and wellness of persons, then from within church walls there is going to have to be wholesale self-examination of the policies and practices that empower oppressive tactics and endanger people. Put another way, if churches (or mosques or synagogues or temples) are going to offer loving, safe spaces to gather and form community, they are going to have to confront their own complicity in violence and exclusion.

We have offered a shift in language and a shift in leadership as two concrete ways to move forward, with questions and homework "challenges" to apply within your context in order to increase the capacity of the faith world to offer care to the activist world. The type of loving care and dynamic affirmation that church can offer would no doubt be useful to those who grow more weary as the tragedies pile up; the wisdom of ancient faith has much to teach us in these anxious times.

But the movement has much to teach as well. For all the ways that religion has shaped the movement, let the movement teach now, and let the church be healed so it can teach anew.

5

Domestic Violence and Pastoral Care in the Age of #BlackLivesMatter

SHARON ELLIS DAVIS

In 2016 I had the opportunity to speak at the Conference on Crimes against Women (CCAW) in Dallas, Texas. The CCAW has been engaged, since 2005, in providing over ten thousand law enforcement officers, prosecutors, advocates, medical professionals, campus administrators, and others with best practices for responding to crimes against women. This conference draws over two thousand attenders from across North America to hear from the nation's leading experts on domestic violence, sexual assault, campus safety, cybercrimes, stalking, culturally specific issues (affecting LGBT people, women of color, people of faith, and immigrants), investigation technology, and more.[1] The overwhelming majority of attendees were White. My assignment was to conduct two workshops around culturally specific issues of sexual and domestic violence. The workshops conducted were titled "Race, Class, & Gender: The Impact of Gender Entrapment on African American Women," and "Faith & Culture: Domestic Violence in African American Relationships."

The conference consists of a few days of workshops with one exception. Day 1 of the conference begins with an invited plenary keynote speaker to set the stage for the various workshops and dialogues to come. The keynote speaker on this day happened to be a White woman who was

1. Conference on Crimes against Women, website (http://www.conferencecaw.org).

a domestic violence survivor. She spoke of her experience (all too familiar to survivors) as a domestic violence victim battered by her now-estranged husband. This story resembled my own story. It was a story of betrayal, shame, and physical and emotional abuse. It was a story of the manipulative tactics of the abuser; of the victim reaching out for help and support from family, friends, and professionals; and finally of the victim leaving the abusive relationship and picking up the pieces of a broken life. It was a story of reconciliation, recovery of self, resiliency, and restoration. I remember repeating an all-too-familiar refrain silently to myself, *This is truly every survivor's story.* And yes, it was, up to a point. This story came to its conclusion as the speaker reflected on how wonderfully the police treated her, on how they followed up about her safety, on how they offered and gave her rides to the police station, and overall on how the police cared greatly for her as a victim. By the end of her speech I was greatly empathetic and grateful that she had not only survived such a horrific event but recovered and eventually thrived. Yet my refrain switched from *This is truly every survivors story*, to *That was not my experience with the police, or the experience of the many African American women survivors for whom I had provided pastoral care and advocacy.* This refrain as well as the keynote speech shaped my introduction to the two workshops I conducted on these two days. Introducing the word *particularities* and its meaning was key to establishing the themes of my presentations related to domestic violence in African American communities.

The word *particularities* became real for me in the 1980s while I was in an abusive relationship with an African American police officer. This experience led me down the path to teaching a seminary course titled Domestic Violence in the African American Community. As a survivor of sexual and domestic violence, I found myself advocating for victims and serving on the board of directors for an agency tasked with preventing violence against women and supporting survivors. Most important, I was able to begin a ministry to victims of domestic violence within the local church setting. However, there was no experience more enlightening than being a survivor of domestic violence whose African American husband was, like myself, a police officer. Although I did not at this time have the scholarly knowledge to articulate the dynamics I experienced within the police department, and although I had no knowledge of the word *particularities* as it related to domestic violence, I unsuspectingly became a living example of how these *particularities* operated. I intuitively learned in the department about racism, sexism, gender bias, and the police code of silence. These

-isms and gender roadblocks negatively influenced my ability to receive the help, safety, and support I needed. I learned how this male-dominated, chauvinistic, and military-style organization served as a source of protection for my abuser and permitted racist and biased behavior toward him as a Black male. I witnessed a system that shielded my abuser from being fulling accountable within a male-dominated system—a system that thus stifled my agency and limited my trust in a system that I believed would protect me. I learned the particularities that exist within a system of male privilege replete with racism and gender bias.

As an African American battered woman survivor, I became energized by the imperative to bring into the classroom and into postdoctoral work information about violence against women. Consequently, I began teaching Domestic Violence in the African American Community in a local seminary. And, for the most part this class was fruitful for the African Americans who attended. However, it was in early 2000, when the course title was changed to Sexual and Domestic Violence and opened for all students, that I learned another valuable lesson.

The class was designed to foster both a theoretical and a practical environment. Course topics included diagnosing the dynamics of violence against women, preventing sexual and domestic violence, and intervening effectively in situations of sexual or domestic violence. It was during one of these classes when I asked a question about particularities. My question centered on African American batterers. It centered on the inclusion of the African American history of oppression and its possible relationship to domestic violence. Focusing more on male batterers, I asked the class about their willingness to engage this topic. One young, self-identified feminist in the classroom, who had been quiet for most of the conversations, gently raised her hand and belted out an angry-sounding "No!" She went further with her comment and stated, "And that is my contribution to this class." I was convinced at this moment that not only were issues of race, class and gender ignored and devalued within the feminist setting, but so were the lives and experiences of African American men and women, who lived with these dynamics and microaggressions daily. Their lived experiences didn't seem to matter. Today, the phrase Black Lives Matter[2] rings true for what I felt, and what I was experiencing the absence of in that classroom.

2. Blacklivesmatter.com/—In 2013, three radical Black organizers, Alicia Garza, Patrisse Cullors, and Opal Tometi, created a Black-centered political will and movement building project called #BlackLivesMatter. It happened in response to the acquittal of Trayvon Martin's murderer, George Zimmerman.

My ambition became to read work by and about people of color and provide scholarship about them, as well as to include experiences from people of color (particularly from African American people) in my own preaching, lecturing, teaching, and training on issues of both sexual and domestic violence and pastoral care—especially in this age of #BlackLivesMatter.

This chapter cannot and should not exhaust the various ways to provide pastoral care especially for African American victim-survivors. Yet, intertwined in this chapter are insights to these particularities and viable pastoral care practices that have been utilized to provide culturally sensitive responses to both the victim-survivor of domestic violence and the perpetrator of violence. The chapter also illustrates the need for advocacy, justice-making, and the prophetic voice—all as important forms of intervention and violence prevention in African American communities. Overall, this chapter will assert how the work of violence prevention and intervention has to be accomplished from the context of oppression. Prevention and intervention in various forms are needed to facilitate healing and restoration for the victim-survivor and accountability for the abuser. Addressing these issues is a great starting point for those who are serious about all Black lives, including the lives of Black women who are victims of sexual and domestic violence. This chapter will focus on two particular and important first steps of pastoral care—first, safety for the victim and accountability for the batterer; and, second, advocacy and doing justice.

In my book *Battered African American Women: A Study of Gender Entrapment*, domestic violence, also known as intimate partner violence, is described as including sexual abuse, emotional abuse, spousal rape, and even economic abuse. It impacts all people but specifically women, children, LGBQT people, and teens.[3] I suggest that the lack of response in the Black church to women's being abused has its origin in the history of slavery, racism, and oppression in America. The necessary response to this oppression—Black liberation theologies and Black empowerment movements—focused more on Black men to the detriment of Black women.[4] This lack of attention on Black women within the Black church and community ignored violence against Black women in intimate relationships and minimized the availability of care for African American battered women, thus creating an environment of silence and increasing the possibility of the continued victimization and traumatization of Black women. Yet, racism

3. Davis, *Battered African American Women*, 4.
4. Ibid., 5.

and the continued systemic oppressions suffered by African American people must be better understood as we continue to examine more effective ways to be inclusive of Black women's experiences and the particularities of pastoral care needed for the prevention of and intervention to stop intimate partner violence within Black families and communities. This is especially true if we are legitimately concerned about keeping Black women safe, about holding batterers accountable, and about doing justice for all within Black families and communities.

Safety for the Victim, Accountability for the Batterer

Safety for victims and accountability for batterers need to be examined together in order to understand their significance—especially given the need for African American battered women to seek out safe spaces, to report physical abuse to police, and to hold batterers accountable.

African American women have often been stereotyped as strong women, as taking on the responsibility of caring for and fixing the brokenness within their families, even while experiencing abuse themselves. In 1979 and 1980, a TV commercial advertising Enjoli perfume featured a cover of the 1962 song "I'm a Woman." The song makes the point that women are strong because they can meet both their partner's needs (by frying his bacon or waxing his car) and their own without breaking a sweat. The commercial closed by calling Enjoli "the eight-hour perfume for your twenty-four-hour woman." The image of the strong Black woman continues to be part of the culture accepted by Black women and promoted by Black men. The images and expectations of Black women are that they are to be superhumans. In her book *Chain, Chain, Change: For Black Women in Abusive Relationships*, author Evelyn White traces how the cultural history of Blacks in America has led Black women to place everybody's needs before their own.[5] White further states, "The images and expectations of black women are both super- and sub-human . . . This conflict has created many myths and stereotypes that cause confusion about our own identity and make us targets for abuse."[6]

Black women, although suffering equally with Black men from the impact of slavery, lynching, Jim Crow, poverty, and so forth have not necessarily been factored into the equation of healing and liberation. In her

5. White, *Chain, Chain, Change*, 19.
6. Ibid., 16–17.

SPIRITUAL CARE IN AN AGE OF #BLACKLIVESMATTER

book *The New Jim Crow: Mass Incarceration in the Age of Colorblindness*, Michelle Alexander gives an excellent depiction of the criminal justice system and how drug laws that facilitated a war on drugs resulted in the mass incarceration of African American men, which resulted in their over-representation in prisons. In addition, she describes how these and other discriminatory laws and systems strip prisoners and ex-convicts of voting rights and of access to housing and employment. All this, she says, has contributed to a new kind of slavery.[7] This slavery she describes as legal ways to further oppress African American men after slavery—hence her book's title, *The New Jim Crow*. As it impacts African American women, Alexander states, "Women, in particular, express conflicted views about crime, because they love their sons, husbands, and partners and understand their plight as current and future members of the racial undercaste. At the same time, though, they abhor gangs and the violence associated with inner-city life."[8]

This same tension can be also applied to battered Black women—women who abhor the violence they are experiencing. Yet Black women are not ignorant of these oppressive systems; they understand the impact of these systems on Black men and the Black family. Consequently, Black women's consciousness leaves them rightfully empathetic, sympathetic, and protective of both the Black man and the Black family. Thus, it also leaves them conflicted in their loyalties and vulnerable to further abuse, and retraumatization.

Pastoral care with African American battered women must consider how the women's conflicted loyalties impact their safety and well-being. Pastoral care should seek ways to enable battered women to understand their right to be free from physical, emotional, and psychological harm, even to the extent of separating from the batterer and possibly spending time in jail. Pastoral care must be sensitive both to issues of racism and to the violation of African American battered women and their God-given right to safety. Evelyn White reminds us of this need. Loyalty, she states, "does not mean that you should continue to endure abuse from your partner."[9] She quotes the following poem by Pat Parker:

> Brother, I don't want to hear about how my real enemy is the system,

---

7. Alexander, *New Jim Crow*, 53–57.

8. Ibid., 204.

9. White, *Chain, Chain, Change*, 22.

I'm no genius but I do know that system you hit me with is called a fist.[10]

In her book *In Search of Our Mothers' Gardens: Womanist Prose*, Alice Walker defines womanism in depth. Her definition is the basis for womanist theological practices. Key to this topic of safety is Walker's description of womanism and women's relationship to the other. She states, women are "committed to the survival and wholeness of entire people, male and female. Not a separatist except periodically, for health."[11]

Womanist theological thought helps the pastoral care profession articulate theologically how Black women can be committed to family and can fight for justice within their communities while at the same time committing to their own safety, survival, and mental health. Statistically,

- "1 in 4 women and 1 in 9 men experience severe intimate partner physical violence, intimate partner contacts sexual violence, and/or intimate partner stalking with impacts such as injury, fearfulness, post-traumatic stress disorder, use of victim services, and contraction of sexually transmitted diseases."

- "1 in 3 women and 1 in 4 men have experienced some form of physical violence by an intimate partner."

- "1 in 7 women and 1 in 25 men have been injured by an intimate partner."

- "1 in 10 women have been raped by an intimate partner."

- "Victims of intimate partner violence lose a total of 8.0 million days of paid work each year."

- "72% of all murder-suicides involve an intimate partner; 94% of the victims of these murder suicides are female."

- "The cost of intimate partner violence exceeds $8.3 billion per year."[12]

These numbers underestimated of the problem, because many victims don't report. Certainly these statistics align with Walker's description of *womanism* in helping Black women make critical decisions about their safety. She

10. Ibid.

11. Walker, "Preface," xi.

12. These stats come from the website of the National Coalition against Domestic Violence: *NCADV* (website), "Statistics; National Statistics." The NCADV website in turn relies on stats from Black, et al., *National Intimate Partner and Sexual Violence Survey: 2010 Summary Report*; Truman and Morgan, "Special Report: Nonfatal Domestic Violence"; Rothman et al., "How Employment Helps Female Victims"; and other sources.

states, "Committed to the survival and wholeness of entire people, male and female. Not a separatist, except periodically, for health."[13]

Safety also calls for developing relationships with local domestic violence shelters. Shelters have often been known in Black religious circles as places that take away your religion and encourage divorce. It is important for pastoral caregivers to dispel this myth and to establish relationships with shelters. Shelters have much to offer victim-survivors and their families in the ways of shelter, support groups, housing, and employment. The faith community can invite shelter personnel to visit the church and can share its resources for prevention and intervention, as the church and shelter develop trust for one another.

Another important factor in safety is for the pastor and faith community to provide theological clarity. Theological clarity must empower the victim-survivor and hold the abuser accountable. Repentance, forgiveness, and divorce are three main issues I have discovered to be roadblocks to victim safety. On many occasions abusers will apologize for the battering, implying that the abuse must be immediately forgiven and reconciliation must be sought. Theological clarity helps the batterer and the victim-survivor understand that being sorry does not equal repentance. Repentance involves expressing contriteness, taking responsibility for the abusive action, and providing restitution. And if the victim-survivor is ready, repentance can also result in reconciliation. However, marriages do die, and some lines that abusers cross cannot be retraced. In those cases, divorce may occur. Pastoral care involves helping victim-survivors understand that divorce from an abuser has not broken the marriage covenant. Rather the violence of abuse broke the covenant. Oftentimes we in the church, quote Mal 2:16 when speaking of God's hatred for divorce. Yet we fail to pay attention to the entire verse, which also states God's hatred for violence. We must ask ourselves, as Dr. Frank Thomas often does, to what end and for what purposes do we privilege some passages of Scripture over others?[14]

The same goes for biblical passages on forgiveness. Forgiveness is often cited as the abused woman's first obligation after undergoing abuse.

---

13. Walker, "Preface," xi.

14. Dr. Frank Thomas is a former pastor now serving as the Professor of Preaching at Christian Theological Seminary in Indianapolis, Indiana. I have listened to many of his sermons and this is a recurring theme in many of his sermons. It is so universal now that many people use it without any reference to a source. Yet, they will mention his name, indicating he was the original source, as most know it to be. Yet, this is said so much, it probably does not need attribution at all. I just love to offer it because of the authority of his voice.

When we encourage premature forgiveness, we are negating the process a victim-survivor must endure in order to make sense of the victimization; forgiveness is not the priority and may come in time but must never be encouraged until the victim-survivor is ready. When I teach courses or lecture on sexual and domestic violence, the issue of forgiveness always tends to elicit long, deep dialogue about the who's, what's, when's, and how's of forgiveness. Pastors and pastoral caregivers must provide this theological clarity to both the victim-survivor and the abuser. Biblical passages prohibiting divorce or enjoining forgiveness need to be revisited, deconstructed, and reconstructed so that they can serve as resources and not roadblocks to safety.

Finally, accountability may include incarceration for the batterer. Unfortunately, often the only resource available for batterer accountability is the criminal justice System. When the abuser enters this system and it becomes the option of choice for the victim-survivor, the pastor and pastoral caregiver must support the victim. Supporting the victim involves being with her during her court visits. Traditionally in the Black Church leadership has supported African American men through the court system. Caring for the batterer is okay as long as his support includes him being held accountable (whatever that might look like) in the end. However, it is vital that the victim-survivor not be alone in court, especially as the batterer is fully supported in this setting. We need more spaces for accountability within our communities if we ever hope to avoid the criminal justice system. Accountability is also available in many areas within culturally specific domestic violence batterers groups that take into consideration the total history of oppression and that seek to make these connections with batterers in order to help break this cycle of violence.[15] In addition, programs of restorative justice seek to decrease convictions and offer new possibilities for accountability and healing. The Black church could serve a tremendous service in this field. Yet, with all these programs for safety and accountability, our work is not over. Pastoral caregiving also entails providing advocacy and doing works of justice.

Advocacy and Doing Justice

The faith community can provide justice by holding the abuser accountable and providing for the victim-survivor. Key to caring for the victim-survivor

15. African American Domestic Peace Project (website: http://www.aadpp.org/).

is providing a safe place for disclosure, offering spiritual support, and hearing and believing the stories of victim-survivors, knowing that their stories are only the tip of the iceberg. However, advocacy as pastoral care also involves speaking out against domestic violence and having members of the faith community become professionally trained in proper advocacy. Advocacy also involves examining the churches organizational structure to ensure that Black women as well as Black men are in positions of leadership and are valued as equals within the faith community. These actions ensure that the faith community itself is leading by example in creating an environment of inclusivity and empowerment. And yet, there is even more work to do.

Mic 6:8 states, "He has told you, O mortal, what is good; / and what does the LORD require of you / but to do justice, and to love kindness, / and to walk humbly with your God?" (NRSV). This passage sums up our responsibility in the African American church and community. As a community that cares for the entire family, our responsibility does not end with caring for the victim's safety and well-being or for the batterer's accountability. We must undertake an ethical analysis of the treatment of Black women in history and the impact of such treatment on violence against women. Traci C. West, in her book *Disruptive Christian Ethics: When Racism and Women's Lives Mater*, attempts to have a dialogue on this subject through combining theory and practice in her engagement. She tells stories of women to put practical meaning to her ethical considerations. She states, "My hope is that this dialogical method of developing Christian social ethics will provide practice in how to conceive of what it means to share power rather than hoard it; how to make the transformation of unjust, marginalizing conditions for women key criteria for evaluating society's healthiness; and how to generate such commitments by Christian faith and practice."[16]

One great and necessary work of the Black church is to end marginalizing practices and conditions for women and commit to practicing equal justice from the inside out.

In addition, we must continue the work of being a prophetic voice against systemic injustice, advocating for the rights of women, volunteering in domestic violence shelters, and advocating for changing the laws and policies that impact mass incarceration, homelessness, and unemployment. These and many other issues in our communities represent important work that must be done. We are never fighting a single battle, and all the ills

16. West, *Disruptive Christian Ethics*, xxi.

within our communities make up what is known as an intersectionality framework for a prophetic voice that seeks to be inclusive of the ways our communities and families are being destroyed both on the inside and on the outside.

Conclusion: What Next?

This chapter has attempted to introduce some ways to provide pastoral care to victim-survivors of domestic violence in the age of #BlackLivesMatter, and to provoke direct actions from pastoral caregivers. It is by no means a comprehensive pastoral care manual but seeks to give voice to the conditions of racism, sexism, gender biases, and the like that impact the safety and well-being of African American battered women. Issues of African American LGBQT persons are left out of this conversation. In my conversations with battered LGBQT persons, I learned that many of the issues they face are the same ones battered women face. However, as particularities are concerned, differences do need to be explored and researched. Although women are battered more than men, this does not mean that lesbians are not battered. And, when lesbians are battered, as pastoral caregivers we must consider their plight as people who live in a society rife with antigay bias. They fear being outed, and they are afraid of rejection by family and friends, including by their church family. As a faith community, the Black church must engage in self-examination of biased practices and misinformed Scripture interpretation, which has led to not only sexism but also to homophobia and damaging practices that leave the gay community vulnerable and isolated. As a faith community, we are not where we ought to be. Yet we are not where we used to be. I pray that a closer examination of ourselves and our practices will bring us closer to offering the kind of pastoral care to victims of domestic violence that is liberating and healing as well as replete with God's kindness and justice for all people—regardless of their race, class, gender identification, or who they choose to love. This is our call to pastoral care in the age of #BlackLivesMatter. Let us learn it! Let us live it!

"We are called to make justice, called to make it right. Called to do the Holy work of turning back the night. Called to investigate each shattered shaken soul. Called to make this world, our world whole.[17]

17. Author Unknown.

6

See Her

Creating a Culture of Safety in the Black Church for Young Women and Girls Living in a Prison Nation

LIZ S. ALEXANDER

The emotional, sexual, and psychological stereotyping of females begins when the doctor says, "It's a girl."

—SHIRLEY CHISHOLM, U.S. CONGRESSWOMAN, NEW YORK 12TH CONGRESSIONAL DISTRICT

Back then, Black churches were a small piece of peace. Church was a world where, even with its imperfections, the offer of equality and common humanity was the sustenance needed to make it through the rest of the week in a society that deemed [Black people] less than human.

—JANELLE GRAY, AUTHOR OF *ECHOES OF THE STRUGGLE*

Young women and girls are the fastest-growing population to enter the criminal and juvenile justice system in the United States. According to the White House Report "Advancing Equity on Women and Girls of Color,"[1]

1. White House Council on Women and Girls, "Advancing Equity for Women and

girls and women between the ages of thirteen and twenty-four represent a growing share of arrests, delinquency petitions, detentions, and postadjudication placements in both the juvenile and criminal justice systems. Nationally, girls accounted for 20 percent of all juvenile arrests in 1992; however, girls account for nearly 30 percent of arrests today. The numbers are even more staggering for girls of color, who are disproportionately impacted by juvenile incarceration when compared to their White counterparts. African American girls, for example, compose roughly 33 percent of the juvenile justice system but make up only 14 percent of the national population. In a newly released report titled *The Sexual Abuse to Prison Pipeline: The Girls' Story*,"[2] this disproportionality was found to be due not to an increase of criminal activity or violence among girls, but instead was due to "an aggressive enforcement of non-serious offenses that are rooted in the experience of abuse and trauma" as well as racialized and gendered policies. In fact, incarcerated girls in general were found to overwhelmingly experience trauma, poor health, family conflict, and residential instability. Additionally, incarcerated girls overwhelmingly reported experiencing significant levels of physical punishment, sexual abuse, and high levels of psychological distress; higher percentages of abuse were reported by girls of color. In the 2005 study titled *Detention Reform and Girls: Challenges and Solutions*, published by the Annie E. Casey Foundation,[3] Francine T. Sherman reports an overreliance on the juvenile justice system to deal with troubled and traumatized children.

Simply put, girls are being criminalized for their victimization.

Victimization and Incarceration

I met Jay, a sixteen-year-old young woman, in 2016 while serving as the director of a project in New York City. My major responsibilities included overseeing the connection of formerly incarcerated youth to employment, housing, and educational resources. While working with Jay, I learned that she had entered foster care at the age of three. She did not disclose much about her mother, but she informed me that her father was in prison. At the time of our encounter, Jay had been in foster care the majority of her life, and since entering care she had been in twenty foster care placements

Girls of Color."

2. Saar et al., *Sexual Abuse to Prison Pipeline*.

3. Sherman, *Detention Reform and Girls*.

before eventually being placed in a residential treatment center (RTC). An RTC group home is a specialized group home for children in foster care with psychological and behavioral disorders. I came to learn that Jay had been diagnosed with bipolar disorder and attention deficit hyperactivity disorder (ADHD). Jay also suffered from mild developmental and cognitive delay. This meant that although she was sixteen, she functioned as a twelve-year-old. Because of her delays, she had difficulty communicating and had poor self-regulation. This often made her a target for bullying by both youth and staff members at her group home, and as a result she would often have violent outbursts. At the time of our meeting, she had been committed to a psychiatric hospital twice and had been incarcerated six times. Unfortunately, for young women and girls involved in the criminal and juvenile justice systems, stories like Jay's is not unique.

In fact, also in 2016, fourteen-year-old Bresha Meadows made national news after she fatally shot her father while he was sleeping, in an act of self-defense. According to medical records, police reports, court documents, and testimonies from relatives and neighbors, Bresha and her family had endured years of physical, emotional, and mental abuse by him. In fact, just two months before the incident, Bresha had run away to her aunt's house because her father had threatened to kill the whole family. According to Bresha's aunt, a police officer who worked with victims of domestic violence, both the police department and child protective services were aware of the abuse but did little to help—all of which is said to have driven Bresha to take matters into her own hands. Bresha was charged with aggravated murder, and if convicted, was at risk of serving life behind bars. Fortunately for Bresha, she received the support of major organizers who rallied for her to be viewed as a victim of domestic violence, and her case received national attention. Ultimately, as a result of the national support, her sentence was reduced to juvenile involuntary manslaughter, and she was sentenced to one year in juvenile detention, six months at a mental health facility, and two years of probation. She was released in 2018, and when she turns eighteen, her record will be sealed and expunged. Jay and Bresha's experiences reveal the prevalence of trauma as a result of adverse childhood experiences as well as the reality of a victimization-to-prison pipeline for vulnerable young women and girls.

Trauma and Adverse Childhood Experiences (ACES)

Adverse childhood experiences (ACEs) are stressful and traumatic events experienced during childhood and that lead to poor life outcomes. Further, a direct correlation has been found between ACEs and delinquent behaviors for justice-involved girls. Research has shown that the higher the ACEs score for children (scores range from 0 to 10), the greater their risk for chronic disease, mental illness, committing violence, and being victims of violence. Roughly 45 percent of girls in the juvenile justice system had experienced five or more ACEs. When compared to boys, girls have disproportionately reported having experienced complex and chronic trauma.[4] Dr. Judith Herman, esteemed physiatrist, researcher, and teacher, describes trauma as experiences or situations that are emotionally painful and distressing, and that overwhelm one's ability to cope, often leaving the person powerless. Trauma is typically outside the range of usual human experience. Complex trauma is exposure to multiple traumatic events. Consistent exposure to trauma has been found to literally change the shape and structure of the brain.[5] Some behavioral indicators of trauma can include acting out (with aggression or anger), withdrawal, sleep disturbance or nightmares, mood disturbances, self-destructive behavior and antisocial behavior—to name a few. Given this, unfortunately, the criminal and juvenile justice systems have proven ill-equipped to address specific and unique needs of young women and girls who have experienced trauma. And because of this, the justice system becomes a revolving door for girls, ultimately creating a pipeline for incarceration within adult facilities.

As a staunch advocate for justice-involved young women and girls, I have seen this firsthand. Two years ago, I was a member of an assessment team organized by the Women's Justice Institute (WJI), which works to promote the decarceration of women and girls by bridging critical gaps between policy and practice and by promoting gender-specific and responsive services. Under a project sponsored by the U.S. Department of Justice and the National Institute of Corrections (NIC), the WJI had won a contract to conduct the Gender Informed Practice Assessment (GIPA) at the largest women's prison in Illinois. As a member of the team, I was tasked with conducting interviews, focus groups, and surveys with correctional staff and inmates. During my time in this role, I visited a housing unit and

4. Sherman and Balck, *Gender Injustice*, 26.
5. Herman, *Trauma and Recovery*, 33–34.

met a young woman who, after expressing her grievances about the conditions of the prison, informed me that she had given the system fifteen years
of her life. At the time, the woman was only twenty-nine years old.

Black Girls and the Prison Nation

Dr. Beth E. Richie, author of *Arrested Justice: Black Women, Violence and
America's Prison Nation*, argues that the investment in incarceration and divestment from the social safety net in the US, has been particularly harmful
to Black women (and girls) in complex ways. When women (and girls) are
victims of violence and have records with law enforcement or social service
systems, their risk of being penalized for nonnormative incidences increases. Ritchie argues that Black women and girls are penalized because of the
tactics used by conservative politicians, and because the women's antiviolence movement addresses violence against women exclusively through law
enforcement, criminal justice legislation, and enforcement strategies. All
this helps to create and sustain a prison nation. "Prison nation" metaphorically describes the state's unwillingness to supply sufficient resources and
opportunities to uplift vulnerable and economically depressed groups. As
a result of this, the social agenda instead enforces law and order, reducing
community and state protection for women and girls.

For young women and girls living in a prison nation, the traumatic and
unhealthy social environments in which many of them live result in behaviors that are criminalized or are mishandled—or both—by other systems.
As a result, girls and young women enter the criminal and juvenile justice
systems. Once they are there, misguided processes pull them deeper into
systems not built to help, heal, or respond to their physical, developmental, emotional, psychological, spiritual needs—systems that often worsen
their situations. Additionally, these systems are built on structural gender
inequality and are particularly harsh on girls of color and LBQ/GNCT
(lesbian, bisexual, questioning/gender-nonconforming, transgender) girls.
These girls not only are unsafe in their homes but are also harmed by the
systems. Richie argues that in a prison nation, social issues are addressed by
criminalization, which has devastating consequences for Black women and
girls overall and for survivors of violence more specifically.

The Black Church as a Place of Safety

Young women and girls living in a prison nation are in crisis. And they have fallen victim to punitive criminal and juvenile justice systems incapable of meeting their needs. Despite this, the plights of young women and girls have been largely left out of criminal and juvenile justice discourse. What can best address neglected girls and women in the juvenile and criminal justice systems is a multitiered program of support, grounded in prevention, intervention, and community-based diversion programs which provide trauma-informed and gender-responsive rehabilitative spaces. Girls also need access to spaces that provide physical, psychological, and spiritual safety.

More than any other demographic, African American women participate in the Black church. Therefore they play a key role in the church's functionality, longevity, and sustainability. Because of this, Black churches have a moral and ethical obligation to be places of respite, refuge, and solace for African American women and girls who are in need of temporary relief, comfort, and safety. The Black church should create and promote a culture of safety that meets the physical, psychological, social, and spiritual needs of young women and girls who are living in a prison nation.

Pastors have a moral obligation to challenge and rethink traditional ways of doing theology in order to address contemporary issues. This will require pastors to critically examine how young women and girls are affected by Christian doctrine. In order to meet the spiritual needs of young women and girls who are suffering from the trauma of violence and involvement in the criminal and juvenile justice systems, pastors must promote a culture of safety in the Black church. Pastors must be grounded in the belief that God is concerned about the quality of life for young women and girls; pastors must reimagine atonement theories; and last, pastors must embrace an ethic of resistance, as Jesus did, in order to resist violence against African American women and girls in the church and in the society.

Faith communities have a legacy of providing safety for vulnerable populations. This is most evident in the sanctuary movement in the United States, when faith communities housed refugees who were fleeing the Central American civil war during the 1980s; as well as in the sanctuary for families movement, when women fleeing from intimate partner violence were provided shelter. These models of sanctuary provide a model of leadership for faith leaders today as they seek to create communities of safety for young women and girls impacted by violence and incarceration.

Employing a systems approach, faith leaders can also advocate for young women and girls by challenging criminal justice legislation and harsh sentencing policies on a legislative level; on an organizational level, they can challenge violent organizational culture; and on an individual level, they can provide one-on-one support and access to resources, not excluding adequate legal representation when necessary.

Although the Black church has historically been a site of sanctuary for African Americans fleeing White terror and oppression, the Black church has also been a site of internalized patriarchy, sexism, and sexual violence for African American women. However, incorporating a culture of safety allows the Black church to focus on redemption and transformation in order to work towards healing and wholeness for women and girls.

Creating a Culture of Safety in the Black Church

A culture of safety is defined as *"the product of individual and group values, attitudes, perceptions, competencies, and the patterns of behaviors that determine the commitments to and the style and proficiency of, an organization's health and safety management . . . characterized by communications founded on mutual trust, by shared perceptions of the importance of safety[,] and by the confidence in the efficacy or preventative measures."*[6] For young women and girls living in a prison nation, a culture of safety consists of psychological safety, social safety, and moral safety. Each component encompasses a sense of support, the establishment of healthy boundaries, tolerance of distress, healthy coping strategies, the association of new meaning to hurtful experiences, and a literal place that serves as protective space.

Psychological safety applies to an individual's self-efficacy. Self-efficacy is the ability to confidently have control over one's behaviors, motivation, and environment. Psychological safety also includes the ability to protect one's self from harm. Self-protection in this context includes the ability to develop healthy boundaries and to protect against those boundaries being crossed. A psychologically safe environment supports self-empowerment, positive self-esteem, authenticity, creativity, and spirituality.

Social safety entails interconnectedness, community, and a sense of belonging. A socially safe environment functions as a community predicated on support, care, mutuality, trust, and accountability. A socially safe environment acts as a therapeutic space that is nurturing, forgiving, and

6. Cox et al., "Trust Relations in High-Reliability Organizations."

tolerant, and that promotes mutual cooperation. For young women and girls, social safety provides a healing space that validates their experiences and offers communal support. Communal supports can include support groups, women's groups, for survivors of violence, prayer groups, and the like. Trust in one-on-one relationships can also serve as a supportive resource for women. Environments that lack social safety are characterized by undue or poorly delivered criticisms, judgment, breaches of confidentiality, and lack of support.

A morally safe environment is an environment where the values of the organization are reflected in the services it provides. A morally safe environment demands transparency, offers services that meet the needs of its clients, and promotes self-efficacy. For the Black church, a morally safe community looks like living out the mandates of Christ to serve "the least of these" and seeking justice. For young women and girls, a morally safe environment offers attentiveness to their specific needs and challenges. The best way to insure that young women and girls are getting their needs met is to listen to them and to allow them space to communicate their needs. Additionally a morally safe environment empowers girls and young women, and provides them resources to meet their own needs, supporting them as necessary.

Establishing a Referral Network

Another strategy for creating and promoting a culture of safety that meets the psychological, social, and spiritual needs of young women and girls impacted by the criminal and juvenile justice systems is to establish a comprehensive referral system. A referral system is "an institutional framework that connects various entities with well-defined and delineated mandates, responsibilities and powers into a network of cooperation"[7] with multiple partners. For example, the Black church can partner with government and community-based organizations, other faith-based institutions, medical institutions, foundations, and public and private organizations. The partnering organizations must be credible, with quality services and proven records of effective outcomes. Referred resources might include "physical safety and shelter, hotlines, legal, health, social services and psychosocial

---

7. United Nations Population Fund (UNFPA) et al., *Strengthening Health System Responses.*

counseling."[8] Another important component of a referral network is a unified data, tracking, and information-sharing system.

In order for the Black church to make effective referrals for young women and girls living in a prison nation, it has to do the following:

- Provide first-line support—being able to provide supportive, validating and nonjudgmental emotional and psychological support

- Assess the needs of young women and girls and develop a safety plan: Be able to understand the needs of women and girls and to recognize signs of immediate danger and trauma symptomatology. Use church resources or resources from the referral network to establish immediate physical safety

- Be knowledgeable about the existing referral system and services, and support young women and girls in identifying the best options: have established relationships with the stakeholders in the referral network.

Establishing a referral network is essential. But pastors can also impact policy through advocacy and community organizing.

An Ethic of Resistance

Pastors must embrace an ethic of resistance, as Jesus did, in order to resist violence against young women and girls in church and the larger society. Ethicist Traci West urges churches to become moral communities that practice truth telling and inclusivity. Moral communities also promote wholeness, and are responsive to violence inflicted on women and girls. Moral communities act strategically to foster communal and institutional change. This looks like "developing and incorporation rituals"[9] that resist violence and challenge patriarchal and sexist norms within the church and society. Such rituals can include litanies around resisting violence against women, prayer vigils, and services to spread awareness of violence and to honor survivors. If pastors are committed to following the mandates of Christ, they are morally obligated to seek justice for women and girls living in a prison nation. The current quality of life for many Black girls and young women, the truth of redemption, and the ethic of resistance point

8. Jennings, preparer. *Community of Practice in Building Referral Systems.*
9. West, *Wounds of the Spirit*, 200.

the way toward reconstructing our theology in order to create a culture of safety for girls and women within the Black church.

Conclusion

Young women and girls are the fastest-growing population entering the criminal and juvenile justice systems in the United States. And given the central role Black women play in the life of the Black church and the devastating impact of criminal and juvenile justice on the lives of young women and girls, Black churches have a moral and ethical obligation to be places of respite, refuge, and solace. They must create and promote a culture of safety that meets the psychological, social, and spiritual needs of women and girls living in a prison nation.

According to Traci West, a respite space is a "place to pause, however briefly, right in the midst of the unrelenting threat of violence."[10] A respite space can offer young women and girls a sense of belonging, validation, and safety. This will require clergy, prayer groups, and individual congregants to be empathetic and affirming while addressing violence in the church and society. For young women and girls, this establishes trust and fosters a supportive environment, which are both critical in the establishment of a respite space. Faith and spirituality are important components of resilience, and a respite space can continue to nurture that resilience as young women and girls navigate a prison nation. Also, incorporating a culture of safety allows the Black church to focus on redemption and transformation in order to work towards healing and wholeness.

I recently had the opportunity to talk with girls in a Close to Home program, a program that allows justice-involved youth to serve their sentences in community rather than in detention. As I engaged these youth, the youngest of them age fourteen, it was apparent that these girls were relegated to the margins, that these girls were overlooked, that these girls were violated, that these girls were sacrificed, that these girls were subjected to juvenile justice policies with harmful racial and gender consequences. But it was also apparent that these girls were resilient, that these girls were brilliant, that these girls were wise, that these girls had an indomitable will to live, and that these girls—our girls—were sacred. And, I "saw" them. And, I believed them. And, I affirmed their existence. And they were beautiful.

10. Ibid., 178.

7

Creating Circles of Peace

*Mindfulness as a Pastoral Response to Health,
Education, and Violence in the Black Community*

Marsha Thomas

For the entire year that I was in the fourth grade I was terrorized by a girl in my class, also named Marsha. How embarrassing is that? She was bigger, stronger, and definitely more streetwise than I ever hoped or even wanted to be. I never quite figured out why she didn't like me, but every day she would jeer at me across the classroom. With her knuckles keenly accentuated by her closed fist, Muscular Marsha would tap the area under her eyes—first the right then the left—while she mouthed the words, "See you at 3:15!" She seemed to derive pure pleasure from seeing how terrified I was as I anticipated being annihilated before I even left the school grounds at the end of the day.

My parents were the original pacifists. My two sisters and I probably got two spankings among us the whole time we were growing up! And, unlike many of my friends' parents, mama and daddy never instructed me to fight back. So, no matter how threatening the *other* Marsha became, no matter how afraid I was, my daily strategy was to appeal to what I hoped existed deep down inside of her—even the smallest kernel of decency and compassion. I utilized every oratorical technique I could muster to try and convince Mean Marsha that beating me up would not benefit her in the least; and that, in fact, it ran counter to the goodness that I *knew* was at the core of her very being.

This sappy monologue continued for the entire school year and, undoubtedly, Massive Marsha became bored out of her mind listening to my philosophical, you're so-much-better-than-this speeches. Eventually (which seemed like an eternity), she just left me alone. And, here is the amazing thing. Not once during that whole time did she ever actually beat me up. In fact, she never even laid a hand on me. But for months I was completely terrorized and traumatized by the constant mental and emotional violence inflicted by this ten-year-old bully. Little did I know at the time that I was a peacebuilder-in-training.

Have you ever said to yourself, "I'm no Martin Luther King Jr. or Mother Teresa, but I want to do *something* to help bring peace to the world!" If so, you have the heart of a peacebuilder! The good news is that you don't need a Nobel Peace Prize to begin the important work of peacebuilding. You don't even need celebrity status, wealth, a degree, or a title. All you need is intention, an open heart, and a willingness to put your words into action. Ps 34:14 says, "Depart from evil, and do good; seek peace, and pursue it."[1]

The nightly news vividly documents unspeakable violence both foreign and domestic. Sadly, gang wars, carjackings, robberies, murders of children, and domestic abuse are all right here, in our faces, up close and personal. But as much as we would like to place the blame of violence out there in the world, on someone else, Thich Nhat Hanh, writer, poet, and Buddhist monk says in his book *Creating True Peace* that "all of us can practice nonviolence. We begin by recognizing that, in the depths of our consciousness, we have both the seeds of compassion and the seeds of violence." Everyone, at one time or another, can experience feelings of anger, fear, insecurity, and the pain of being disrespected. Our deep emotional and psychological wounds harbor those seeds of which Hanh spoke and, when tended and watered, they become the root of all the violence out there.[2]

Hurt people hurt others. And very often, hurt people hurt themselves, as well. For some, the wounds are so deep that it may seem to them that the only outlets for their anger, rage, or frustration are putting a fist through a wall or, worse yet, a bullet into someone's head, or engaging in any of a wide range of self-destructive behaviors. Truly, those of us who

---

1. Ps 34:14 (NRSV).
2. Nhat Hanh, *Creating True Peace*, 1–2.

are peacebuilders-in-training cannot bring healing and wholeness to a hurting world if we have not yet found our own inner healing. If we want peace "out there," we must make the decision again and again to actively seek peace and happiness within. Imagine what the world would be like if every adult reset the compass of our lives and were guided by kindness and compassion in all that we did?

In order for us to begin to counteract and heal the violence that exists in our communities and in the world, we must become aware of the painful places within ourselves that harbor those seeds of violence. Anger can arise from many different sources: e.g., from feelings of helplessness, feelings of powerlessness, perceived and real discrimination, poverty, and other challenging and humiliating life circumstances. Anger can also be the result of acts of violence and anger directed toward us at any point in our lives. Over time and without intervention, this cycle of violence and anger can take a huge toll on our overall health and well-being; and our capacity for experiencing deep satisfaction, happiness, joy, and peace.

Just before graduating from seminary in 1988, I would learn that I harbored a seed of violence that was as destructive as anger. Suddenly, I lost the hearing in my right ear, and after a series of tests I received a misdiagnosis of multiple sclerosis. Not one of the seven University of Chicago physicians or other health professionals who examined, tested, probed, and cat-scanned me ever asked, "What's going on in your life?"

The symptoms I experienced were my body's way of sending me an unmistakable message which prompted me to do some serious self-reflection about what was *really* going on in my life. I realized I was totally stressed out! At that moment, I gained a healthy respect for what stress could do to my body, and I immediately began to explore ways to begin to turn things around. I evaluated the situations and the people in my life, and took appropriate action to either "edit or delete!" I became deeply curious about the ways my faith in God's healing power, combined with yoga, progressive relaxation, meditation, and commitment to live in the present moment could help reduce my stress and empower me to live a healthier, more peace-filled life. That was the beginning of my interest in and commitment to learning as much as I could about holistic health and the mind, body, spirit connection.

Over the next year I became a certified yoga instructor, modified my diet, and began exploring Eastern meditation practices. My life changed for the better, and I am still reaping the benefits of those practices to this day.

As I began to research stress-reduction techniques, I discovered the work that Jon Kabat-Zinn, PhD, began in 1979, when he started the Stress Reduction and Relaxation Program as a pilot project at the University of Massachusetts Medical Center. The participants in his eight-week course were referred by physicians and other healthcare providers for help coping with all kinds of illnesses—heart disease, cancer, AIDS, chronic pain, irritable bowel syndrome, skin problems, and chronic anxiety and panic—among other diagnoses. Since his stress-reduction program was based on the principles and practices of Buddhist meditation, he wondered if people would come to his program for help.

But it's now forty years later, and the practice of mindfulness has gained worldwide acceptance because studies show that people who practice mindfulness experience a reduction in symptoms; and they tend to become more accepting of themselves and their limitations; more confident in their ability to handle physical and emotional pain; and less anxious, depressed, and angry. They are able to handle the entire range of life experiences much more skillfully.

Kabat-Zinn describes mindfulness this way: "Mindfulness means paying attention in a particular way: on purpose, in the present moment, and non-judgmentally. This kind of attention nurtures greater awareness, clarity, and acceptance of the present-moment reality. It wakes us up to the fact that our lives unfold only in moments. If we are not fully present for many of those moments, we may not only miss what is most valuable in our lives but also fail to realize the richness and the depth of our possibilities for growth and transformation."[3]

Chronic stress is the result of unrelenting assaults on our mind, body, and spirit, and can cause serious problems such as headaches, muscle aches and pains, sleeplessness, and eating disorders—to name a few. When stress is high and we are not functioning at our best, our inability to deal with life's daily demands creates the conditions for violence to be directed "out there" or inward toward ourselves—or both! When stress is not managed well, many of us turn to negative ways of trying to cope. We overeat, drink too much alcohol, use illegal drugs, abuse prescription drugs, and engage in risky sexual behaviors. These are just a few of the ways that we "water the seeds of violence" within ourselves.

"Because the roots of toxic stress lie deep in the nervous system, we need tools that go beyond the conceptual mind to directly target that

3. Kabat-Zinn, *Wherever You Go, There You Are*, 4.

system. To transform our habitual responses, we need to regularly practice our skills when we are not in 'fight-flight-freeze mode.'"[4]

Practicing mindfulness was a health-saving vehicle for me at a time when highly trained doctors didn't have a clue about what was wrong with me. If I had followed the path of traditional medicine, I would no doubt eventually have been prescribed medication for a disease that I didn't have. Mindfulness was free, effective, and without side effects. Misconceptions about the practice of mindfulness meditation, as well as knee-jerk reactions to the term, can serve as unfortunate barriers to folks in the Black community having access to unconventional approaches that can lead to stress reduction, calm, emotional balance, impulse control, focus, resilience, heartfulness, and compassion.

One important thing to remember is that mindfulness is not a religion. While it is true that mindfulness meditation has its roots in Eastern spirituality, mindfulness is a secular practice that has no connection to any established religion or deity. Mindfulness and prayer are not religions but practices that can help us move through life with a greater sense of awareness, purpose, grounding, and connectedness.

Ten years ago at the invitation of a colleague, I developed a program called Creating Circles of Peace, in response to the pervasive gang violence in the African American community of Roseland on the South Side of Chicago. My vision was that we would provide a safe place for adults, parents, and parents-to-be, regardless of faith tradition, to gather together to think, pray, and "hold space" for each other as we shared our stories and our feelings about how violence had impacted our lives. After all, how could we ask our youth to stop the violence if we hadn't yet done the inner work necessary to heal the wounds from our own experiences of violence?"

In order for us to create circles of peace we must first shine the light of inquiry on our inner conflicts, because this is the only place where we can truly effect change. As we become more peaceable, members of our families will experience a new environment of calm and respect. And, as individual members of our families become happier and more respectful to each other, that will manifest in healthier communities where cooperation and respect are the order of the day. The desired result will be healthy, loving communities contributing in their own ways to peace in the world.

My hope was that along with other components of my program, mindfulness could be introduced as a way to help create and maintain an

---

4 "Why Mindfulness Is Needed in Education."

environment of peace and resilience in the lives of Roseland residents de-spite the extremely challenging and seemingly hopeless conditions under which they lived.

Unfortunately, my program went nowhere. To this day, I wonder if the local pastor in charge of the various peace initiatives in that community rejected my program because he saw the word meditation as heresy op-posed to his Christian principles and practices. That kind of close-minded, fear-based response serves only to limit the possibilities of greater collec-tive peace, health, and wholeness.

The pastor's rejection of a practice that had helped me so tremen-dously was a wake-up call that *semantics matter*! It suddenly became clear why those involved in the work of mindfulness in this country almost forty years ago began to secularize the practice by dropping the word *meditation*. As a result of the secularization, a gradual shift in perception has swung the door open for millions of everyday folk and professionals around the world in fields such as education, business, medicine, sports, psychology, and, yes, even religion, to reap enormous benefits from the practice of mindfulness.

Just as in the Roseland community in Chicago ten years ago, today, there are thousands upon thousands of mothers and fathers and aunts and uncles and grandparents and other caretakers in communities of color who deal with the seemingly never-ending struggles of daily life, which result in unbelievable stressors adversely affecting their minds, bodies, and spirits.

Unfortunately, adults are not the only ones adversely affected. Too many of our children are troubled and traumatized! And, not only do our Black and Brown children have to deal with adversity at home, but they also experience overt and covert racism at school—or at the very least cultural insensitivity on the part of teachers who may be ignorant of the circumstances of our kids' lives. Their hardships, difficulties, and danger-ous surroundings affect not only their ability to focus and learn but their very ability to act in socially responsible and acceptable ways in the school environment and toward their peers.

Cynthia Mendoza, of brownmamas.com/, writes: "A report in *Social Science & Medicine* says that young people who experience racism or racist treatment are more likely to struggle with mental health issues such as de-pression and anxiety both as children and later as teens. The lead researcher in that report stated that 'the review showed there are strong and consistent relationships between racial discrimination and a range of detrimental health outcomes such as low self-esteem, reduced resilience, increased behavior problems and lower levels of well-being."[5]

All of these factors make it extremely hard for a child growing in poverty to achieve academic and social success. That is not to say that success in school or life is impossible. It does mean, however, that educators and parents must take specific actions to help their less-advantaged students fulfill their potential.[6]

Many of our children are angry and don't know why; or if they know why, they have no idea what to do with those emotions. Mindfulness gives them a way to become aware of those emotions, to be told that it is okay to have angry emotions, and then to practice putting space between feeling those emotions and reacting to them in ways that won't cause harm to themselves or others. We've all heard the phrase, "Take a deep breath before you do something you'll regret!" If you've ever followed that sage advice, you were practicing mindfulness!

So, the question is, what tools and strategies do we need to provide to our children to help them deal with the effects of all the stressful things that are going on around them at home, at school, and elsewhere?

Megan Cowan, cofounder of Mindful Schools, writes, "Just as it is good for children to move to expend and release energy, it is also good for them to practice stillness. It supports focus, self-awareness and impulse control. When children deliberately sit in stillness and don't respond to every urge to move, they are building the critical skills of body regulation, resilience and choice around when to act and when not to."[7]

Without specific instruction in cultivating resilience, focus, and body regulation, our Black and Brown kids cope with what life has thrown at them in the only ways they know how: with resistance, anger, and rage; by acting out, disrespecting adults, bullying peers, joining gangs, doing drugs, and worse. They deserve more from us! Just as they are taught reading, writing, and arithmetic, our children need and deserve social-emotional intervention at the earliest possible age. We owe them intentional and consistent instruction and support in developing social skills, in learning to recognize and accept their emotions, and in training their minds not to react to every situation or internal or external stimulus. This is not psychobabble. These are serious survival tools.

5. Mendoza, "Mindful Meditation Should Be Required for Black Kids."

6. See Jensen, *Teaching with Poverty in Mind.*

7. Cowan, "Role of Stillness in Mindfulness."

Knowing their history is certainly another critical part of their training. They need to learn from role models whose lives speak to the incredible things that a trained and disciplined mind can accomplish. For example, Nelson Mandela, one of the most well-known and beloved leaders of South Africa, and an enduring model of resilience, named this poem from the Victorian era as one of the elements that helped him survive twenty-seven years in prison.[8]

Invictus[9]
by William Ernest Henley

Out of the night that covers me,
Black as the pit from pole to pole,
I thank whatever gods may be
For my unconquerable soul.

In the fell clutch of circumstance
I have not winced nor cried aloud.
Under the bludgeonings of chance
My head is bloody, but unbowed.

Beyond this place of wrath and tears
Looms but the Horror of the shade,
And yet the menace of the years
Finds and shall find me unafraid.

It matters not how strait the gate,
How charged with punishments the scroll,
I am the master of my fate,
I am the captain of my soul.

As Peter Maxwell notes, "According to people closest to him, Mandela often recited this poem from memory when he felt low or lost. During his long incarceration, whenever he was permitted, he wrote and reread this piece of literature to boost his spirit, and to keep his mind active. He shared this poem with his fellow inmates whenever possible."

8. Maxwell, "How Did Nelson Mandela Survive 27 years in Prison?"
9. Henley, "Invictus" (https://www.poetryfoundation.org/poems/51642/invictus).

Pema Chödrön offers this insight: "Meditation is about seeing clearly the body that we have, the mind that we have, the domestic situation that we have, the job that we have, and the people who are in our lives. It's about seeing how we react to all these things. It's seeing our emotions and thoughts just as they are right now, in this very moment, in this very room, on this very seat. It's about not trying to make them go away, not trying to become better than we are, but just seeing clearly with precision and gentleness."[10] The perpetuation in the Black community of the stigma around Eastern-inspired rituals is not in our best interest emotionally, physically, or spiritually. Learning to be in the present moment via mindfulness practices can help adults as well as children put critical space between anger and potentially negative responses to that emotion, and can mitigate the devastating effects of stress on our bodies—as evidenced by the well-documented work of John Kabat-Zinn and anecdotally by myself, my clients, and many others in the mindfulness community.

Mindfulness strategies taught very early in life could have important implications for African American individuals, families, and communities if those strategies are taught very early in life. What are murder, rape, and robbery but anger, hopelessness, desperation, and bullying—on steroids? Believe me, I am not ignorant of the reality that many factors contribute to the hurtful and horrific behaviors in some people; but what we are talking about here is offering additional tools to help everyone in communities of color to better cope with the stresses of life, and we are offering options for responses other than violence to oneself or others.

One of the most important things I've done with my retirement time and energy has been to work at an elementary school in Indianapolis as an instructional assistant in a special education classroom. We are an International Baccalaureate School—kindergarten through fifth grade—serving a racially and culturally diverse population. Our entire school district is very supportive of neuroscience education for staff and of social-emotional learning practices for our kids. My awesome and supportive principal didn't hesitate to give me the go-ahead when I approached her about teaching the Mindful Schools Curriculum after I had completed the six-week online course.

Mindfulness has consistently gained traction over the last decade as a way to teach our children strategies that help them to become more focused, calm, and able to make better decisions. And school administrators

10. Chödrön, *Wisdom of No Escape*, 16.

have become more aware through cultural responsivity and implicit bias trainings that they need to change their perspectives and approaches to the behaviors and attitudes of our Black and Brown children. They need to find responses other than school suspensions, which, in many school districts occur for Black and Brown children at rates three to four times higher than their state's average for all students.[11]

Last semester I offered the Mindful Schools Curriculum to a class of thirty fourth graders and to a class of twenty-eight kindergartners. In our twice-weekly, sixteen-session Mindful Schools series, I taught the children to make the connection that mindfulness can help them to be more aware of their emotions, their physical indicators and their responses to various emotions. With each session, we increased our time of silent mindful breathing—starting at thirty seconds and working our way up to five minutes. All the while we were training the mind to focus on the breath, which is our base or anchor to the present moment. We also practiced mindfulness in areas of our daily life: e.g., eating, walking, seeing, listening, and interacting with kindness and compassion with friends on the playground. The children also practiced mindful responses to seeing someone being bullied and to being bullied themselves.

After just eight weeks, I observed that these students had a greater awareness, understanding, and ability to practice generosity, heartfulness, gratitude, kindness and caring on the playground, deep breathing, and mindful sitting. These practices are foundational to helping them develop focus, impulse control, and resilience. I also find it incredibly rewarding and fun to teach mindfulness to our kiddos on the autism spectrum. Of course they have varying capacities for stillness and quiet, but it is amazing what can happen with consistent practice and with no expectations of them to perform, achieve, or master anything—just to accept whatever appears in the present moment.

I have been inspired by our students to resurrect, renew, and refine my once-rejected Creating Circles of Peace program. (Delayed doesn't mean denied!) It is now called SuperKids for Peace. I am currently teaching the principles of peacebuilding in a third-grade classroom of twenty students— and they look forward with enthusiasm to our mindful time together twice a week. We will cover the following topics in our sessions over a sixteen-week period:

11. Loveless, "Racial Disparities in School Suspensions."

- Cultivating a Mindful Body
- Mindful Listening
- Sharing Mindfulness with My Family
- Twelve Qualities of a SuperKid for Peace
- Giving and Receiving Compliments
- Developing Resilience
- Getting in Touch with Emotions
- Inclusion and Being Your Best Self
- Kindness and Compassion
- SuperKids for Peace Affirmation and Peace Pledge
- Our Class Peace Project

Every topic is designed to teach peacebuilding through the lens and practice of mindfulness.

The question for some in this discussion might be, shouldn't we train our Black and Brown children to be warriors in the fight against discrimination and institutional racism, against those who blatantly, and without consequences, defy the truth that Black Lives Matter? Won't mindfulness make them soft at a time when we need to be angry for the cause?

The civil rights movement was led by Rev. Martin Luther King Jr., a man of incredible resilience and resolve who spoke of love and peace, and who embraced the path of nonviolent resistance. His approach demonstrated that anger at racial injustice and inequality could be channeled into productive and effective avenues for change. Resilience and nonviolence are qualities that can be cultivated, developed, and strengthened through challenging experiences mediated by conscious mindfulness practice. Hot tempers, competition, grasping, and trash-talking have had their chance. It's a new day, and there's a powerful movement afoot. Its name is mindfulness.

PART 2

*Caring for Body and Soul
in the Black Community*

8

Rethinking Interpretive Tools
for a Liberating Spiritual Care

Afri A. Atiba

The Discovery

I remember when I sat down in my first Introduction to Bible class in semi-nary. I had no idea what I would subsequently learn in that class, and others to follow. The professors were quite straight-faced and serious when they would say such things as Moses didn't write the first five books of the Bible, and there are three Isaiahs. The only students that seemed to have alarmed looks on their faces were the African American students, of which I was one. However, I was intrigued by the information, and I wanted to know more about the Holy Scriptures. Most of my fellow Black students began to shut down: they couldn't hear more of what they deemed as the desecration of the Word of God. I, on the other hand, decided to continue studying the word in this manner, with my eyes wide open, thinking that this might be the key to a better understanding of who God was or was not.

I took every Bible class that was offered, Old and New Testament, and I began to study the languages, and to my surprise, I discovered that I had been bamboozled, hoodwinked, and flat-out lied to. I learned that the Scriptures did not say exactly what we thought they said, and that translators had taken, or been given, the first opportunity to interpret what certain words, phases, and even whole stories meant. I was flabbergasted, as I learned who wrote the Scriptures, when they were written, what their sources were, and what types of literature were contained in them. It didn't stop there, I learned about the culture, the history, and mind-sets of the biblical writers. The most intriguing information was hermeneutics: simply put, who did the interpreting and declared what the Scriptures meant. All this learning was the key to my liberation.

I believed that learning to read the Bible critically and understanding hermeneutics would liberate not only me but the African American Christian community as well. The surprise element was that this type of Bible reading would also change my theology.

The Issue in the Practice of Ministry

Pastors and Bible teachers in a large number of African American churches have primarily clung to traditional interpretations of the biblical text. These interpretations are either literal or conservative reads handed down by theologians of past generations. Even though these interpretations have some value in the context of denominational beliefs, they can also conflict with contemporary reality. Although pastors, Bible teachers, and laypersons have interpreted biblical texts in accordance with their spiritual, cultural, and social context, given the state of the African American church, pastors, teachers, and laypeople need additional tools to challenge some traditional meanings oppressive to individual African Americans and to African American communities. Taking part in critical Bible study, not in the sense that it criticizes the Bible, but in the sense that it carefully and deliberately engages the text, will help African Americans ascertain meaning that can free them to interpret text for contemporary situations.[1] Even some seminary-trained African American pastors are perplexed about how to challenge traditional interpretations of biblical texts. I contend that an interpretive bridge is needed to connect critical biblical scholarship to ecclesial Bible study.

An interpretive bridge between academic biblical scholarship and churches can be particularly liberating in congregations with parishioners who are racially or economically marginalized, or both. Some marginalized populations have little access to scholarly and intellectual resources, which can limit their ability to interpret the Bible in ways that allow them

1. Brown, *What They Don't Tell You*, 5.

to conceptually extract meaning from more than a literal read. The Bible plays an important role in the lives of marginalized Christian groups, and I am convinced that it is precisely the inability to critically interpret Scripture, that has contributed to keeping numerous minorities on the margins of society.[2] Moreover, African Americans' interpretations of the Bible not only contribute to marginalization but also in many ways can be deemed self-detrimental. Such interpretations and literal reads of the Bible have contributed and continue to contribute to the internalization of racism, sexism, and homophobia in Black churches.[3] Many minorities fail to understand how the Bible itself is often used to marginalize them. A literal understanding that the Bible is the Word of God that liberates all its readers is, in my opinion, a serious misunderstanding. Minority communities, chiefly African American communities, need resources that will assist them in understanding the Bible within its historical, literary, and current theological context.

Historical and Sociological Context: The African American Church

African American Christian education, which includes the study and interpretation of the Bible, was rooted in racism. Long before the emancipation of slaves in 1863 White slave owners realized that Christian education for Blacks was contrary to the dominant views of chattel slavery. A baptized person during this time would potentially or theoretically have had the cause to claim authority and freedom to live and grow within their Christian family. Many slave owners saw a threat to their dominance in this and so sought to make "Christian education a means to the end of maintaining the institution of slavery and placating the conscience of the church."[4] Grant Shockley states that slave owning Bible teachers took out, rearranged, or phased out biblical texts with "freedom" implications.[5] Most

2. Weems, "Reading Her Way through the Struggle," in *Stony the Road We Trod*, 57–77. Weems starts her compelling argument stating that even though marginalized groups regard the Bible as a meaningful resource, it is often used to reinforce their marginalization. She concludes with the point that marginalized readers have to restore the voices of the oppressed in the kingdom of God by resisting "those elements of tradition that have sought, even in the name of revelation, to diminish their humanity."

3. I am using Black Church and African American Church interchangeably.

4. Shockley et al., "Christian Education and the Black Church," 8.

5. Ibid, 8.

illiterate Blacks had little understanding of how they were being manipulated with the Bible. When the slaves heard their owners' interpretations of the biblical text, they heard justification of slavery.

Because slaves were not allowed to learn to read, they relied on these aural interpretations given to them through Bible reading or sermons from the slave masters. The slaves in turn memorized portions they felt were beneficial for them and rejected others that they felt were not. African Americans appropriated scriptures, unconsciously adopting a "reader response" biblical hermeneutic.[6] If this had not been the case, Eph 6:5 — "servants be obedient to them that are your masters . . ." — would have been adhered to as all other literal interpretations of the Scripture; however, Blacks like Howard Thurman's grandmother understood Eph 6:5 as not being the "Word of God."[7] Given the tools to read the text critically as a strategy for liberation, African Americans can become more aware of their own internalized racism, sexism, and heterosexism. Biblical authority today can be reassessed in light of these early African American liberationist readings.[8]

The resistances to critical biblical interpretation within the African American church today tend to take on two dimensions. The first dimension demonstrates interpretations that can lead to various forms of abuse, and the second dimension acknowledges the inability to link cultural experiences with the Scripture as a source of empowerment and agency. A study conducted in 2009 by the Pew Forum on Religion and Public Life revealed that 55 percent of African American Christians surveyed interpreted Scripture literally.[9] Such a high number of literal interpreters means that the traditional interpretations and understandings of the text continue, which can conflict with contemporary reality, and in some cases can be dangerous.

While visiting a neighborhood church, I observed a young man drag his very unhappy wife up to the altar after the pastor of the church had

6. Braxton, *No Longer Slaves*, 29. Braxton states, "Reader-response theory suggests that meaning does not reside solely in the text . . . [It] is a product that is created from the encounter between text and reader."

7. Thurman, *Jesus and the Disinherited*, 30–31.

8. Braxton, *No Longer Slaves*, 29.

9. Sahgal and Smith, "Religious Portrait of African-Americans," 1. In this article the analysis states that "among African-Americans with less than a high school education, nearly two-thirds (63%) are members of historically black churches, as are about the same number (60%) of African-Americans who are high school graduates. Among African-Americans who have completed college, however, fewer (53%) are members of historically black Protestant churches."

finished preaching that wives should obey their husbands. He declared that this is plainly stated in Eph 5:22, and that this is the Word of God and should be obeyed. It was obvious from the look on the woman's face that she had had a rough night with her husband and had no desire to be in church with him, let alone to be dragged down the aisle to the altar. I suspected abuse, yet the pastor had no regard for the woman's distressed demeanor. It was the Word of God, and she must submit to her husband's wishes regardless. Instances like these point to the dangers of having a limited understanding of a critical biblical analysis.

Second, because most African Americans traditionally use only a literal reading of the Bible, they are not aware of the agency their community has to interpret scriptures from their own cultural experiences. They also do not understand how traditional biblical interpretations have influenced their responses to societal issues. For instance, regarding homosexuality, a broad-based coalition of gay-rights organizations and homosexual advocacy groups reported in 1994 that 1.51 percent of the total U.S. population, or 4.3 million Americans in total, identified as gay, lesbian, or bisexual.[10] In spite of this statistic, homophobia is still a big issue in the African American community and in the Black church. Overall, about four in ten African Americans (41 percent) thought that homosexuality should be accepted by society, while 46 percent said that homosexuality should be discouraged. By contrast, among the public overall, those who said that homosexuality should be accepted outnumbered those who said it should be discouraged (50 percent to 40 percent).[11] Since Black men are discriminated against by society in general, few Black men want to experience the extra discrimination of being gay. In addition, homosexuality is denounced by the majority of Black churches, which see it as a sin according to traditional interpretations of the biblical text. A combination of these factors causes many Black men to keep their sexual orientation a secret. Black men who have sex with men identify themselves as "on the down low" instead of labeling themselves as gay. In the vast majority of cases, the woman in the relationship is unaware of her partner's activities and continues to have, in many cases, dangerous, unprotected sex. This fact contributes to the statistic that African American women have the highest rates of AIDS in the United States. If the stigma of homosexuality is addressed in the church with the aid of

10. Gagnon et al., "National Health and Social Life Survey," 287.

11. Ibid., 146.

critical biblical interpretation, lives lost senselessly because of AIDS might be spared.

Even though some African American scholars such as Brown, Reems, and Braxton have challenged the universality of the historical-critical method and began to point to culturally specific reader-response interpretations, ecclesial-liturgical readers in African American communities have moved little from literal interpretations. This means that even though biblical scholarship, especially by Black scholars, is constantly improving, the majority of African American church communities do not benefit from it. This in turn thwarts the liberating efforts of the scholarly community. Thus, a bridge is needed to connect the two.

Theological Interpretative Implications

Exploring the Bible for any reason other than grounding one's faith, in any traditional setting, can be a touchy endeavor, particularly within the African American church. Why would anyone want to challenge God's word? Why would anyone need to? African American pastors and church leaders regard the Bible as a foundation for Christian theology and faith. Even though Christian leaders consider the Bible to be sacred text, not all of them give it the same regard when constructing their theologies.

Some believe the Bible is fundamentally the Word of God, that God is the author and therefore the Bible has no flaws; it is inerrant—completely without error. This interpretive approach is mainly found in minority and evangelical churches, leading to more rigid, exclusive theologies. Others take a more modern approach to the biblical text, believing that it is the product of humans, and that even as a holy document it still can contain errors and contradictions. Those with this more modern approach tend to have more liberal theologies. Several mainline denominations fall into this category. Finally, there are those who regard the Bible minimally, using it only to support the theology or practices they adhere to. This approach can be found in some New Age Christian congregations.[12] Regardless of what approach is taken, Christians have to understand that all Scripture is given its meaning by readers and communities of readers, and that no scripture has one static, fixed, or rigid interpretation.

Stephen Fowl is a Christian theologian who argues for a new Christian interpretation of the Scriptures, and that such interpretations involve

12. Head, *Absolute Beginner's Guide to the Bible*, 16–17.

a complex interaction of Christian convictions, practices, and concerns.[13] He discusses the need for Christian interpreters to give some place to the Spirit: first, by bearing witness to the work of the Spirit in the lives of others; and second, by recognizing that the Spirit in others causes friendship and spiritual bonds. This recognition, he states, brought about the inclusion of Gentiles to the early church in Acts 10–15, and it can be used to support the contemporary argument for the inclusion of homosexuals.[14] I agree with Fowl, as I do with Paul, who wrote to the Corinthians admonishing them to be ministers of a new covenant, "not of the letter, but of the Spirit; for the letter kills, but the Spirit gives life."[15] African Americans no longer need to accept interpretations that victimize them, but rather can interpret the Scriptures in a way that helps them build an inclusive community of liberating spiritual care.

Fowl also argues for an ad hoc use of professional biblical scholarship in relation to Christian interpretation. While he believes that it is useful he contends that it is not necessary, because not all of it will be equally useful all the time. I understand Fowl's point that not all biblical scholarship is useful,[16] but I think that a systematic approach to biblical criticism can be useful for minorities, particularly to those who have never been introduced to a critical biblical approach. Biblical criticism coupled with the Spirit of God, plus the convictions, practices, and concerns of African Americans will guide Black readers of the Bible toward interpretations that will liberate and empower them, and that will lead them to a theology of justice and inclusion.

Methods for Interpreting Scripture

The historical-critical method was introduced in the early part of the nineteenth century as a way of understanding the Bible within its own context and culture. Its main aim was to bridge the gap between ancient writings and modern readers.[17] The method entailed a process that focused on the historical and theological context of the scripture, in an attempt to draw meaning out of the text (exegesis). Eisegesis, its opposite, is reading meaning

13. Fowl, *Engaging Scripture*, 8.

14. Ibid, 121.

15. 2 Cor 3:6.

16. Fowl, *Engaging Scripture*, 179.

17. Segovia, "Bible as a Text in Cultures," 24.

into the text, and came to be understood as a misreading of the text.[18] The historical method eventually became understood as the scientific method of determining the one true, objective meaning of the text.

The historical-critical method lay unchallenged until the latter part of the twentieth century when literary critics began to focus on the text as text rather than historical "windows to the world,"[19] and ideological critics began to identify power relations in the text. Feminist and womanist scholars have challenged the gender constructions in the text, while liberationists, both Latina/o and Black, have challenged the effects of the political, social, and racial economy of biblical translations. The historical-critical method was shown to be highly patriarchal and middle-class in its approach, debunking the myth of the method's scientific objectivity.[20] However, in spite of century-long trends in scholarly circles, the historical-critical method of interpretation has yet to reach minority ecclesial circles.

In addition to the historical-critical method of biblical interpretation, scholars use several other methods for making meaning in the biblical text. They range from the traditional literary criticism to form criticism to source criticism and redaction methods to more contemporary feminist or womanist criticism, reader-response criticism, canonical criticism, postmodern criticism, and so on.

In light of the many new interpretive tools, the historical-critical method has come of age and is no longer the only method that renders truth of meaning. Given this phenomenon, I still suggest that the historical-critical method be used as the first of two methods in ecclesial settings, not because it renders so-called true meaning to the text, but because it gives readers a clearer understanding of where to start. This method helps answer basic questions such as Who were the original authors? When did they write this material? To whom were they writing? What was the sociopolitical background that helped to produce the text? All these questions are helpful in establishing differences between the text in its context and in our own. Thus, I start with the historical-critical method as one of my primary resources to aid in theological inquiry. Second, I include literary criticism; the basics of literary criticism give insight into what type of literature is being read. Knowing the type of literature starts the meaning process. One would not look for history in a parable, or law in love poetry,

18. Ibid., 25.

19. Ibid., 25.

20. Ibid., 26–27.

for instance. Brad Braxton recommends the "reader-response" method. With reader-response criticism comes "the rise of the importance of the reader in the creation of meaning[, which] entails the relative decline of the importance of the author as the sole arbiter of what the text really means."[21] Meaning now is coming not from the author only, but from the relationship and communication that happens between the author and readers. The Bible is a book full of all types of beautiful literature, but if one thinks that it is simply the Word from God, all of which is historically true, then all sorts of problems can emerge. Some of these problems feminist and womanist Bible critics have pointed out clearly in the text.[22] Considering the amount of sexism in the church, I also emphasize techniques for reading the biblical text from a feminist or womanist perspective.

I suggest these primary interpretive methods for several reasons. First, when one discovers the world of the writer of the text, the cultural context and social norms of the writer, it gives one knowledge of the writer's world, which sheds new light on the meaning of the text. The writer's world is often a world that is very different from the reader's. Thus, readers see the absurdity of projecting their modern assumptions onto the world of the biblical writers. Second, a basic understanding of what type of literature one is reading in the biblical text also lends the text new meaning. In addition, when students discover that some texts come from other sources in the ancient world, that in itself can liberate them from an exclusive, imperialistic understanding of the biblical text. Third, all Bible students should have the liberty to interpret biblical scripture from their own cultural and social contexts, in conjunction with their communities.[23]

In light of the social context that bears on the lives of minorities today, I believe that these hermeneutical tools can work in conjunction with other educational means that can help to strengthen our society. Education is the primary source for liberating minorities and giving power to the powerless. Education opens the door to all of the human sciences, physical sciences, history, diverse cultures, and so on. If Christian education does not align itself with secular education, the Church stands to continue to loose participants, mainly the youth. In particular, critical Bible study as a part of Christian education cannot be underestimated as a viable tool for the growth and life of the church. The biblical hermeneutical tools, which I

21. Braxton, *No Longer Slaves*, 30.

22. Trible, *Texts of Terror*; and Weems, *Battered Love*.

23. Braxton, *No Longer Slaves*, 30.

have proposed will equip people of faith with the agency to use Scripture as an instrument of liberation for the body, mind, and soul.

Conclusion—Interpretation for a Liberating Spiritual Care

Over the centuries biblical passages have been interpreted to reflect the culture and society that rendered the interpretation. In African American churches traditional biblical interpretations have directly corresponded to traditional responses that have helped to keep them within the margins. And as much as tradition has its place, traditional values and ethics have to be examined for indiscretions and discriminations. Every generation is gifted with the Scriptures and has the right to allow the Spirit of God to give fresh insights into the meaning. The biblical text should always be regarded as sacred, but its sacredness lies in the spirit of the interpretation and the power of the interpretation to produce a radical transformation of the human spirit.

In this era of #BlackLivesMatter, biblical interpretation within the Black church has to be addressed in a new way. Biblical scholars have had for decades the methodological tools to understand how sacred texts can be interpreted. Early scholars deemed that the historical-critical method was the best tool for getting at the most correct meaning. Literary scholars added that meaning could be inferred by the intent of the literature. Today, many postmodern biblical scholars contend that the author's meaning can never be completely ascertained, and that all meaning comes forth from the reader. I maintain that all these methods have interpretive value and should no longer belong solely to the academy but can become liberating tools in every Christian education program within the church, particularly within the African American church, where #BlackLivesMatter.

9

Breaking Bread and Breaking
the Silence in Black Churches

Let's Talk Mental Health

Rochelle Johnson

Introduction

Jesus left that place and went away to the district of Tyre and
Sidon. Just then a Canaanite woman from the region came out and
started shouting. "Have mercy, Lord, Son of David, my daughter
is tormented by a demon." But he did not answer her at all. And
his disciples came and urged him, saying, "send her away, for she
keeps shouting after us." He answered, "I was sent only to the lost
sheep of the house of Israel." But she came and knelt before him,
saying, "Lord, help me." He answered, "It is not fair to take the
children's food and throw it to the dogs." She said, "Yes, Lord, yet
even the dogs eat the crumbs that fall from their masters' table."
Then Jesus answered her, "Woman, great is your faith! Let it be
done for you as you wish." And her daughter was healed instantly.
(Matt 15:21–28, NRSV)

I recognize that placing this scripture in conversation with statistics on mental health and Black churches can be problematic. Especially since some clergy, without considering biological or environmental factors, equate mental health distress with demonic possession and spiritual weakness. This practice has done harm to some parishioners who believe wholeheartedly that their suffering isn't caused or influenced by biological or environmental factors, and as a result fail to seek professional help. Untreated mental health distress has devastating consequences for the mind, body, spirit, and community. In 2017, mental health again played an outsize role in the shooting deaths by police: 236 people, or nearly one in four of those shot, were described as experiencing some form of mental distress at the time of the encounter.[1] In this scripture the disciples' and Jesus's initial response mimic the literature findings on the church experience of some mentally distressed parishioners. The published results of an anonymous survey with 293 participants appeared in an article titled "Demon or Disorder: A Survey of Attitudes toward Mental Illness in the Christian Church." Analysis of the results found that while a majority of the mentally ill participants were accepted by the church, approximately 32.9 percent of mentally ill participants reported a negative interaction. Negative interactions included abandonment, equating mental illness with the work of demons, and suggesting that the mental disorder was the result of personal sin. Analysis of the data by gender found that women were significantly more likely than men to have their mental illness dismissed by the church or to be told not to take psychiatric medication. The negative influences of the antipsychiatry movement of the 1960s and 1970s are still found in the Christian community today.[2] Some mentally distressed parishioners experience a feeling of being invisible, silenced, and shamed in the church. In our scripture Jesus isn't positive, but eventually he uses his body in a helpful way: it functions as a catalyst for transformation and healing. A Kohutian perspective offers a theoretical framework within which we can conceptualize the healing aspects of the interaction between Jesus and the Canaanite woman. Kohut theorizes that during our childhood, if our relational experiences, with our caregivers are optimal, then they function as a selfobject need fulfillment and allow for the development of a healthy self. Kohut believed that these needs didn't cease as we matured,

1. Sullivan et al., "Nationwide, Police Shot and Killed Nearly 1000 People in 2017."
2. Stanford, "Demon or Disorder," 447.

but instead remained throughout our lifetime. Sheppard summarized five selfobject needs:

1. Mirroring: the need to feel recognized, affirmed, and confirmed as a whole person; the need to feel accepted and appreciated.

2. Idealizing: the need to experience oneself as an extension or part of a respected, strong, and admired person.

3. Kinship/twinship: the need to feel that one is essentially like those important in the developmental milieu.

4. Adversarial: need to oppose a benign force who will remain present, caring, and encouraging in the face of opposition.

5. Efficacy: the need to experience oneself capable of impacting one's environment.[3]

Later in this chapter, I will put four of these concepts in conversation with the scripture from Matthew. I am a former member of a Catholic church, located on the South Side of Chicago. It was not uncommon for the priest to end a service with an altar prayer during which he would say, "I bind up the spirit of depression." It is my hope that if a parishioner self-identifies as being in mental health distress, the clergyperson will resist the temptation to only "bind it up in the name of Jesus!" As a child, I attended Christian Youth Baptist Church on the South Side of Chicago. At the present time, I am a member in discernment serving at Covenant United Church of Christ in South Holland, Illinois. In between the Baptist church and my current place of worship, I have called a few other faith-based institutions my church home: an Apostolic Church of Christ church, a Church of God in Christ church, and a nondenominational church. So my experience with churches spiritualizing—and mishandling—mental health diagnoses isn't limited to the Catholic Church. If I had a dollar for every church sermon in which I witnessed the alleged instantaneous death of anxiety or depression at the altar, I would be rich. At the altar, a prescription was given without a full understanding of the person's or persons' experience. This is a risky practice because it leaves room for misinterpretation and faulty conclusions being drawn. Individuals and families left the altar with a false sense of security. In this chapter, I am arguing for Black clergy caregivers who are caring for mentally distressed parishioners to use a relational approach and

3. Sheppard, *Self, Culture, and Others*, 117–18.

collaborate with mental healthcare providers. According to the literature most churches, regardless of race, aren't equipped to handle mentally distressed people in a manner that will be effective long term. My focus is on Black churches for a three reasons:

1. Black people are overburdened by mental health distress due to oppression and a lack of resources.

2. Stigma related to mental illness is especially problematic among African Americans.[4]

3. Blacks are more likely than other groups to take their mental health concerns to a Black church.

Broadly speaking, traditional mainstream psychological or psychiatric literature will opt for the terms *mental illness* or *mental disorder*, in keeping with a psychomedical paradigm whereas critical social-scientific or user-centered literature tends toward the terms *mental health problem* or *mental distress*, reflecting a psychosocial paradigm.[5] I too subscribe to a psychosocial perspective that considers the impact that life events and oppression, in its many forms (racism, classism, sexism, genderism, heterosexism, ageism, and so forth) can have a person's mental health. I reject the notion that a suffering parishioner can be fully understood and cared for from a purely biological or purely spiritual perspective. This writer subscribes to a holistic care approach that considers biology, spirituality, social factors, and African American history. When the Canaanite woman sought help for her daughter's condition, historical and social factors were in the midst of her experience. Individuals like the Canaanite woman, such as low commoners, Gentile outsiders, traveling foreigners and the like, were to be avoided, ignored, or excluded.[6] When the disciples requested that she be "sent away," they were motivated by social and political norms. A relational approach creates space for engagement that allows for connection and understanding. A dual-disciplinary approach creates space for holistic care. The World Health Organization defines *mental health* as a state of well-being in which every individual realizes his or her own potential, can cope with the normal stresses of life, can work productively and fruitfully, and

4. Catalano et al., "Disproportionate Use of Psychiatric Emergency," 1667.

5. Coppock and Dunn, *Understanding Social Work Practice*, 8.

6. Gullotta, "Among Dogs and Disciples," 337.

is able to make a contribution to her or his community.[7] The church and the field of psychology share a common goal; the promotion of well-being.

Call and Response

Central to African American religious culture, the role of first respond-er is driven not only by biblical teachings but also by the long-standing history of racial discrimination and injustice in this country.[8] Therefore, it is understandable that a Black person or a Black family experiencing mental health distress would first express concern to the Black church. However, this poses a problem because mental health distress is beyond the scope of clergy training. On the flip side, mental healthcare providers, who are trained to deal with mental health distress, are not as well prepared to identify and address spiritual concerns. The church functioning without collaboration with mental healthcare professionals may serve as a barrier to effective mental healthcare. Mental healthcare professionals functioning without collaboration from Black clergy may serve as a barrier to effective mental healthcare for some Black people. Although advancements have occurred in the integration of spirituality and professional counseling, the actual practices have been limited in scope.[9] A recent survey of care, referral, and consultation practices among clergy in New York City found that a majority was not confident in its ability to deal with a variety of problems, including alcohol and drug abuse, depression, domestic violence, severe mental illness, and suicide. Over 21 percent of the clergy surveyed were Black. . . . Less than half the clergy surveyed had training in Clinical Pastoral education (CPE), and those who did tended to feel more competent in dealing with all types of problems.[10] However, despite how well-intentioned, in the absence of a collaboration between mental healthcare professionals and Black clergy, neither churches nor mental health agencies are equipped to provide effective long-term mental healthcare for parishioners in Black churches.

In addition, it is believed that because African Americans' mental ill-nesses go untreated or treated inadequately, their disease burden is greater

7. World Health Organization, *Mental Health*.

8. Trader-Leigh et al., *Understanding the Role*.

9. Frame et al., "Counseling African Americans," 19.

10. Moran et al., "Study of Pastoral Care," 263.

than that of White Americans.[11] A few years ago I had the pleasure of working with a seventeen-year-old young man I will call Jackson. He resided with his divorced mother in a mixed-income community. They attended a Baptist megachurch on the South Side of Chicago. The church congregation was predominately Black. Oftentimes he would report being hassled by other young men in the community for being a "nerd." Once he was physically assaulted, and in a separate incident he was robbed of his cell phone. In response to any boundary setting, Jackson would become physically aggressive, primarily directing his anger toward his mother. He had poor school attendance and utilized his paternal grandparents' credit cards without permission. Eventually his risky and aggressive behavior required inpatient care at a Chicagoland area psychiatric facility. Upon discharge he was referred to my office. Written on his discharge papers was a diagnosis of borderline personality disorder, psychotropic medication prescriptions, and a referral for outpatient psychotherapy and outpatient psychiatric care. The psychotherapeutic approach I used with Jackson included trauma-focused care, relational psychotherapy, and behavior management. He was clinically depressed and anxious, and his energies were being utilized to regulate his emotions. He reported feeling that he didn't have the ability to graduate from high school, nor did he believe that he was employable. Jackson's risky, aggressive, and isolative behaviors functioned to ease his emotional pain. In other words, with every swipe of the credit card, with every tantrum and act of rebellion, he was trying to feel better, raise self-esteem, and ease the pain of depression and anxiety. The risky and aggressive behaviors were a dysfunctional pattern that he needed help unlearning. His dysfunctional behaviors helped him regulate his emotions and work at resolving internal conflicts. The isolating behavior and suicidal thoughts provided an escape route from a life that at times felt overwhelming. During our first session, Jackson's mother reported seeking biblical counseling from a minister at the church. The counselor offered prayer and a Scripture reading but never mentioned psychotherapy as a treatment option. Later, when she reflected on that session, this angered Jackson's mother; she realized that the church wasn't equipped to care for her son. I worked with Jackson for about four years: we held individual sessions as well as family sessions with his grandparents and biological father. Most of our work focused on setting appropriate boundaries, establishing effective communication between caregivers, and working through Jackson's early childhood

11. Wang et al., "Recent Care of Common Mental Disorders," 289.

traumas (i.e., being separated from a parent at an early age, witnessi domestic violence, and living through his father's near-death experience). Eventually, he had more energy, his self-esteem improved, and he gained the necessary coping mechanisms to manage negative emotions in a way that would be effective in the long term and reduce potential harm to himself and his relationships. He began to contribute to the community in a more helpful way. He secured a job in retail, and within six months he was promoted to a manager's position. He was a spokesperson for two mental health workshops, sharing his story with community members. Lastly, he enrolled in a GED program. His relationship with his family (with his parents and grandparents) improved. Psychotherapy became an effective vehicle for change. A clergyperson who encounters an adolescent and their caregiver may not be informed about familial mental health history, community stressors, family dynamics, or emotional barriers. A church milieu isn't conducive to the type of interview that would gather such information. However, a mental health professional is trained to conduct a psychosocial assessment that would produce such information, and works in a more conducive environment. As it pertains to mental health, at best, a clergyperson may utilize their encounter to serve as a helpful selfobject that is internalized as an affirming, accepting, and strong person. A resource that is supportive and willing to utilize its resources to colabor with the parishioner. In addition, the clergyperson is equipped to address spiritual concerns that a mental health professional isn't trained to address.

Black Churches

According to Douglas, no single entity can be pointed to as the Black church. It is a diverse groupings of churches that reflects the rich complexity of the Black community. It is defined by its historical and social- cultural significance. Historically, it emerged as a form of resistance against White racial oppression.[12] Historically the role of the Black church and Black clergy has been to provide support to the Black community for mental healthcare services. Clergy are considered the first line of contact for mental healthcare services because of availability, accessibility, and trustworthiness.[13] This may contribute to the underutilization of the traditional mental healthcare system by Black parishioners. In addition, given that Black clergy are

12. Douglas, "Black and Blues," 113.
13. Allen et al., "Being Examples of the Flock," 11.

viewed as the first line of defense for mental health distress, their attitudes toward seeking professional help may help to determine whether a parishioner seeks professional help or not. Researchers in one study concluded that the following concerns impacted clergy decision whether or not to refer parishioners to mental health providers or not: (1) If clergy shared the same values as the mental healthcare professional, then clergy would refer; (2) if clergy trusted the mental healthcare professional, then clergy would refer; 3) finally, if clergy knew that their relationship with the mental healthcare provider was mutually beneficial—that is, if the mental healthcare professional would make referrals to clergy—then clergy would refer.[14]

Stigmatization

Black people are more reliant on faith in God and less reliant on seeking professional mental healthcare. The stronger their faith, the less likely they are willing to admit experiencing negative emotions, or to seek professional help. This reluctance is born out of a fear of being perceived as spiritually weak for needing secular help.[15] Stigma, shame, or both keep to congregants from seeking help from a mental-health professional. Stigma is defined as a set of negative and often unfair beliefs that a society or group of people has about something.[16] In a study conducted by Cooper-Patrick et al., stigma was for Black patients a significant barrier to getting treatment For African Americans, the idea of seeking professional help is culturally unacceptable among family members and peers.[17]

Horrid History

Maude White Katz provides a catalog reference from a medical college in South Carolina that included this paragraph: "No place in the United States offers as great opportunities for the acquisition of medical knowledge, subjects being obtained from among the colored population in sufficient number for every purpose, and proper dissections carried on without

14. McMinn et al., "Psychologists Collaborating with Clergy," 567–68.

15. Davey and Watson, "Engaging African Americans in Therapy," 40.

16. Greenstein, "I Stop Stigma By . . ."

17. Cooper-Patrick et al., "Identification of Patient Attitudes," 435.

offending any individuals in the community."[18] This is just one example of a horrid practice in the medical field, which treated Black bodies like lab rats. So, it is understandable that Black Americans are less likely to use mental healthcare services. Interpersonal and social trust is an important influence on the relationship and interactions between a patient and a healthcare provider. It is more so important for non-White groups.[19] Having mental healthcare referrals readily available is one step in providing holistic pastoral care. However, equally if not more important is the relationship the clergy has established with the referral source. This alleviates some of the clergyperson's anxieties about a values conflict with the mental healthcare professional. Such a relationship also may alleviate some of the parishioners' anxiety about the mental healthcare professional as well. The recommendation that the parishioner see a mental healthcare professional will come across as more genuine if the clergyperson has a relationship with the secular provider. Second, the clergyperson can serve as a spiritual resource for the mental healthcare provider. Clergy should work with providers to make mental health services accessible and affordable. Clergypersons should ask agencies or private practice providers to offer a sliding scale to its membership. They could work to create an environment hospitable to their parishioners: i.e. invite the agency staff or private practice providers to visit the church and become familiar with Black church culture.

Relationship

"Have mercy on me, Lord, Son of David; my daughter is tormented by a demon" (Matt 15:22, NRSV). The Canaanite woman needed to be connected to someone she felt was stronger than herself. So she tried to connect with Jesus, a respected and admired person. Clergy are respected and admired members of the Black community. Parishioners experiencing mental distress and choosing to reach out to clergy may be hoping to connect to a stabilizing presence that they view as stronger than themselves. Clergy should know that more often than not just being fully present with a member can be healing. Clergy can create a holding environment in which they feel in sync with another human being; held, soothed with calming voice tones, and heard in a deep way. "[Jesus] answered, 'I was sent only to the lost sheep of the house of Israel.' But she came and knelt before him, saying, 'Lord, help

18. White Katz, "She Who Would Be Free—Resistance," 66.
19. Cooper-Patrick et al., "Identification of Patient Attitudes," 436.

me.' He answered, 'It is not fair to take the children's food and throw it to the dogs.' She said, Yes, Lord, yet even the dogs eat the crumbs that fall from their masters' table" (Matt 15:22, 24–27, NRSV). This verbal and physical exchange between Jesus and the Canaanite woman is a pivotal moment upon which the outcome is predicated. The woman is oppositional with Jesus, yet he functions as a "benign force" that remained physically present and in communication with her. Although, his words were probably not pleasing to the woman's ears, he communicated nonverbally that he cared by remaining physically present and continuing his verbal exchange with the woman. In other words, he remained in relationship with the woman. She was being adversarial with Jesus, yet he remained in dialogue with her. Walker-Barnes notes credible pastoral care for the StrongBlackWoman is that which does not avoid, minimize, rationalize, or otherwise dismiss her experience, but is willing to "sit with" the discomfort of the realities of racism, sexism, and classism.[20] Although, this chapter isn't specifically focused on the StrongBlackWoman, the message is applicable; credible care is marked by a willingness to remain in relationship despite the uncomfortable realities. It is not uncommon for persons experiencing mental distress to have poor interpersonal relationship functioning in other areas of life. This makes the relational experience with clergy or ministry leaders even more valuable. "Then Jesus answered her, 'Woman, great is your faith! Let it be done for you as you wish.' And her daughter was healed instantly." (Matt 15:26–28, NRSV). The Canaanite woman's engagement with Jesus was empowering: she experienced herself as capable of shifting Jesus's attention away from cultural norms and practices and toward her particular situation, thus meeting an Efficacy need. Mirroring occurred when Jesus recognized her personhood: she was not a dog; she was a "woman." Not only was she human, but she had great faith. I am not suggesting that mentally distressed persons or their caregivers need the clergyperson to sustain a healthy sense of self. But I am suggesting that when two or more human beings come together and a reciprocating encounter occurs, the opportunity is present for either person or both persons in that moment to function as a selfobject need. A coconstructed between space is created that has the potential to be healing. It's the relationship that heals, the relationship that heals, the relationship that heals.[21] The Canaanite woman was changed by her encounter with Jesus, and Jesus was changed as well. This experience

20. Walker-Barnes, *Too Heavy a Yoke*, 165.

21. Yalom, *Love's Executioner*, 91.

can be cobeneficial—an opportunity for both parties in an encounter to experience healing and growth.

Safe Space

In conclusion, Black churches have a unique opportunity to utilize their reputation as reliable resources to promote a holistic approach to mental health distress in the Black community. Such an approach promotes care for the whole self: mind, body and spirit; it promotes self-care and self-understanding. The Black church can create a safe space by breaking the silence on mental health distress, working to destigmatize mental health distress and making it acceptable to ask for professional help. Black churches can help parishioners attain long-term, effective solutions to mental health distress, not only by collaborating with mental health professionals, but also by establishing reciprocal relationships with these professionals.

how one transcends from their limitations and becomes one with their Father.

10

My Mind's Made Up

Barriers to Accessing Mental Health Services
for the African American Community

CHARLENE HILL

She walks into my office. She looks around. She settles into a chair. She waits. With a few questions from me she begins to share her story. She is like the kid first learning how to skate. But she is a natural, and I feel myself following her. She unfolds, sharing layers of her story and what brings her to my office. She wants to talk. She wants to unload her burden. She wants to be heard. She wants help. She wants resolution. Her story keeps spilling before me, natural and slow and coherent. I wish there were more time. I hate to cut her off. The hour is gone. She looks at me startled. And she asks what I have heard so many times: "So, Doc, am I crazy?" I would laugh except I can look in her eyes and tell she is serious. I instead censor my response. You are far from crazy. You are overdue for someone to hear your story. I look forward to working with you.

There are real barriers to African Americans seeking out and accessing mental healthcare. In this chapter I would like to discuss a few of those barriers.

Barrier #1—You Have to Be Crazy to See a Therapist

There is a perception in the Black community that you have to be really sick to seek help. It follows that if you seek mental healthcare, something is really wrong with you that is observable by others and needs fixing. You go to a therapist only when you have metaphorically driven off the road and you are headed for a cliff. At the brink of disaster, then and only then can we excuse you for seeing a shrink. There is no other reason to see a head doctor unless you clearly have big problems. By the time some have come to counseling, the problem is fairly complex, and there have been years of buildup.

Perception is very important to African Americans. I was once was at a sports game and I saw these White men dressed up in crazy outfits. I said to a friend, a brother would never be caught in such an outfit. My friend responded, no a brother is much too cool for that outfit. Because of our experience in America, image matters very much to African Americans. African Americans spend lots of time on how they look and even the car they drive. We may not have much else going for us, but we can look good. One client says her day is impacted by how she dresses.

The importance of image has been passed on to our youth. From my sessions with youth, I know that the concept of cool is very important to African American young people. I see youth who get into physical altercations. When we unpack how they ended up fighting, it often involves not wanting to be perceived as a punk. If someone approaches you in such a way, for image you have to fight because you image is at stake. Being cool also impacts how often a child may speak up in class for fear of being perceived as not cool. So it is no wonder many do not seek counseling because of the stigma associated with counseling as something reserved exclusively for crazy people.

However, seeking a mental health counselor is a form of self-care that allows one to see and hear one's self in an unbiased space. Someone outside of you listens, able to see your blind spots, and provides feedback. I love to say counselors are the front seat passenger, empowering the client to drive his or her own future with some pushing and prodding and sometimes making suggestions. The world we live in is complicated and stressful, and whether you need someone for a few months or years, it's okay. You don't have to be crazy before venturing to seek help.

Barrier #2—Our Faith Is Strong Enough to Heal Us of Anything

One day a church member came to me and she was clearly in psychological pain. She has been diagnosed as bipolar, and she takes her medicine regularly. Because she is consistent and sees her psychiatrist quarterly, she lives a better life, and she knows it. She recalls life before medicine and her life now with medicine. But she had been talking to her friends, and they told her that if she had enough faith, she wouldn't need medicine. Faith would heal her. They challenged her to try and trust God. She was already trying and trusting God, but they equated faith with not needing medicine. So she came to me asking for some way to fight back in a fight in which she had been defeated. Her question was more a plea than a question as she asked, do I have to stop taking my medicine? I encouraged her to stay on her medicine and to see God as giving her the knowledge to alleviate her struggles with the support of medicine. I affirmed that she was faithful, and that she had a chemical imbalance that warranted medical assistance.

A few years ago I heard a gospel artist share the healing story of her sister. She had a sister who needed glasses. Her eyesight was relatively poor, and so her sister's lenses were very thick. During one revival a preacher visited who claimed to have the gift of healing people with vision challenges. He announced his gift and instructed those who wanted to be healed to get in line. It seemed like a good time for this gospel artist's sister to get in line. He also collected their corrective ware because they would not be needing it after their healing. The preacher went through laying hands on each person in the line. When it was all over, the family of the nearly blind girl watched as she groped around trying to find her way back to her seat. When service was over, the mother of the girl told her to go get her glasses.

In some of our spiritual understandings is a belief that God can heal one instantaneously. In the gospel are references to God healing people because they had faith. If one can only have enough faith, then one can be healed. But it is a deep misunderstanding to attach healing solely to faith because it implies that those who are not healed do not have enough faith. I have ministered to people who have felt deeply hurt because they somehow blamed themselves for their own mental struggles.

Clearly instances of miraculous healings do happen. These are often exceptions and not the norms. There are instances where someone with stage 4 cancer is healed. These stories encourage our faith. And we embrace these stories. But this notion that healing happens at the command of one person whenever the person chooses to use it has been harmful to the church. It has been used to leave people with physical and mental challenges crippled.

We need to hear all stories as we garnish wisdom. Imagine that for every miracle story there are one hundred regular stories. It could be your story. Stories of people who need time to unfold, share, and slowly recover. Stories of people who have experienced unimaginable horrors that send them running. Stories of people who with faith can look back like the Sankofa bird to really be able to look forward to all the future holds for them.

Barrier #3—The Strong Black Race

I grew up hearing and seeing that my grandmother was a strong Black woman. She was a Thornton lady. She was the only daughter and youngest among nine children. She had had two husbands and I daresay some other men. Way before my time, I heard, she's been in a few fights but only in defense. She always had a penny, and she raised her four daughters and worked full time. I could go on and on about my grandmother, but mostly I want to say she was the epitome of a strong Black woman. She once said to me, your generation makes so much more money than I ever had and you have nothing to show for it. She had no luxuries, and she came out more than okay.

For African Americans, if being strong means you don't need counseling, than inherently we are implying that mental healthcare is for weak people. It is for the crazy people. It is for those who have been to war or raped. It is for those who have had really extreme experiences. But it is not for us who are the product of centuries of slavery, racism, oppression, and all kinds of evil heaped on, that was built into the foundation of America.

I remember one client explaining she almost lost her baby. She had been raised to act like a proper woman. So when she was ready to deliver her baby, she conducted herself as a proper woman. During the childbirth she was in immense pain, but she refused to scream. When she finally did start screaming, they realized that something was wrong. The doctor ended up giving her a C-section. Later, the doctor explained that if she had expressed her pain sooner, they would have known something was wrong sooner.

This lady's experience reminds me of how we have put obstacles between us and our mental health. We equate being strong with not showing vulnerability. I recall peers often saying, "That's what White women do." There was almost a sense of superiority that we could endure way more than our weak counterparts. We knew we were not White women, and we were much stronger. We should not cry. We should not wear our feelings on our sleeves or recognize that we are the lady on the table refusing to hollah. I have worked with countless African Americans who cannot cry because very early on they were given the message that the crying was not okay and is what weak people do.

Without taking anything away from our ancestors and what they had to do in their context, for African Americans today It takes incredible strength to talk about our experience in America. It takes incredible strength to bare one's soul to another. It takes incredible strength to pause and examine one's life. I think Marvin Gaye was on to something in his "Inner City Blues." There he sings that life makes him want to holler. "This ain't living," he sings, describing the world that is given to African Americans. The way I see it, if anybody should see a therapist, it's Black people.

Barrier #4—You Can't Let Your Left Hand Know What Your Right Hand Is Doing

I grew up with my mother using a lot of idioms, most of which I did not understand. But like parents who buy their children's clothing one size bigger to increase longevity, I grew into an understanding with time and age. There was this sense in my family that your business should be guarded, and to be careful who you shared pertinent information about yourself. There was a real distrust of anyone who wasn't family.

Because of our history, Blacks are often suspicious of Whites. And with the current Republican administration and public display of racist overtures, those sentiments of "us and them" and "they cannot be trusted" lurk like a demons constantly whispering in our ears. No matter how friendly and kind they are, there is a suspicion about their motives. And since the face of healthcare and mental healthcare is White, like the face of poverty is Black, there is a distrust of them. What will they do with my information? Could this come back to bite me in the face? What do they know about my struggles? What good is their book knowledge going to do me? Half of them are crazy. They can't tell me what to do; they don't have a clue. I been doing okay thus far; why talk about it now? Talking doesn't change anything.

There is a real distrust of the other in the Black community. For many years the pastor was that one trusted person, and even s/he has come under scrutiny. For Black people, trust is important and is gained through relationship. In our history people knew your people, and that said something about you. My grandmother was a Thornton, and those were strong people. My mother can go anywhere, and once she says my grandmother's name, it opens doors. Relationships are the bridge to trust among African Americans, and a counselor or outsider is perceived as a stranger and not worthy of sharing my personal business.

Furthermore, history has plenty of examples that provide a lens to why Blacks are distrustful and suspicious of others, especially of Whites and White institutions. For example, in the medical world we have not always been treated well. Famous studies include the Tuskegee syphilis experiment, conducted from 1932 until 1972. The purpose was to observe the natural progression of untreated syphilis in rural Alabama under the guise of providing free medical care to African American men. The 622 Black men were told the study was going to last six months, but it lasted forty years. After funding was lost, these Black men were never told that they were not being treated. The men infected with the disease were never told they had the disease, and none was treated with penicillin, even after the drug was found to be successful in treating syphilis. Instead they were told they were being treated for "bad blood," a catchall term for various medical conditions, including syphilis.[1]

As recently as 2010, the nonfiction book *The Immortal Life of Henrietta Lacks* is another example of the medical field's treatment of Black people. Henrietta Lacks's cells were used for research and commercial purposes unbeknownst to her family. While the medical field heralded that consent was not needed to use these cells, her cells had been used all over the world, gaining a notoriety, without her family knowing. Lacks's cells were unique: they could be kept alive because they kept dividing. Up until then cells

1. See Wikipedia, "Tuskegee Syphilis Experiment."

died within a few days. But her cells could divide multiple times without dying—hence the phrase "the immortal cells." The cells remaining alive allowed biomedical research breakthroughs including the polio vaccine. In the '70s, many of her cells became contaminated, so the family was sought out to supply additional cells, but still no mention was made to her family that her cells had been used.

Such occurrences in history have made African Americans suspicious of the other. We know that discrimination literally kills. We know that they don't really care about us. Just two years ago Ethel Easter in Houston, Texas, didn't like how her doctor was treating her and put a recorder in her hair. Later when she listened to the recording, she heard the staff making lewd comments about her. And so, African Americans are understandably suspect about who they can trust. In order for African Americans to place trust in someone, that person will need to have been inspected as if under a microscope. How often race has impacted the quality of care we receive sends chills throughout our communities. Therefore African Americans may well say that healthcare (including mental healthcare) doesn't work, or that medical professionals can't tell them something they don't already know.

I remember my graduate education. I could sense a large gap between my privileged classmates and me. There was so much I did not know. I found myself needing tutorial help with one of my classes. I wasn't even swimming but taking in large gulps of water. While White students gladly were getting tutoring, for me tutoring was for dummies. And so I never sought out tutoring. In graduate school, a Black, upwardly mobile professional woman observed I could use some tutoring and reached out to help me. Actually she insisted. So I did get to feel stupid. And for many Sundays, at Mrs. Loeseth's insistence, I showed up at her home. I did not want her help, but she insisted on giving it.

In graduate school, I could see that my peers had been exposed to a world I didn't even know existed. They were confident and sure of themselves while I was just honored to have made it in. They were asked their opinions and exercised their voices early on while I was taught to be quiet in the presence of adults and to speak when addressed. But in graduate school there was a whole new mode of operation for which I was not prepared. I knew that my peers had more even if I could not articulate what was that more. And I knew how hard it was to ask for help because it said something about me.

I learned in graduate school there is much I do not know, and it's okay to not know, but it's not okay to do nothing about what you do not know. Jesse Jackson says it well: "Democracy does not guarantee that all of us can dunk the ball. It guarantees all those can have the right to dribble. It assumes an even floor, an even playing field. And today, that even playing field is not there."[2] The truth is the playing field is not equal, through no fault of our own. Early on Blacks and White are socialized differently about the world and our space in the world. I was an above-average student, and I was experiencing the impact of race on my upbringing, which left me trying to catch up on the playing field.

When people have been put down in a society and devalued and described negatively, their egos are fragile, and many experiences they have may be perceived as slights against themselves; these slights are often real and sometimes perceived. African Americans are too busy to ask for help—too busy trying to survive and keeping up their guards in a racially hostile context. Among African Americans, asking for help—mental help, academic help, or any kind of help—is seen as weak and reflects negatively on the person seeking help. It would take me a decade to begin to shift my own understanding of help when I pursued another graduate degree, which yielded a much more positive experience. Asking for help was no longer a sign of weakness to me but a sign of strength. I was shocked when another White student shared with me and said that I asked the questions she was afraid to ask. I transformed from being the quiet kid to insisting I be heard. I wanted to learn, and I knew not knowing had nothing to do with my intellectual capabilities.

While there are many barriers to African Americans' receiving mental healthcare, more and more are seeking out help. Ironically, in this present Trump era, with despair encroaching, we are more in need of therapeutic spaces. The real irony is that if anybody needs the gentle presence of an empathic listener sage, it is Black people. African Americans were taken from their native land and treated horrifically both in America and in the Caribbean. They were packed on boats like sardines and let up for air after days of being chained underneath. When they were very sick, their bodies were tossed in the ocean; others willingly jumped overboard. Once on dry land they were improperly clothed, groped, and placed on auction blocks to be sold. The institution of slavery continued to get worse, mutating, over the

2. Jackson, interview by Henry Louis Gates Jr., on "The Two Nations of Black America."

generations. African Americans were robbed of their culture and treated as less than human beings. We were taken against our wills, we were put in inhumane conditions, we were stripped of any say-so over our bodies and our lives, we had our children taken from us, and we were whipped for any insubordination. If we showed any self-agency, we received physical punishments—including but not limited to having body parts cut off, experiencing whippings, and being left for dead. We were raped and made available to the whims of masters, their wives, and their children. We were sold and moved to suit the economic pursuits of slave owners. We were forbidden to be educated and taught an oppressive rendition of the Bible that rendered us helpless and dependent. Even after slavery, the Deep South and other places enforced enslaving systems and practices with different names. Black bodies were lynched on false allegations. Plantations continued, and the system kept us in debt. There were cross burnings in response to miraculous Black economic growth or to assertions of Black agency against all odds. Jim Crow and segregation along with violence and fear worked hard to keep Black people in our place. All the way up to today we have seen and are seeing Black bodies killed by Black hands and by police hands, and we are not hearing an outcry

The criminal system and the lack of a good lawyer lead to our men serving time beyond the crime and finding guilt in the face of innocence. Gaps are growing wider between those that have and those who do not— gaps in healthcare, education, economics, and access to services. And we have by no means recovered from all that was done to our people. We need our stories—our laughter, our pain, and our tears—to be heard.

In the novel *The Salt Eaters*, by Toni Cade Bambara, the protagonist asks, "Are you sure, sweetheart, that you want to be well?" of a woman who has tried to commit suicide.[3] The healer is trying to help the woman, who was once on the ledge and fell off. An underlying sentiment in the healer's question is that not everyone wants to be well. Not everyone wants to be well. Or maybe a more gentle truth is, not everyone is willing to do the work that will make themselves well. Wellness requires something of the person that wants it. For one, you have to let go some of the myths that surround seeking mental healthcare. You have to work at and invest time into maintaining mental health. You have to desperately want wellness enough that you are even willing to let others help, no matter how awkward you feel. Letting someone in requires incredible strength. Toni Cade Bambara

3. Bambara, *Salt Eaters*, 3.

goes on to say "There is a lot of weight to being well."[4] There are some good mental health workers that can help you better navigate your wellness journey.

We are psychologically struggling to breathe amd the social calamity and enormity of being Black in America. We are containers of deep trauma and pain. We need trained professionals to hold our stuff. We need careful hands to prod and journey with us. We need to begin the hard work of resisting medicating ourselves with shopping, gambling, drinking, and other addictive behaviors: we need to stop walking down dead-end roads. We often look good on the outside, but it's important to address our internal well-being and to answer the question, do we want to be well? If you yearn for hope, healing, and health, then make up your mind to reach beyond yourself. Mental health professionals do know something that you do not know. You just have to find the right one for you. There are counselors who look like us, who understand us, who have good hearts and capable hands and seasoned ears. With quality mental health professionals, we can cover old ground and make new maps and plot new mental health territories for our next generation.

4. Bambara, *Salt Eaters*, 5.

11

Give Us What Magic Johnson Got!

Spiritual Care for Black Lives Living with HIV
and AIDS in the Era of #BlackLivesMatter

MICHAEL J. CRUMPLER

I must admit, I barely knew Magic Johnson before 1991. But, nevertheless I felt the full weight of his sobering HIV disclosure as if it were my own. I remember knowing it was a big deal, but not fully knowing why. How had he gotten it? He must be gay, right? I pretended not to care, lest in my curiosity my own closeted truth become disclosed. As he stood there next to his wife, blinded by the flashing camera lights, naked before the entire world, I felt what he felt. Magic Johnson's reality made it real not just for me, but for everyone. It was no longer a gay disease, a prostitute's disease, a junkie's disease, or Africa's disease. It was now our disease as we witnessed a Black, successful celebrity athlete, admired and respected by all, living our worst nightmare in public guise. If Magic could get it, any of us could get it. If any of us could get it, then I knew that I certainly *would* get it. Fifteen years later, when I did get it, my dad comforted my mom by reassuring her that I would live a long healthy life because, "See! Look at Magic Johnson." Those words provided quite enough hope to get her through that day.

#BlackAndGay and HIV Positive

What Was Then

Iconography is alive and well among Black folk. Living, breathing iconography has always played a vital role in the Black American experience. If iconography is *"the visual images and symbols used in a work of art or the study or interpretation of these,"* the black experience in America is to be understood as a succession of icons who overcame the shackles of White supremacy.[1] We love our heroes. We need our heroes. From Frederick Douglass and W. E. B. Du åBois to Martin Luther King Jr. and Malcolm X, from Jesse Jackson to Jesse Owens, from Hank Aaron to Mohammed Ali to Barack Obama, these are the visual images and symbols of Black hope for a future yet to be fulfilled for generations of Black people. The road to Black liberation and empowerment has been pioneered through the lenses of the trials, tragedies, and triumphs of American Black nobility. The life and legacy of Magic Johnson is no minor contender among such icons.

Back then, as a Black, gay seventeen-year-old, I had never seen anyone who looked like I felt. I was completely void of any vision of who I might become or what I might experience in a world in which my life seemed destined for disdain. But when Magic came out as HIV positive, in one fell swoop I gained an unlikely role model. The shame on his face and the shock on everyone else's was the first marker of what life might be like on the day that my positive diagnosis would be revealed. Would my family stand in solidarity? Would my sexual transgressions be consumed by insatiable skeptics? Would my peers shudder in disgust? As it went with Magic, might it go with me?

This Is Now

Interestingly, as it went with Magic, so it did not go with me. The failure of Black iconography is that our lives rarely reflect the lives of our idols. Every year thousands of young Black men leave the ball court in despair, having fallen short of NBA stardom. Every season, America's aspiring top models fall too short of Tyra's ultimate top-model stature. Likewise, many Blacks diagnosed with HIV rarely achieve the health of Magic Johnson. The consolation that Dad shared with Mom was of no comfort to me. Sure, I was

1. *Oxford Living Dictionaries: English,* "Iconography."

relieved that Magic's story was enough to stave off the questions she had for me. But I knew that I was no millionaire. I knew that I was not married with children. I knew that I had no superstardom to mask the realities of being HIV positive. As time passed, it was as if the threat of AIDS on Magic's life evaporated. Fifteen years later, after the epic advances in the field of HIV and AIDS, when I received my diagnosis, Magic's story was farthest from my mind, and death was my only hope as I sat gazing through the clinic window.

HIV and AIDS Basics for Black Lives by the Numbers

Nearly thirty years after the Magic press conference, more than 1.1 million Americans are living with HIV, and 1 in 7 do not know it. In 2016, 39,784 people were diagnosed with HIV. Black gay and bisexual men are the most affected.[2] Of the twenty-six thousand annual infections among all gay and bisexual men in recent years, ten thousand affect black gay and bisexual men. That is, 38 percent of new infections among gay and bisexual men affect Black men. While HIV infection has decreased among White and Latino gay and bisexual men by 10 percent and 14 percent respectively, infections have increased by 4 percent for Black gay men.

HIV Diagnoses in the United States for the Most-Affected Subpopulations, 2016[3]

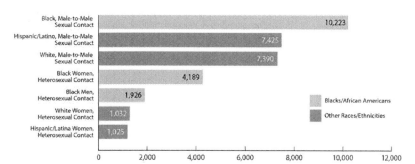

Black men who have sex with men are not the only story here. Black heterosexual women might contend that HIV and AIDS is no longer a

2. HIV.gov/ (website), "U.S. Statistics."
3. Center for Disease Control and Prevention (CDC), "HIV among Women."

gay disease as 72 percent of women living with HIV are Black.[4] In 2016, Blacks overall represented 12 percent of the U.S. population but accounted for 47 percent of HIV diagnoses. In 2014, African Americans make up 43 percent of all people living with HIV in the United States. In 2015, Blacks accounted for 52 percent of those who died from complications related to HIV.[5] These numbers reveal that #BlackLivesMatter extends far beyond racialized policing. Or does it?

Black and Positive and Criminal

The greatest threat to Black people living with HIV and AIDS in the United States is HIV criminalization. Any conversation involving the matterment of Black lives must include the disproportionate rate at which Black men are jailed for living while HIV positive. Thirty-eight states have laws that could criminally prosecute people living with HIV and AIDS. These laws penalize those living with HIV who willfully transmit HIV or who fail to disclose their HIV diagnosis before sexual intercourse, and these laws originated long before HIV and AIDS were considered treatable, manageable illnesses. The penalty for infraction is up to thirty-five years' imprisonment and registration as a sex offender.[6] Due to the lack of education about HIV and AIDS and the overwhelming stigma surrounding them, fear sustains such laws and places Black people at compounded risk in that we are already the most vulnerable to be harmed by HIV and mass incarceration.

Just as it came as no surprise to Black people that the Black dead body of Michael Brown lay bleeding in the middle of Canfield Drive for four hours, neither should it come as no surprise that nearly half of all bodies infected by HIV and AIDS in the United States are Black. In a White supremacist construct, it is well established that those living while Black are impacted tenfold by nearly every social ill than our White counterparts. Whether the malady is heart disease, infant mortality, or median income, the statistics prove that Black lives matter less than White lives. The compounded oppressions of mass incarceration and being HIV positive reveal the inhumanity of criminalizing HIV, especially during the dawn of

4. Black AIDS Institute, website.

5. Center for Disease Control and Prevention (CDC), "AIDS among African Americans."

6. Movement Advancement Project, *LGBT Policy Spotlight: HIV Criminalization Laws.*

prevention and treatment methods that greatly reduce the probability of transmission.

#BlackHIVPositiveLivesMatterToo

Since 2014, racial bias in policing has become common kitchen table conversation. After the many marches, rallies, and protests that have followed Sanford, Florida; Ferguson, Missouri; Staten Island; Cleveland; Charleston; Baltimore; Baton Rouge; Charlotte; Minneapolis; and Waller County, Texas, we have become accustomed to what to do when a Black body falls victim to state-sanctioned White violence. Despite the repeated exonerations, we know that police officers are rarely held to account for fear for their lives when encountering unarmed black men. Yet, we have become accustomed to tweeting, posting, looting, rallying, and marching whenever an unarmed Black body is slain by state-sanctioned violence. Conversely, we are not as astute when Black lives are assaulted by a system that ignores the impacts of HIV and AIDS in Black communities. Our protests and our rallies become strangely muzzled when faced with the problem of HIV and AIDS for Black people—which begs the question, why do black people tolerate disproportionate Black HIV and AIDS infections in the age of #BlackLivesMatter?

The Triple Threat—HIV and AIDS and Black Stigma— We Are Killing Us

Truth be told, compared to most of the social ills that plague Black bodies, racialized murder by police is somewhat of a soft pitch. Even among Black people there is a slowness to rise up in protest of our victimization. It was not until I was convinced that Trayvon, Michael, Eric, or Sandra were unarmed with hands raised that I felt justified to rally in their defense. White policemen executing unarmed Black folks pleading, kneeling, running for their lives ought be an easy argument in the case against Black lives. But when it comes to the sexual proclivities of those same Black bodies, Black people are much less likely to join the movement for Black viability. Faced with the legacy of lynchings, mass incarceration, and disproportionate rates of poverty, Black people find it difficult to confront systemic social ills that plague our communities. It is easy for us to blame ourselves for being in the wrong place at the wrong time, surrendering to a Jim Crow prison system engineered for Black entrapment, or succumbing to sexual temptation with someone already infected with HIV. Ever since the abolitionist ethics of Booker T. Washington, the Black psyche has conceded that blaming ourselves for our social ills is easier than indicting a system engineered to undermine Black viability.

HIV and AIDS and Black Respectability

In 1995, hundreds of thousands of Black men descended upon the National Mall to protest our own propensity to live fully into the African American ideal originally enforced by the oppressor under antebellum Christendom, long before we achieved our emancipation. At the peak of the HIV and AIDS epidemic, with Minister Louis Farrakhan presiding, legions of Black men joined together to reaffirm our Black dignity. Farrakhan summarized his epic gathering in the *Final Call*: "The Million Man March, in one day, helped to defeat all of the evil propaganda spread about Black men throughout the world."[7] Rather than a sacred outcry against anti-Black oppression, Minister Farrakhan attributed his march to a vision from God due in part to the need to warn Black men of the self-defeating plagues of gangs, crack cocaine, and gangsta rap.[8] While the Million Man March may have offered a subtle critique of White supremacy and free market capitalism, the greater indictment was on our inability to live fully into Black self-affirmation.

A similar message was promoted through Bill Cosby's Black conservatism. Ever mindful of the plight of Black America, rather than condemning white supremacy wholesale, Cosby found it more appropriate to "grab the city's black men by their collars and shake them out of the torpor that has left so many of them—like so many of their peers across the country—undereducated, overincarcerated, and underrepresented in the ranks of active fathers."[9] Mr. Cosby took this show on the roads that stretch from the rust belt America to the Deep South, preaching the gospel of Black respectability, saying, "Men, if you want to win, we can win. We are not a pitiful race of people. We are a bright race, who can move with the best. But we are in a new time, where people are behaving in abnormal ways and calling it normal."[10] Even as Bill Cosby's legacy has fallen into ill repute and scandal, his message of Black revivalism has not.

7. Farrakhan, "Million Man March."
8. Ibid.
9. Coates, "This Is How We Lost to the White Man."
10. Ibid

These gospels of Black paternalism intended to inspire moral courage and Black spiritual individualism are peddled across the Black community as the reason for our oppression and are cited by Whites to justify recklessly abandoning the problem of HIV in the Black community. Such ideologies have allowed the rates of HIV and AIDS among Black people to soar, even as these rates have declined drastically among Whites. The disease of Black respectability, fueled by a protestant social ethic inherited from our oppressors, prevents us from confronting the HIV and AIDS epidemic head-on. The notion that those impacted were infected due solely to moral and spiritual failing perpetuates shame and prevents us from seeking HIV testing and treatment that will inevitably eradicate the disease within privileged populations, leaving Black lives in dire straits.

Theology of Black Shame

The disproportionate impact of HIV and AIDS upon Black people is a consequence of the theology of Black shame. Not only have the gospels according to Minister Farrakhan and Bill Cosby infiltrated the Black community, but also the theology of White supremacy has infused Black folk religion. Central to the social compact of the slave and slave master was the heresy that God is on the side of the oppressor, demanding the oppressed to obey them. No other text from the Christian Scriptures affirms this more than, *"Slaves, obey your earthly masters with fear and trembling, in singleness of heart, as you obey Christ."*[11] Such obedience was incumbent upon the oppressed in order to achieve salvation on earth and in the hereafter. Furthermore, one's obedience to his master correlated directly to one's obedience to Christ. The inevitable outcome of such a compact is failure, in that slavery is inherently dehumanizing—the oppressor never sees the oppressed as fully human. This dehumanization leaves the slave suspended in a self-defeating quest for survival and believing that "if I am the model slave I will be rewarded by my God and my master, but if I fail I will be condemned." This results in a perpetual state of Black shame. This notion is further deconstructed by the Father of Black liberation theology, Dr. James H. Cone, who writes:

> White Americans try to convince themselves that they have been innocent onlookers of that history, but black Americans evaluate

11. Eph 6:5 (NRSV).

the history of this country differently. For them, white Americans have pursued two principal courses of action with regard to blacks. First, they decreed that blacks were outside the realm of humanity, that blacks were animals and that their enslavement was best both for them and for society as a whole. And as long as black labor was needed, slavery was regarded as the only appropriate "solution" to the "black problem." But when black labor was no longer needed, blacks were issued their "freedom," the freedom to live in a society which attempted to destroy them physically and spiritually. There is no indication before or after the Civil War that this society recognized the humanity of black persons.[12]

The hope of Black liberation theology is deliverance from Black shame. Black shame reinforces the misnomer that blackness not in service to White supremacy has no value. Black liberation informs Black people of our own innate power in a culture that refuses to recognize our humanity. Unfortunately, this information has limited reach in a society where the same theology that enslaved the slave is empowered by privilege to the demise of Black lives. While a few Black icons are able to escape the claws of shame by living into our inherit humanity of Black liberation, the many among us are unable to see beyond the marred Black image reflected in the mirror of White supremacy.

Challenged by the mandate of Black respectability, Black people diagnosed with HIV and AIDS immediately become mired in a yoke of Black shame that has plagued Black people from generation to generation. As if being Black isn't shameful enough, Black people living with HIV and AIDS possess a more crippling shame that inhibits self-care. Black lives are lost unnecessarily when Black people, not wanting to admit that they are HIV positive, do not seek treatment and so we see increased HIV transmission levels. Therefore, an HIV icon the likes of Magic Johnson lacks efficacy in the lives of everyday Black people living with HIV and AIDS. The legacy of Black shame can be eradicated only by a power greater than the feel-good stories of a few fortunate Black lives whose experience is insulated from the everyday struggles that accompany the Black experience.

12. Cone, *Black Theology of Liberation*, 14.

#BlackLiveswithHIVandAIDSMatter—
Spiritual Care for Black People Living with HIV and AIDS

What I loved most about the comfort that my mother found in the miracle of Magic's survival is the hope. Despite the sloppy politics of celebritizing HIV and AIDS, the grace and dignity with which Magic, Carmen, and their gender queer son E. J. have navigated their circumstances is undeniable. No magic pill was unveiled when Magic Johnson disclosed his status. What was unveiled to us was hope. Prior to Magic, our only hope was drug cocktails, kaposi sarcoma lesions, and facial wasting. The doom of dying White gay lives left little hope that Black lives would survive the plague. Magic Johnson changed that.

Our HIV-AIDS icon renewed in the Black community our faith in modern medicine. The Johnson family gave the Black family a model for how to talk about HIV. Magic Johnson moved HIV/AIDS beyond being a distinction without a difference; we came to realize that Magic had HIV, not AIDS. Absent of a working theology or spiritual resources for confronting the disease, Magic Johnson gave Black people a framework for talking, listening, and responding to HIV and AIDS. While the church and state were knit together in silent complicity against Black lives infected with HIV and dying of AIDS, Magic Johnson's still, small voice taught us how to overcome the fear of people who are positive, and gave us the courage to live positively with HIV.

But just as the Black Lives Matter movement decries the paternalistic activism of Al Sharpton and Jesse Jackson, Malcolm X and Martin, the #BlackLiveswithHIVandAIDSMatter movement needs no Magic. Black people living with HIV and AIDS in 2018 are detached from the riches of Magic, Carmen, and E. J., and feel exempt from the #BlackLivesMatter mantra. While the Black community has an HIV hero in Magic, Black people living with HIV and AIDS have no heroes. Black people living with HIV and AIDS simply need Black allies, Black advocates, and Black healing from Black people, rooted and grounded in the Black spiritual tradition.

Spiritual Care of and from Black Allies

The problem with Black liberation and Black power is the many who are left living in Black bondage and Black powerlessness. The theologies of Black respectability leave behind the many whose bootstraps are tattered and broken. The White theology of free market capitalism has limited space for Black self-respect and responsibility. HIV and AIDS further marginalize Blacks who are otherwise capable of accomplishing the American dream. The Black Lives Matter movement argues to Blacks and Whites alike that Black lives are innately esteemable, worthy of dignity, and sacred regardless of circumstance. To chant #BlackLivesMatter is to prosecute a system that indicts Black people for being Black and uplifts White people for being White. All who take up our chant, whether Black or White, are our allies and co-agents of change in the movement of Black lives.

Providing spiritual care to Black people living with HIV and AIDS involves being an ally who understands the nature of the disease and the nature of being Black in America. HIV and AIDS treatment and prevention have long centered on White HIV transmission as mainstream. LGBTQ activism has leveraged White privilege to navigate systems and build institutions that have filled the void left by a church and a state content to see gay men dead.

Allies come in all colors and understand how these colors engage anti-Black racism. Black allies understand the nuances of Black invisibility in the White gay community and the need for HIV and AIDS care for Black women. Black allyship eases the burden of navigating inherently racist systems while also navigating the complications of living with a disease.

Spiritual Care of Black Advocates Who Are Black

While Black allies and advocates exist in all colors, here I will lift up Black advocates who are Black. The Black church, Black music, Black leadership, Black media, Black athleticism, and Black business all serve a special place in the souls of Black folk. Nike, Beats, Harpo, BET, AME, Tidal, Ebony, Motown, and FUBU are among the many institutions that reflect Black affirmation. Black affirmation is the mirror that reflects Blacks beauty and greatness. A Black person who fails to see her reflection is blind.

Progress for those living with HIV and AIDS, while nothing short of a miracle in medical and social science reform, has by and large left Black communities behind. Black people serious about overcoming the stigma of living with HIV and AIDS are forced to transgress the boundaries of race in order to establish relationships with advocates beyond our Black neighborhoods. Such advocacy is inept in dealing with the intersections of race, class, gender, and sexuality unique to the Black experience. Black people living with HIV and AIDS are forced to endure the microaggressions of White supremacy perpetrated by those we depend on for survival.

Black advocates who are Black, in close proximity to the lived experience of Black people advocate for people living with HIV and AIDS through the lens of Blackness. This requires that Black churches, Black institutions, and Black cultural icons join the movement Black Lives with HIV and AIDS Matter. Just as Black voices have embraced efforts to combat diabetes, sickle cell disease, and heart disease, so Black institutions must sponsor a platform for normalizing the prevention and treatment of HIV and AIDS. When the NBA stumbled in its attempt to stand with Magic Johnson, the Black community realized the risk of disclosure. A more steadfast show of solidarity with Magic Johnson's plight would have decentered the story of a superstar and created a platform for the everyday experience of people living with HIV and AIDS.

Healing in the Black Spiritual Tradition

The backbone of the Black community is the Black spiritual tradition. Long before abolition, Black slaves were spiritually emancipated from the heresy of antebellum Christendom by reimagining the religion of their oppressor. According to Dr. James H. Cone:

> The task of black theology, then, is to analyze the nature of the gospel of Jesus Christ in the light of oppressed blacks so they will see the gospel as inseparable from their humiliated condition, and as bestowing on them the necessary power to break the chains of oppression. This means that it is a theology of and for the black community, seeking to interpret the religious dimensions of the forces of liberation in that community.[13]

This transvaluation of Christian values is what has sustained Black people through the horrors of slavery, lynching, and Jim Crow. Generations of Black mothers and fathers believed in their bones that the Christian faith of their White masters was from the antichrist. Illiterate in Western religion, victims of the transatlantic slave trade hewed from the horror of their a experience a faith that worked. Long before #BlackLivesMatter, they unearthed the hermeneutic of a Black Jesus in solidarity with their suffering. What White supremacy used for evil, they used for good.

13. Ibid., 5.

Spiritual care for Black people living with HIV and AIDS must include a theology of Black healing. This will involve a revolutionary reversal of what HIV and AIDS means in the lives of Black people. Advances in treatment on par with prevention options allow people who are HIV positive to live lives indistinguishable from the lives of people who are HIV negative. The rise of PrEP (Pre-exposure prophylaxis) in the gay community have brought about a sexual revolution that is allowing for serodiscordant sexual partners to engage in responsible sex without reservation.

The opportunity for people with HIV and AIDS to live sexually fulfilling lives provides hope for healing from the stigma and shame of contracting HIV. Taken further, HIV and AIDS do not have to be wished away or invisibilized in order for positive people to fine joy. Black people have demonstrated the opportunity for healing amid suffering. The spiritual heritage of Black liberation has empowered Black people to persevere tragedy by experiencing embodied resurrection. The songs sung by Nina Simone and James Brown, the survival networks of Harriet Tubman and Marcus Garvey, the lived experiences of James Baldwin and Harry Belafonte have broken us free from the chains of a hereafter. Black healing for people living with HIV and AIDS involves finding joy and meaning in the dexterity of the disease shared with others who are positive. Black healing happens when Black people come together in the spirit of our ancestors, interpreting our HIV and AIDS infection out a history of suffering that has attended the Black experience.

Black healing for Black people living with HIV and AIDS eliminates stigma in that it removes the chasm between Black people struggling to live with HIV and AIDS and black people who are just struggling to live. Black healing places HIV and AIDS in tandem with the heritage of Black power and Black liberation that is always on the march to dismantle White supremacy. Black healing for Black people living with HIV and AIDS tunes our ears, hearts, and minds to the soul-stirring tunes of the juke joint, to the liberative anthems of the Black freedom movement. Spiritual care for Black people living with HIV and AIDS embraces those who died off in the early days of HIV and AIDS as ancestors in the freedom struggle alongside our Black iconic nobility, who died dreaming of the day when their Black progeny would no longer experience the shame or fear of living with or dying of AIDS or HIV.

12

When Life Doesn't Seem Worth Living

Congregations Engaged in Suicide Intervention and Prevention during the Era of the Black Lives Matter Movement

Delois Brown-Daniels

During the era of the Black Lives Matter movement, an undertackled topic within congregations and ministries is suicide intervention and prevention. Suicide registers high among the taboo topics in churches and within society. The social stigma of suicide makes the topic among those that people would rather not talk about. People opt, albeit reluctantly, to risk suicide happening rather than to have it addressed.

The Black Lives Matter movement has placed Black suicide within the national spotlight. The population most vulnerable to suicide is the African American transgender community, according to a survey sponsored by the National LGBTQ Task Force, in which 49 percent of the African American respondents who are members of the transgender community indicated that they had attempted suicide. Suicide within the overall Black community has garnered attention through the multifaceted platform of Black Lives Matter. The National Suicide and Black Church Conference along with the National Organization of People of Color against Suicide are two groups committed to addressing suicide within Black communities.[1]

A recent article by Justin Moyer in the *Chicago Tribune* registers the vulnerability to suicide for Black children under the age of eighteen. Moyer writes, "Nationwide, suicides among black children under 18 are up 71 percent in the past decade, rising from 86 in 2006 to 147 in 2016, the latest year such data is available from the Centers for Disease Control and Prevention. In that same period, the suicide rate among all children also increased, up 64 percent."[2]

In 2015, 2,504 African Americans died by suicide in the United States: 2,023 males (80.79 percent) and 481 females. As will be noted below, Black males commit suicide at a rate four times higher than the rate for Black females. There is clearly a crisis within the Black community in the United States. It is affecting Black men, Black children, and the Black transgender individuals. The statistics related to suicide are staggering. For more than a decade, suicide ranks among the top ten causes of death for all Americans, including African Americans. For children between the ages of ten and fourteen, it is the third leading cause of death. For youth and young adults between fifteen and thirty-four it is the second leading cause of death. Each year an estimated thirty-four thousand Americans commit suicide. One million people in the United States attempt suicide every year. These numbers illustrate the magnitude of this crisis that congregations and the society fear addressing.[3]

Suicide victims include Black celebrities such as the famous singers Donny Hathaway and Phyllis Hyman, and the TV host Don Cornelius of *Soul Train*. Among those who attempted suicide is Donna Summer, the popular singer. Summer's autobiographical account of her own suicide attempt captures in words the inner struggles related to suicidal thoughts and plans. In a hotel room during a concert tour, Summer describes her being suddenly "overcome by an overwhelming sensation of profound despair and uselessness." She names feeling "emotionally destitute" and as if her life was a lie and a fake. She desperately wanted to escape "this insanity." She recalled:

---

1. Harrison-Quintana et al., *Injustice at Every Turn*.
2. Moyer, "Researchers Unclear Why Suicide Is Increasing," para 7.
3. Thornton, "Reality of Suicide in the Black Community."

> I had thoughts that kept repeating in my head, rolling like the TV screen, that I couldn't turn off. I had failed God. I was worthless, I couldn't be forgiven. I was doomed for hell.
>
> Believing I was without God made me feel truly and completely alone and utterly desperate. Those dark thoughts forced me out of bed. I walked over to the big, heavy window, threw it open, and hoped the weight of my loneliness would send me crashing eleven stories to the sidewalk below.[4]

Having plotted her suicide, she began to execute the plan by placing her right foot outside of the window. Her left foot "somehow got caught as the drapes bunched around the curved radiator pipes." As she frantically tried "to shake the curtain" off her left leg, she found herself interrupted by the entry of the hotel maid into her room. Both Summer and the maid were stunned. Without either initially saying a word, the maid broke the silence by stammering: "Oh, Mrs. Summer, can I come in and clean your room now?"[5]

Being unexpectedly interrupted, Summer remembers:

> Flooded with shame, I was shocked back to reality. A rush of panic shot through my whole body, jolting me back to my senses. I knew I was in a bad place in my head, which God knew as well. But He'd put those drapes there for me to get caught on, providing enough time for Him to send in the maid to save me from jumping. In that instant my head began to spin. I was humbled . . . I needed to get medical help, real help.[6]

The Role of Congregations in Suicide Prevention

Congregations can assume a key role in confronting suicide. Research exists that indicates that religion is among the positive factors within suicide intervention and prevention. In order for congregations to engage effectively in suicide intervention and prevention, church members must learn and understand simple assessment tools, suicide warning signs, suicide risk factors, recommended pastoral guidelines to help suicidal people, and how to make referrals for suicidal people to mental healthcare professionals.

4 Summer, *Ordinary Girl*, 137–38.

5. Summer, *Ordinary Girl*, 138.

6. Summer, *Ordinary Girl*, 138.

Once a congregation has been trained to intervene or prevent suicides, that congregation must fashion a community in which suicide can be
discussed in an open and informed manner. A congregation must create a
caring culture with communal norms of care that exhibit the best practices
related to suicide intervention and prevention. It is important to clearly
delineate the work of laypeople, clergy, and professionals trained in suicide
intervention and prevention, whether a psychiatrist, clinical psychologist,
social worker, pastoral counselor, or crisis counselor.

Concepts and Definitions

Key terms for this topic are *suicidal thoughts*, *attempts*, and *completion*,
along with suicide *warning signs*, *risk factors*, *intervention*, and *prevention*. *Suicidal thoughts* happen, or *suicidal ideation* occurs when people
contemplate suicide—from imagining what suicide is like to fantasizing
how it would end their problems to coming up with ways at attempting
it. A *suicide attempt* entails trying to commit suicide. *Suicide completion*
is the committing of suicide. *Suicide warnings* are specific behaviors, such
as journaling about suicide, that alert one to something unusual going on
with an individual. *Suicide risk* points to identifying people as prime can-
didates for suicide attempts or for committing suicide itself, because their
profiles include a number of risk factors. *Suicide risk factors* range from
certain stressors to family history. *Suicide intervention* employs strategies to
work with a person having attempted suicide or suicidal thoughts. *Suicide
prevention* employs strategies that address in their early stages the plights of
people having suicidal thoughts; suicide prevention also entails educating
congregations, families, significant others, and individuals about suicide
warning signs, suicide risk factors, and screening tools related to stopping
suicides.[7]

---

7 See Barnes, "Suicide," 444–60.

Black Suicide Statistics

Table 1[8]

Suicides by Black Males and Females per 100,000 African Americans

YEAR	BLACK MALE	BLACK FEMALE
1970	8.0	2.6
1980	10.3	2.2
1989	12.2	2.4
1999	10.5	1.7
2016	10.5	2.4

For almost a half century, the Black male suicide rate has been over four times higher than the suicide rate of Black females. Since 1980, it has been consistently above ten per one hundred thousand while the Black female suicide rate has been consistently below 2.5 and during 1999 it registered below two per one hundred thousand.

The differences in the suicide rates between Black males and Black females could possibly be related to the "sisterhood" or strong social network that unites various sectors of Black women, whether in the women's auxiliaries of the congregations, sororities, fraternal orders, and women social clubs as well as fictive and actual kinship groups. Since veterans as a cohort have high suicide rates, and since a higher percentage of men are veterans, the unaddressed behavioral health challenges especially facing war veterans may account for part of the difference. The higher male to female ex-offender population may also be a contributing factor. Among these factors and others, the drastically lower percentage of men than women who belong to religious congregations may account for a higher suicide rate among men since religion has been identified as a preventive factor.

Table 2[9]

Suicides Per 100,000 Black Males and Females Ages 24–44

8. Early, *Religion and Suicide in the African-American Community,* 12 for 1970, 1980, 1989; Curtin et al., 4–5, for 1999; National Institute of Mental Health, "Suicide" (esp. Figure 3) for 2016.

9 Spates and Slatton, "I've Got My Family and My Faith," 1; also see Spates, *What Don't Kill Us Makes Us Stronger*; and Borum, "African American Women's Perceptions."

Year	Males	Females
1989	20.5	3.8
1999	15.5	2.5
2014	15.0	3.0

Among Black men and women, the age cohort with the highest suicide rate is between the ages of twenty-four and forty-four. While the numbers are significantly above the male and female averages, there has been a noticeable decline in the rate among Black men by 25 percent between 1989 and 1999 and lesser decline between 1999 and 2014; yet there was a clear increase in suicides for this age cohort among Black females between 1999 and 2014.

While the suicide completion rate among Black males runs higher than among Black females, the suicide attempt rate, among suicide survivors is higher for Black women than for Black men. Black women attempt suicide at a rate of 117 out of one hundred thousand whereas Black men attempt suicide at a rate of 77.6 out of one hundred thousand.

Religion as a Positive Factor in Suicide Prevention

Key research studies indicate that religion can play a positive role in suicide intervention and prevention. These studies distinguish between religious affiliation, participation, and doctrine in their findings: religious affiliation involves identifying with a faith tradition, religious participation entails attending religious services (and practicing a spiritual discipline), and religious doctrine encompasses beliefs in God, life, and so forth.

These studies suggest religion may inhibit a person from acting on suicidal ideas by providing access to a supportive community, shaping a person's beliefs about suicide, providing a source of hope, providing ways to interpret suffering. Additionally, I would argue that religion provides positive reasons to live; it offers people purpose in life.

These studies include people across races, nationalities, genders, sexual orientations, and world religions. For instance, African Americans commit suicide at a lower rate than White Americans; the higher rate of religious affiliation and participation by African Americans than by White Americans might serve as a positive factor preventing suicide. Men commit suicide more than women; possibly the lower rate of religious affiliation and participation among men might be a factor in the higher suicide rate among men. Consequently, White males make up the cohort with the highest suicide rate within the United States. Research shows that the highest suicide rates are among the "nones," which are those who lack any religious affiliation.[10]

Regarding sexual orientation, one study "surveyed lesbian, gay, or bisexual adults . . . along with heterosexual matched controls . . . Those with a religious affiliation reported fewer suicide attempts than those with no religious affiliation; both in the whole sample . . . and in the lesbian, gay, or bisexual." Marriage equality, according to one study, reduced teen suicide attempts among the LGBTQIA community. This Johns Hopkins University study linked the "legalization of same-sex marriage" to a marked "decrease in adolescent suicide." Researchers compared data from "32 of the 35 states that legalized same-sex marriage between 2004 and 2015," the year the Supreme Court ruled that same-sex marriage was constitutional. "The researchers found that suicide attempts by high school students decreased 7 percent in states after they passed laws to legalize same-sex marriage." The study noted that "among LGB high school students" there was a 14 percent decrease in suicide attempts.[11]

In nuancing these findings, Robin Gearing and Dana Lizardi contend that research "also indicates that the relationship between religion and suicide risk is complex. Different religious affiliations provide different degrees of protection." While religion functions as a preventive to suicide, each world religion offers a ranging degree of prevention related to their religious ways of believing, belonging, and behaving. Among world religions, the lowest suicide rate is among Muslims followed by Jews, Hindus, Roman Catholics and evangelical Protestants; mainline Protestants have the highest suicide rates among those affiliated with a world religion.[12] To add further nuance to these findings, some studies indicate that certain religious expression within particular context can serve as a risk factor for suicide. The driving question is, why is religion sometimes associated with increased suicide risk? A few studies have identified patterns of "negative religious coping," which may include "deferring all responsibility to God, feeling abandoned by God, blaming God for difficulties, experiencing

---

10. See Barnes, "Suicide," 444–60.

11. Segal, "Same-Sex Marriage Laws Linked to Fewer Youth Suicide Attempts"; also see Raifman et al., "Difference-in-Differences Analysis."

12. Gearing and Lizardi, "Religion and Suicide," 334–37.

spiritual tension or doubt, or experiencing conflict and struggle with God."[13]

Other studies focus the role that moral objections against suicide may play in deterring suicide acceptability. They stress the "unique association" between moral and religious belief against suicide and lower suicidal behavior. These studies often note that "the life-saving beliefs associated with religious commitment may protect against suicide." Consequently, low moral objectives increase suicidal acceptability. In this case, according to certain studies, "individuals with low moral [objections] and religious objections to suicide are more likely to have a lifetime history of suicide attempts." Religious beliefs are central to these studies in serving as a "protective factor against suicide."[14]

Religious participation as it regards attendance at religious services can play a key role in suicide prevention. In his book *Religion and Suicide in the African-American Community*, Dr. Kevin E. Early argues that congregations can create a "religiously based normative climate" and play a "crucial role in pulling together the social fabric of the black community." The Black church, according to Early, crafts a religious "tradition shaped out of suffering"; this religious engagement of suffering has nurtured resiliency and supplied "strength, identity, coping skills, and a reason for living" to Black congregants and the Black community.[15]

Dr. Steven Stack in his study, "The Relationship Between Culture and Suicide: An Analysis of African Americans," engages Early's research. Stack distinguishes between religious beliefs and religious participation. He concludes that "only one indicator of religiosity (church attendance) significantly lowers suicide acceptability for both Black men and women." According to Stack, then, African American congregations might play a vital role as networks of support, serving as a means of "emotional and other support."[16]

Dr. James M. Shopshire, a Black sociologist of religion, contends that religion reduces "suicide by its collective function of fostering intensified relationships, strong social bonding, and shared values." Quoting Brainbridge and Stark, Shopshire states: "Religion has the power to comfort people who otherwise would be plunged into depths of despair, power relevant

13. Lawrence et al., "Religion as a Risk Factor."

14. Gearing and Lizardi, "Religion and Suicide," 333.

15. Early, *Religion and Suicide in the African-American Community*, 1, 2, 44, 45.

16. Stack, "Relationship between Culture and Suicide," 253, 266.

for suicide." He adds: "Religion provides a measure of hope and the feeling that once present sufferings are meaningful, compensating to some extent for the deprivations and difficulties experienced in the mundane world." According to Shopshire, congregations need to understand themselves and act as part of a network to provide nurturing, caring, supporting ministries that transform, enable, and encourage persons from within for the missional activity of reaching out and caring. The congregations become centers for refuge and relief but also participant groups in the work of identifying and proclaiming the new possibilities and advocating and resourcing church-based and community-based ministries for those suicidally at risk or potentially at risk.[17]

Identifying Signs of Potential Suicide Victims: Assessment Tools

Assessment tools aid congregations in identifying warning signs and risks factors associated with potential suicide victims. These assessment tools help identify whether someone needs to have a referral or immediate assistance.

Dr. Donna Holland Barnes, an African American expert on suicide, identifies these three theoretical constructs to explain suicide: a sociological one, a psychological one, and a medical (psychiatric) one. According to Barnes, the sociological framework offers what Dr. James Shopshire called social reasons for suicidal acts. These social reasons focus on how the person fails to relate constructively to society. The psychological construct "uses negative internalization—internal drives found in low esteem and an internal negative locus of control—to explain suicidal thoughts and attempts." The third construct, the medical or psychiatric model, interprets suicidal acts in terms of "mental illness."[18]

Dr. Alvin Poussaint, the renowned Black psychiatrist, in a book co-authored with Amy Alexander, a journalist, utilizes the list of suicide risk factors included in a 1999 surgeon general's report of Dr. David Satcher, the eminent Black physician and public health administrator, employing Barnes's distinctions. The sociological risk factors on Satcher's and Poussaint's lists include[19]

17. Shopshire, "Sociological Perspective," 25, 28, 35.
18. Barnes, "Suicide," 445.
19. Poussaint and Alexander, *Lay My Burden Down*, 23.

- barriers to accessing mental health treatment

- relational (i.e., death or divorce), social, work, or financial loss

- easy access to lethal weapons, especially guns

- cultural and religious beliefs—for instance, the belief that suicide is a noble resolution of a personal dilemma

- influence of significant people—family members, celebrities, peers— who have died by suicide, both through direct personal contact or inappropriate media representations

- local epidemic of suicide that have a contagious influence

- isolation, a feeling of being cut off from other people.

The psychological risk factors include these

- previous suicide attempt

- family history of suicide, hopelessness, and impulsive or aggressive tendencies

- unwillingness to seek help because of the stigma attached to mental and substance

- abuse disorders, suicidal thoughts, or both

The medical or psychiatric risk factors include these

- physical illness

- mental disorders, particularly mood disorders such as depression and bipolar (manic-depressive)

- disorderco-occurring mental and alcohol and substance abuse disorders.

These risk factors predispose a person to suicidal thoughts, attempts, or completed acts. In addition to risk factors are warning signs. Stacey Freedenthal identifies a list of warning signs that includes entertaining frequent, intense suicidal thoughts; talking or writing about suicide; making preparations for suicide; and suicide attempts or rehearsals.[20]

Within a congregation the clergy, parish nurses, or pastoral care teams trained in caregiving might be taught how to pose particular questions as

---

20. Freedenthal, *Helping the Suicidal Person*, 90.

a preliminary conversation with people who exhibit warning signs or risk factors. Freedenthal and others suggest four key questions:[21]

1. How religious a person are you?

2. How do your religious beliefs help you to cope with stress, if at all?

3. Are there ways that your religious beliefs or community add to your stress?

4. What does your religion say about suicide? Do you agree?

While the pastoral conversation or interview is meant to be brief, the aim of the four questions is to determine the interviewee's religiosity and how religion might be a resource in suicide prevention.

The first question inquires about how the interviewee self-identifies in regards to religion and provides an opportunity for the interviewee to talk about the role of religion in her or his life.

- How important is religion to this person?

- To what degree does religion shape this person's identity?

- How often does this person engage in religious practices such as prayer, meditation, Scripture reading, and attending religious services?

- How deeply does this person live out religious beliefs in behavior?

While the question seems to anticipate an individualistic response, it is also inquiring about whether the person participates in a religious service; it also seeks to know whether religion is important in the lives of those in the person's network of significant others, ranging from parents to other kin to the spouse or partner to friends; this network of significant others reenforces the religion within the individual.

Since stressors are risk factors in people contemplating or attempting suicide, the second question seeks to get the interviewee to speak out loud about how religion has help them cope with stress in the past, if it has helped them at all.

- During crises in the past, did religious practices, ideas, and services help them to persevere or cope?

- Did a sermon inspire the person?

- Did hearing certain religious music encourage the person?

21. Ibid.

- Was there a particular pastor, deacon, or lay leader that the person found helpful when she or he talked or prayed with him or her?

If the religious resources available to the person were not utilized, then a follow-up question might be, how could these resources possibly be of help?

Realizing that religion in certain cases for particular people can contribute to suicidal thoughts, attempts, and completion, the third question explores this concern.

- Does the religion foster within the person an unhealthy amount of guilt?
- Is the congregation an unforgiving community that undermines the person's self-worth?
- Do the interactions between people in the congregation and the individual increase the person's anxiety, adding to the person's depression, and overall exacerbating the person's emotional well-being?

The responses to the question help the interviewer recognize that encouraging the person to embrace the congregation wholeheartedly might possibly be counterproductive.

Since all world religions teach against suicide, the fourth question asks about the faith tradition's teaching about suicide; yet it asks in an open way so that the interviewer does not assume that the person's particular faith tradition is actually against suicide. Assuming that it is, then the interviewee gets to speak this out and to state whether they concur with this teaching. If a religion affirms life and living, then the religious person's articulation of this belief can inform attitudes and behaviors. So even if the person has suicidal thoughts, she or he is less likely to act on those thoughts because of the religious sanction against suicide and the religious value placed on life and living.

During the era of #BlackLivesMatter, these four key questions inquire about the religiosity of the suicidal person in order that the inquirer might have a sense to what degree religion might be a source of resilience, support, and life-affirming beliefs.[22]

22. See American Psychiatric Association Foundation, and Mental Health and Faith Community Partnership Steering Committee, *Mental Health:*.

Conclusion

Suicide has received added attention as the Black Lives Matter movement focuses needed attention on issues and challenges that diminish the lives of African Americans. As the above discussion demonstrates, religion has played and can continue to play a vital role in empowering African Americans to access inner strength as well as social support within their faith communities to fight for justice.

13

#BlackHealthMatters

Addressing Food Oppression in the Black Community

Danielle J. Buhuro

"Do you want fries with that?" This simple question that McDonald's workers ask patrons to convince them to purchase more has catapulted the $20 billion company now serving sixty-eight million customers a day, in 119 countries across more than thirty-five thousand franchises.[1] What's worse is the methods fast food companies will employ "to target kids from groups already more likely to suffer from obesity—including the poor, rural Americans and black Americans."[2] According to a new study by researchers at the University of Illinois at Chicago and Arizona State University, fast food restaurants are more than 60 percent more likely to advertise to Black children in low-income communities, using popular movie-themed toys and kid-friendly gimmicks, rather than White children in upper-class neighborhoods.[3] This disparity causes higher rates of obesity, high blood

1. Abel, "What McDonald's Can Teach Us."
2. Ferdman, "Disturbing Ways That Fast Food Chains."
3. Ibid.

pressure, and diabetes among Black children as they grow into adulthood.[4] As a result, the Centers for Disease Control and Prevention asserts that while African Americans are making strides in becoming healthier, statistics show that chronic illnesses continue to remain high among African Americans compared to other ethnicities, in particular to White Americans.[5] African Americans' largest health Achilles heel is heart disease, followed by stroke and cancer, which all consistently result from systematic social factors: lack of home ownership, obesity, lack of exercise, poverty, smoking, inability to afford doctor visits, and unemployment.[6] Of these factors, obesity is the most detrimental I reason because it specifically leads to a slew of chronic illnesses, including heart disease and stroke.

I argue that African Americans living with chronic illnesses have three pastoral needs that a chaplain, clergyperson, or pastor can help to meet. First, I contend that African Americans impacted by obesity, diabetes, heart disease, stroke, cancer, or combinations of these need ample and quality social support. According to the *Journal of Health and Social Behavior*, persons living with chronic illnesses and limited to no social support have higher mortality rates.[7] For example, according to the American Society on Aging, "an uplifting conversation that introduces hope and joy into the morning may influence physical activity, healthy food selection, or the choice to engage further in proactive social relationships later in the day or week. Open communication with a physician may encourage stronger engagement in answering health questions. A social service agency that provides volunteers to maintain landscaping or home maintenance enables many older adults to live in long-term neighborhood social networks. The range of examples is broad, and the individual variation almost infinite."[8]

I invite chaplains, clergy, and pastors to help hospital patients, parishioners, and community members reflect on their current social relationships by asking the following thought-provoking questions:

- Do you live alone, or do you isolate yourself from others?

---

4. Center for Disease Control, National Center for Chronic Disease Prevention and Health Promotion, "African American Health."

5. Ibid.

6. Ibid.

7. Umberson and Montez, "Social Relationships and Health."

8. Qualls, "What Social Relationships Can Do for Health."

- Do you have empathic, nonjudgmental support from biological family members or family of choice?

- Do you spend ample time with your family?

- Are you a part of a fraternity, sorority, Eastern Star chapter, masonic lodge, motorcycle/car club, and/or other social service organization?

- Are you a part of an affirming, progressive community of faith?

- Do you receive affordable and adequate resources from a particular social service organization?

If persons are unable to answer these questions in the affirmative, pastoral care providers can help patients and parishioners process how to build these relationships; they should refrain of course from evangelizing, proselytizing, or leading one to a specific social organization, and should avoid conflicts of interests.

Health disparities have become the new Jim Crow[9] for African Americans. Furthermore, while they may desire to practice healthy nutritional strategies, most African Americans live in "food desserts," implicating socioeconomic subjugation in what some are calling "food oppression."[10] The African American community must be willing to speak truth to power and ask the following questions: Where are the healthy produce markets in neighborhoods primarily African American and poor? Why is it that a bottle of filtered water costs more than a can of soda? Why is it that a salad costs more than a cheeseburger at a fast food chain? The prophetic call of pastoral care to communities of color, particularly in Black communities, pushes us to respond to the above questions.

I extend a prophetic invitation for faith communities to establish health ministries open to all, especially to people outside the church in the wider community, that can foster proper nutrition and exercise. Imagine the infinite possibilities that could arise from faith communities partnering with local park districts and exercise facilities to offer free or affordable exercise programming to persons living in low-income African American neighborhoods! Thus, I invite clergy to unite with local government, holding politicians accountable to ensure that local park districts remain funded—whether by local, state, or national government agencies. I invite

9. Jim Crow is the time period in the United States from 1865 to 1954 in which local legislation primarily in southern states upheld racist practices against African Americans.
10. Ferdman, "Disturbing Ways That Fast Food Chains."

clergy to hold local government accountable for ensuring that markets selling healthy produce are created and developed in underserved communities, and I urge clergy to oppose the development of new fast food vendors
in these communities.

In addition to having social needs, persons with chronic illnesses have
emotional needs. When one is diagnosed with a chronic illness, sometimes
feelings of shame, guilt, depression, and sadness arise.[11] Chaplains, pastors,
and other clergy must help persons living with newly diagnosed chronic
illnesses move toward hope. Pastoral caregivers can validate the feelings
of those they help, can encourage patients or parishioners not to rush
through the grieving process but to sit with their emotions. Those in the
caring professions can help persons living with chronic illness to experience hope by encouraging these ten self-care interventions outlined by the
South Gippsland, Australia, General Practice Alliance (a group ensuring
that the voices of what we in the U.S. call primary-care physicians are heard
in government and society):[12]

1. All or nothing thinking: You see things in black and white categories.
   If your performance falls short of "perfect," you see yourself as a total
   failure.

2. Overgeneralization: You see a single negative event as a never-ending
   pattern of defeat.

3. Mental filter: You pick out a single negative detail and dwell on it exclusively so that your vision of all reality becomes darkened, like the
   drop of ink that discolors the entire beaker of water.

4. Disqualifying the positive: You reject positive experiences by insisting
   they 'don't count' for some reason or other. In this way you can maintain a negative belief that is contradicted by our everyday experiences.

5. Jumping to conclusions: You make a negative interpretation even
   though there are no definite facts that convincingly support your
   conclusion. a) Mind Reading: You arbitrarily conclude that someone
   is reacting negatively to you, and you don't bother to check this out.
   b) The Fortune Teller Error: you anticipate that things will turn out

11. American Psychological Association, "Coping with a Diagnosis of Chronic
Illness."

12 General Practice Alliance (South Gippsland, Australia), *Self Care Strategies*,
16–17; see also Burns, *Feeling Good*.

badly, and you feel convinced that your prediction is an already established fact.

6. Magnification (catastrophizing) or minimization: You exaggerate the importance of things (such as your mistake or someone else's achievement), or you inappropriately shrink things until they appear tiny (your own desirable qualities or the other fellow's imperfections). This is also called the "binocular trick."

7. Emotional reasoning: You assume that your negative emotions necessarily reflect the way things are: "I feel it, therefore it must be true."

8. "Should" statements: You try to motivate yourself with "shoulds" and "shouldn'ts," as if you had to be whipped and punished before you could be expected to do anything. "Musts" and "oughts" are also offenders. The emotional consequence is guilt. When you direct "should" statements toward others, you can feel anger, resentment and frustration.

9. Labeling and mislabeling: This is an extreme form or overgeneralization. Instead of describing your error, you attach a negative label to yourself: "I'm a loser." When someone else's behavior rubs you the wrong way, you attach a negative label to him: "He's a pain in the neck." Mislabeling involves describing an event with language that is highly colored and emotionally loaded.

10. Personalization: You see yourself as the cause of some negative external event which in fact you were not primarily responsible for.

I extend a prophetic invitation to faith communities to implement mental health services for persons living with chronic illness in order to address their long-term emotional needs. Unhealthy nutritional practices speak to the psychological health of a person. Mental health services could help persons living with chronic illness to address psychological concerns that are leading to poor meal choices. Further, African Americans still struggle with unresolved psychological trauma since the days of African enslavement in the United States from 1619 to 1865; this trauma causes some African Americans to self-sabotage through unhealthy, emotional eating.

Last but not least, persons living with chronic illnesses have existential needs. Persons newly diagnosed with a chronic illness experience what could be considered a life-changing event in that these persons may be unable to return to their normal daily activities or to their previous careers. Persons newly diagnosed with a chronic illness partake in developing a new life identity, meaning, and purpose. Chaplains, clergy, and pastors can help facilitate this process of discernment by asking the following questions:

- Aside from your current gifts, what are your other skills and talents?

- Aside from your current profession, what are other career paths that you've been interested in?

- Do you have a grandchild(ren)? How can you become more involved as a grandparent?

- What social service activities give you joy and peace? How can you become more involved with them?

- Are you open to going back to school, or enrolling in a certificate program in a new subject?

- How can you become more involved in a religious faith community and volunteer more in a local ministry program?

In conclusion, addressing food oppression leading to chronic illness in the African American community calls for more than pastoral, sacrilegious responses. We need practical resolutions that address the root causes of problems, not simply pastoral band aids. The church's response to challenging politics and implementing health resources is a start. What else would you add? The combination of reflection and action is key. African American health depends on it. African American life depends on it. African American survival depends on it.

PART 3

Caring for African American Marriages, LGBT Partnerships, and Families

14

Finding a Mate the Same Hue as You

A Systemic Review of Mate Selection Barriers among African Americans, Spiritual Resources, and Therapeutic Interventions

HEATHER C. LOFTON

The pursuit of finding a mate is researched using the term *mate selection*, and this chapter will continue using that term for definitive clarity.[1] Prov 18:22 proclaims, "He who finds a wife finds a good thing, and obtains favor from the LORD."[2] Prior to embarking upon the "covenant" and "sacred bond" so eloquently and biblically defined, as marriage, all active and nonactively seeking human beings navigate the process of finding a mate. The selection process has cultural grounding, encompassing traditions ranging from arranged marriages to polyamory. Noting the historical and current trends on marriage among African American men and women, one can venture to say that seeking a spouse irrefutably involves sociocultural determining factors.[3] While both scientific and religious conceptual frameworks emphasize the universal and essential nature of healthy

1. Hughes and Hertel, "Significance."
2. Prov 18:22 (NRSV).
3. Hill, "Marriage."

intimate-partner relationships, sociocultural influences on mate selection in the Black community require further exploration. Focusing predominately on the United States (U.S.) African American population, I will analyze the process of mate selection, provided generational and systemic social climate transitions. Now, historically, the undertaking of mate selection among African Americans was rooted in the constraining elements of slavery.[4] Contemporaneously, African American men and women seeking a mate are combating increasing incarceration rates for African American males, the objectification of African American females (e.g., through the image of the strong Black woman [SBW]), violence within and against the Black community, and mental and physical health disparity trends.[5] Many of these compelling factors hampering the mate selection process appear to be anchored in the intersections of racism, sexism and classism.[6]

Observed through the restorative tenants of the Black Lives Matter movement and social research on mate selection, inherent relationships can be detected within and between the aforementioned social constructs and events, consequently claiming the Black community and potentially, systemically compromising the sustainability of mate selection among African Americans. As overwhelming as that notion is, the quest for solutions seems even more grandiose. How, where, and when can we intervene? Movements such as #BlackLivesMatter encourage all people to come together and find solace within relational structures (e.g., the couple, the family, the neighborhood, the workplace, or the church) that share the same purpose of reclaiming community power and privilege and ultimately preserving the lives of a historically oppressed and marginalized population. Black relationships are an important ingredient in the repair process and sustenance of the Black community, and these unions are at risk.[7] In order to intervene with resilient solutions, this chapter examines current spiritual and therapeutic guidelines backed by research, and interventions for combating barriers to mate selection.

---

4. Ibid.

5. Charles and Luoh, "Male Incarceration"; Messner and Sampson, "Sex Ratio"; Abrams et al., "Carrying"; Bell, et al., "Afrocentric"; Bentancourt et al., "Defining Cultural Competence."

6. Bell et al., "Afrocentric."

7 Johnson and Loscocco, "Black Marriage."

Current State of Mate Selection

Present-day trends among men and women getting married, not specifying race, show an overall delay of marriage, as the average age for getting married for both men and women has increased.[8] Between the years 1980 and 2012, the statistics on marriage reveal the average age at first marriage for women has extended by 21 percent, from twenty-two years old to twenty-six years old, and for men the average age of first marriage has risen from twenty-five years of age to twenty-nine years old.[9] Not accounting for technological and other societal advancements, what else could contribute to the delay of marriage?

The theoretical construct of mate selection is currently researched in relationship to the term *marriage market*.[10] A marriage market defines the pool of available individuals for marriage, matched by common factors.[11] Components such as educational attainment, socioeconomic status, race, religion, and sexual orientation are some determinants of marriage market eligibility.[12] In a study surveying the desired personal characteristics of an ideal African American marriage partner, results show that both Black men and Black women seek a mate that presents with affluence; Black men and women both want to choose from a pool of a "well-educated, financially stable, monogamous, spiritual, religious, self-confident, and reliable individuals."[13] Yet, given the current social climate exposing alarming violence rates, unemployment rates, and educational and health disparities, these desired personal characteristics for a Black mates seem unavailable. For the African American population, mate selection constraints can potentially inform the significant decline in marriage rates among Blacks. Analyzing these findings from a cultural perspective, specific concerns within the Black community have the potential to influence processes, such as mate selection. For example, violence has increased within and against the Black community.[14] Gang and gun violence and police brutality have flooded the Black community so that defining Black identity apart from

8. Sassler, "Partnering."

9. Arroyo et al., *Crossover in Median Age*, 1–2.

10. Sassler, "Partnering," 557–75.

11. Goldman, et al., "Demography."

12. Ibid.

13. King and Allen, "Personal."

14. Desmond et al., "Police."

these forces (for example, by finding a mate) has become more difficult.[15] The Black Lives Matter movement was founded on the unjust killings and overall unjust treatment of Black men, women, and children. Dissecting the severity of the oppressions Black people experience exposes the damaging effects such events have on constructs such as mate selection.

Mate Selection Barriers

Educational Attainment

The current state of mate selection among African American men and women living in the U.S. is researched in relationship to educational attainment. Historically African Americans have had a triumphant journey with education. Dating back to slavery, Africans were not allowed to develop literacy; learning how to read and write were forbidden.[16] Maintaining a sense of resilience, slaves would surreptitiously find ways to learn and excel, with the goal of strengthening the community and utilizing education as a survival tactic.[17] Leaders such as Booker T. Washington, Benjamin Banneker, and Benjamin W. Arnett have paved the way for current scholars, essentially creating an educational shield of protection for the generations to come. While the salience of education in the Black community has significant roots, sustaining the academic success of Black men and women is systemically challenged, potentially compromising other elements of their growth and development, such as finding a mate.

African American women are now one of the most educated demographics in the U.S., superseding Black men.[18] According to the National Center for Educational Statistics, between 2009 and 2010, Black women earned "68 percent of associate's degrees, 66 percent of bachelor's degrees, 71 percent of master's degrees and 65 percent of all doctorate degrees awarded to black students."[19] This education gap between Black women and Black men plays a part in the decreasing number of African American marriages.[20]

15. Ibid.; Chambers and Kravitz, "Understanding."
16. Bertocchi and Arcangelo, "Racial Gap."
17. Ibid.
18. King, "Multiple."
19. Osborne, "Black Women," lines 1–4.
20. McDaniel et al., "Black."

Although these statistics have a victorious ring to them, a question about the academic trajectories of Black males arises: why are Black females surpassing Black males in educational attainment? In addition, while Black women are becoming the most educated population in the U.S., they still fill a very small percentage of white-collar jobs. In addition, while Black women are becoming the most educated population in the U.S., they still fill a very small percentage of white-collar jobs.[21] This then exposes the complication of highly educated yet underemployed Black women finding partnerships with undereducated and underemployed Black men. What are the long-term affects of this apparent and burgeoning pattern? Could the gap in educational attainment between Black men and women inadvertently influence the mate selection process and potential marriage market? The unresearched yet obvious answer is, of course. The current observed and speculated dialogue around dating in the Black community invites comments like this: "Where are the eligible Black men?" and "That woman doesn't need a partner; she can do it on her own." Given their vulnerable position, Black men, it is conjectured, are being systematically and permanently incapacitated by unjust social structures and events.

The Strong Black Woman Persona

While African American women are seemingly excelling, at times the journey is not a smooth path, and in many instances Black women tackle constraining social pressures as well. Black women have for centuries endured the multiple oppressions of being Black and being women. Despite historical restrictions of socially constructed, debilitating images such as the welfare mother, the jezebel, and the sapphire, Black women maintain matriarchal status within the Black community.[22] The development of the strong Black woman (SBW) schema is an image that encompasses the stigma of historical hardships endured, portraying a woman who can complete all tasks and withstand all trials, without breaking a sweat.[23] The concept of *strength* the in the Black female community has maintained a sense of perseverance, mental endurance, power and prayer, while solidifying the experience of intersecting oppressions.[24] In popular culture, the SBW is a

21. Brewer, "Theorizing."
22. Gilkes, "Liberated."
23. Abrams et al., "Carrying."
24. Walker-Barnes, "Burden."

powerhouse. She is often displayed as the CEO of her own company, the head of her household, and a pillar of her community. While this image has so many salient messages, the experience of the stressed out and emotionally drained SBW is not as popular. The other side of the SBW may feel quite alone in her experience. Although it is not researched, could the SBW be a response to the scarcity of available men? Rarely is the SBW image paired with a partner. Standing in solidarity with women's rights and not suggesting that women couldn't fulfill such roles and requirements without a mate, there is an unmistakably large number of Black women transcending societal limitations and barriers, with a small number of men to share that experience with.

Violence in the Black Community

The multifaceted nature of #BlackLivesMatter exposes the intersections of race and gender, in addition to the systemic and patterned components of the violent events that preceded the movement. Violence against and within the Black community is an anteceding factor maintaining mass incarceration of Black men in America.[25] Gang violence and police brutality are the current trending acts of violence that harm the Black community's perpetually at-risk social status.[26] Violence within the Black community has been researched, and the critical influence such acts have on employment and family structure has been acknowledged.[27] Exposing the relationship between high rates of crime within the Black community and structural deprivation of social status, researchers have already uncovered the determining affect that the persistent mass incarceration of Black men is having on the production of female-led families and households—which has a cyclical affect on family disruption.[28] Further analyzing these findings and hypothesizing with the researched correlations between violence, mass incarceration, unemployment, poverty and family disruption cultivates a potential bond between violence in the Black community and mate selection.

Discussing the modern trends on mate selection and the overall health of Black unions stimulates a conversation about the influences of the current social climate and the perceived structural barriers to maintaining

25. Western and Wildeman, "Black Family."
26. Messner and Sampson, "Sex Ratio."
27. Sampson, "Effect"; Messner and Sampson, "Sex Ratio."
28. Sampson, "Effect"; Western and Wildeman, "Black Family."

the fragility of Black relationships, marriages, and families. Although violence in the Black community is predominately researched (revealing the alarming, increasing incarceration rates of Black men), Black families face significant pressures because in gun violence, gang violence, and in police brutality. These pressures must be investigated further.

Mass Incarceration of Black Men

Parallel to the increased rate of African American female educational attainment are the distressing increases in African American male incarceration rates. Black men have a long-standing history with the U.S. prison system, which consequently has systemically and structurally damaged the Black male identity, individually and relationally.[29] Harming the Black community in its entirety, Black male incarceration puts both the Black family and Black intimate partner relationships at risk.[30] Although 12 percent of Americans identify as African American, 35 percent of African Americans have been to jail, and 37 percent have been to prison;[31] sometimes they are arrested for crimes such as walking while Black. While Black lives (and specifically Black men's lives) receive sparse social and governmental protection, the repercussions for such displacement are weakening opportunities for educational attainment, economic stability, employment, and mate selection.[32] Encouraging a detrimental domino affect, limitations in one area inform the status of the next. For example, African American men who are subject to the prison system are researched in association with poverty and limited access to adequate education, which then has the potential to constrain their future of occupational success.[33] While these social journeys of Black men and women run parallel to each While these social journeys of Black men and women run parallel to each other, social factors affecting African American men are creating a discrepancy for Black women between available and eligible mate options.

29. Western and Wildeman, "Black Family."

30. Charles and Luoh, "Male Incarceration."

31. Zeng, "Jail," 1.

32. Lopoo and Western, "Incarceration"; Western and Wildeman, "Black Family"; Charles and Luoh, "Male Incarceration."

33. Pettit and Western, "Life Course"; Western and Wildeman, "Black Family."

Spiritual Resources and Therapeutic Interventions

While the development of the Black Lives Matter movement was a response to the unjust killings of individuals such as Trayvon Martin, Michael Brown, Tamir Rice, and Philando Castile, the movement is also a means of community resilience. The individuals in community with these slain men and boys were daughters, sons, sisters, brothers, mothers, and fathers. Each young man who was murdered was removed form his Black family structure so that the vulnerability of Black families, Black marriages, and Black lives was perpetuated. Although mate selection may not overtly appear to be challenged by the affects of violence, police brutality, racism, or sexism, you now have an understanding of the perceived concomitant risks of finding a mate. How can we begin to transition the glaring trends of mate selection in the Black community? With no intent to discourage, awareness can promote action. Through education, awareness, access, and action, the Black Lives Matter movement offers an intervening push toward the eradication of not only violence against minorities, racism, and sexism, but also the wide range of limitations these events put on the community. It is imperative to be aware of and to have access to resources that can aid in combating the multifarious constraints of these systemic issues. Provided the cursory review of historical structures and the current state of mate selection and barriers within the black community, a review of spiritual guideposts and therapeutic interventions aligns with all-conquering quest of the Black Lives Matter movement.

Spirituality and Mate Selection

The Bible introduces the first array of couples, the journeys of their individual selves, the divine nature of their meeting, and the trials and tribulations of their unions. The lessons on how to achieve partnership, commitment, and love are compounded in the stories of couples such as Isaac and Rebekah, Zechariah and Elizabeth, and Joseph and Mary. Within each couple's relationship are the plights to achieve relationship success, combat relational hardships with faith, and transition through life with a united front, protected and guided by God. For instance, Zechariah and Elizabeth teach us that faithful prayer and humble patience with God, will serve as a guidepost towards God's will for their relationship.[34] In their case,

34. Luke 1:1–25 (NRSV).

Zechariah's prayer was for a son, and his faithful service and trust in God's will ultimately blessed himself and Elizabeth with John.[35] They each prayed for the success of their union and the development of their family, and their prayers were answered, but not without great trials, weaknesses, and sometimes even doubt. During this current troubling time in society, when peace, love, partnership, and community are being tested, the unions that preceded our time teach us that such events require prayer. While prayer is a means to discuss with God what you believe you need, want, and are ready for, God requires commitment to his will.

Isaac and Rebekah remind us that love and relationships require commitment.[36] God gives us the power to decide, and we decide to love. Isaac did not meet his wife until the day of their wedding, but they decide to commit to each other and to love one another. Last, alongside prayer and commitment is the command for action. After all, God is always listening and guiding us toward his will, so once we have committed to the task, be ready to act. We learn from Joseph and Mary that *love* is a verb, and that relationships require action. Action can be accomplished both individually and together. Joseph and Mary faced formidable challenges during and after the birth of Jesus—challenges that place stress on their relationship.[37] They show each other the love present in their relationship in order to fight the hostilities and uncertainties of the world. Their union exudes respect, trust, prayer, commitment, and action.

These relationships, among many in the Bible, serve as guideposts for building and maintaining a relationship but also the journey towards finding one.

History of Mate Selection

Although the process of mate selection used to involve elders, parents, and servants choosing a mate for a child, the sought-after union was always a part of God's will. Now these biblical mating practices are no longer used regularly, but some cultural elements of mate selection within the Black community remain rooted in spirituality. In fact, a variety of historical mating practices dates back to slavery; these practices have greatly influenced the current mate selection behaviors among Black men and women.

35. Ibid.
36. Gen 24:2–66 (NRSV).
37. Matt 1: 18–25 (NRSV).

Whereas slaves were not allowed to engage in anything ceremonial or ritual based such as a wedding, mating traditions and behaviors were centered on necessity and rested on the sanctity of spirituality.[38] During slavery, men, women, and children were taken from their homes, spouses, and families, never to return—and presumably unable to ever find any resemblance of such a bond ever again. While Black people were held against their will and forced to live a life of servitude, relationships and family were means of survival.[39] Therefore finding a mate during slavery did not necessarily accommodate personal interests and subjective fancies, such as physical appearance, stylish clothes, or even the idea of love at first sight. The desired attributes of a partner were predominately based on culturally constructed partner roles and characteristics.[40] Quite gendered, the roles entailed the ability for a man to provide, and protect, and of a woman to serve, nurture, and support.[41] Many, if not each of those role-based qualities can be found in the mate selection requirements of Black men and women today; unfortunately, along with these traits can be found the consistently vulnerable status of Black families and marriages. So, how can we continue to learn from Isaac and Rebekah, Joseph and Mary, and, Zechariah and Elizabeth? During this immobilizing time for Black individuals, couples, and families, in what ways can we continue to promote resilience through prayer, commitment, and action when the focus is finding a mate?

Spiritual Resources

Within the Black community seeking clergy for personal prayer and assistance has diverse meanings and purposes. African Americans have been researched in relationship to seeking clergy for personal healing, physical healing, and relational healing.[42] The biblical grounding of relationships encourages the use of assistance when preparing for and preserving an intimate partner relationship. Seeking clergy members for interpersonal help begins with making sure you're one with God. Clergy members encourage commitment to another person, yet not without a personal commitment

38. Hill, "Marriage."
39. Dill et al., "Fictive Kin."
40. Cherlin, "American Marriage."
41. Ibid.; Pinderhughes, "African American Marriage."
42. Giger et al., "Church and Spirituality."

to Christ first. This commitment then motivates the need to seek a partner that you can share your faith with.[43]

Seeking clergy to address various personal concerns has helped protect help-seeking behaviors within the Black community. Help-seeking behaviors are the actions and attempts targeting access to assistance for a presenting problem.[44] Given the historically poor relationship to mental and physical healthcare institutions, Black community members have found comfort, resolution, and many times solutions to major life events from the aid of the church. The relationship between the Black community and the Black church, is quite close. Possessing a tender vulnerability, Black men, women, and children find sodality in the church setting, developing a sincere sense of trust, confidentiality, reliability, and hope.[45] The life events and stories requiring healing and guidance from clergy are bountiful. Needing prayer and requesting guidance, healing, or both is not specific to physical ailments, death, and divorce, but also might relate to the transitional time of finding a mate.

Spiritual Premarital Counseling

In order to place ease and reassurance on the quest for a mate, we must put our faith in God. While the current and universal state of mate selection is an impaired entity alone, adding a drop or two of melanin invites a host of additional constraining factors. Maintaining the use of spiritual guidance, in addition to prayer, what can individuals do to aid the process of finding a mate? The use of spiritual counseling and spiritual premarital counseling have both been researched in relation to Black couples, conclusively highlighting the positive outcomes both resources provide.[46] Operating within regimented parameters, spiritual counseling can guide not only the process of finding a mate, but also preparation for the journey.[47] In fact, in the African American community, Black clergypersons report that adequately addressing premarital content, utilizing a skills-based approach in marriage counseling, and considering marriage preparation are crucial elements of

43. Waite and Lehrer, "Benefits."

44. Rickwood and Thomas, "Conceptual Measurement Framework."

45. Giger et al., "Church and Spirituality."

46. Weaver et al., "Marriage and Family Therapists"; Hine and Boyd-Franklin, "African American Families."

47. Stanley et al., "Community-Based."

ministry.[48] Spiritual counseling as it relates to the lives of Black men and women, has a rich history. Individuals and couples have been confiding in church clergy for centuries, praying for the perfect man or woman or seeking a healing hand for relational turmoil: this resource remains quite available and an asset to the potential needs of the current Black community.

Therapeutic Interventions and Mate Selection— Marriage and Family Therapy

Responding to systemic constraints, the Black Lives Matter movement not only wants to eliminate violence against minorities, specifically African Americans, but also calls for overall societal resilience. Now that we follow the trends that place Black marriages and Black families at risk, the next step is intervention. In addition to the realms of spiritual guidance via spiritual counseling and premarital counseling is an additional field of study designed to meet the needs of a community through the subsystems within the community (i.e., individuals, couples and families). Marriage and family therapy is a growing form of therapeutic intervention that recognizes the systems to which individuals belong, and how they interact. A level of integration occurs among marriage and family therapy theories and treatment models—an integration serves the cultural elements of individual and relational needs.[49] In order to address the challenges of mate selection, utilizing a resource that analyzes relationship structures to solve problems has potential to promote positive outcomes. Provided a variety of systemic interventions, marriage and family therapists align with individual, couple or family needs—all while working from an integration of treatment models that will best serve. In addition, therapists are able work with clients of diverse backgrounds, encompassing differing socioeconomic backgrounds, different races, genders, and sexual orientations.

Preparing for a mate is indeed a part of the mate selection process. While the goal is to find a mate that checks off the majority of your desired traits, men and women also have to make sure they meet their own expectations as well. Research supports that marriage preparation has been found to improve marital satisfaction, increase spousal commitment, and contribute to a 31-percent decrease in the divorce rate.[50] A small 37 per-

48. Wilmoth and Blaney, "African American Clergy."
49. Awosan et al., "Understanding the Experience."
50. Stanley et al., "Community-Based."

cent of diverse couples in the U.S. disclosed receiving a form of premarital counseling, and "86 percent strongly agreed and encourage couples to engage in premarriage preparation (i.e., therapy, premarital counseling), while 46 percent agreed or strongly agreed premarital counseling should be required by law before receiving a marriage license."[51] While therapeutic and educational programs addressing intimate partner relationships and preparation are traditionally accessible only to White, middle-class couples, more diverse resources are available today then ever before.[52] For African American men and women struggling to find a mate and discouraged by the current social climate, now is the time to get a sense of the resources available, not only for exploring a relationship with someone else, but also for exploring the relationship you have with yourself.

Conclusion

Now that you have a brief but comprehensive understanding of the historical factors of mate selection, the current state of finding a mate, and spiritual guideposts and therapeutic interventions for counteracting the many societal restrictions afflicting the Black community, we must follow the word: "Now faith is the assurance of things hoped for, the conviction of things not seen."[53] The Black Lives Matter movement has exposed the inadequacies of a system that was designed to serve and protect. The systemic affects of violence in the Black community are multifaceted, altering not only the life of a Black individual but also the sustainability of Black couples and Black families. While the process of mate selection within the Black community is in a vulnerable proposition, be reminded that Black love is still attainable and beautiful when maintained. After all, "Two are better than one, because they have a good reward for their toil."[54]

51. Ibid.
52. Halford et al., "Strengthening."
53. Heb 11:1 NRSV.
54. Eccl 4:9 NRSV.

15

The Talk

Black Fathers, Black Sons—Letters to Survive

JAMIE D. HAWLEY AND DERRICK FLOYD

By almost every measure, the group that is facing some of the most
severe challenges in the 21st century in this country are boys and young
men of color

—President Barack Obama

Just a boy from the hood that
Got my hands in the air
In despair don't shoot
I just wanna do good

—Jay-Z

Black Fathers Matter!

—God

In this chapter the authors (both fathers of Black sons, both educators,
both pastors, and both spiritual care providers) have been asked to focus
on Black fatherhood and raising sons in the age of #BlackLivesMatter.

While we have been asked to focus on Black males and fatherhood for this chapter, it is important to note that the challenges faced by Black fathers and the social disparities of raising Black boys are in many ways the challenges of Black women and the disparate challenges of raising Black girls. My coauthor and I are sons, brothers, uncles, and nephews. We are college graduates, counselors, educators, pastors, and chaplains. What we are most proud of is having the privilege to be our sons' Dad. We approach this task by writing letters to our sons.

The Talk

Jamie D. Hawley

Dear Son,

It breaks my heart into a million pieces to have to write to you these words, and yet I know that they are necessary to keep you alive. These words are necessary because sadly we live in an age where human beings are still ranked, valued, judged, marginalized, and deconstructed according to race, gender, class, and sexuality. We live in age where your skin, kissed by God, was marginalized, demonized, criminalized, and viewed as threatening all before you were born. More and more Black and Brown communities are under the siege and assault of gentrifying. Gentrification is dangerous. It perpetuates violence against Black people to make White people feel "safe." You must know that your assertion will be viewed as aggression. Your self-pride and dignity will be viewed as uppity. Thinking critically will be viewed as being noncompliant. Your curiosity will be interpreted as being challenging. Your country's social contract with White supremacy, racism, and cultural (In)competence means that all of your lives are at risk . . . your social, political, financial-economic, and physical life. I must tell you that they'll shoot you on credit. They will shoot first and ask questions later. They'll kill you and dismiss your entire life, using a three-word, cold, cal- culated, and cookie-cutter dry script, "I felt threatened." Your feelings will not matter. Reason and rationality will not matter. Facts will not matter. And to some, to many, your very life will not matter. It is because of the sin of Whiteness and America's longtime love affair with imperialist White supremacist capitalist patriarchy that I lift my voice as your father to join in what has become an international declaration. After the cold-blooded murder of a child who looked like you do now, who dressed like you do now, who was as innocent as you are now, and who was gunned down by a racist vigilante when he was the exact age that you are now Black Lives Matter! It is what I shouted on the streets of Ferguson, Mo, one week after the murder of another Black child. Black Lives Matter! It is what you and I shouted as we marched through the streets of Washington DC after the murder of Sandra Bland. Black Lives Matter! Black Lives Matter! Black Lives Matter!

Born in the Struggle

I was there as the pregnancy test turned pink. I was there when your mother began spotting in the middle of night and threatened to miscarry again. In panic and fear I drove her to the closest civilian emergency room. Little did I know that coming to the hospital would be my daily routine for the next month or so. I took your mother to the doctor's office every other day to have blood work drawn to monitor if the pregnancy was progressing, if you were progressing. The doctor placed your mother on bed rest for the next two trimesters. The doctor graciously allowed me come back every odd day to find out the results. She said to me with a nod and a wink "I can't tell you the results of your wife's test, but if you should happen to look over my shoulder as I'm entering the results in her medical record, then I can't help that." It still seems odd to some but nevertheless true that I went to the doctor's office literally more times than your mother throughout the pregnancy. I had to know that you were okay. And every day your mother and I rejoiced in knowing that you were still actively fighting to come into this world.

I was there when you were born. I was there when the doctor informed your mother and me of the health anomalies you were born with. I was there to be your primary care provider, to feed you in the middle of the night, to change your diapers. Why wouldn't I be? You changed my entire world. You made me something that I had never been before: a father.

June 2001

You were two months old. You and I made the pilgrimage from Florida, where we resided at that time, to Texas, where your grandparents lived. I drove the distance because given your heart condition, flying was not safe. Being with and caring for you felt quite natural to me. Which is why I thought nothing of being pulled over by a Louisiana police officer one day and being interrogated. I was sure that I was not speeding. I was certain that my license plates and registration were current. As the officer approached my vehicle wearing a cowboy hat he demanded in a deep southern drawl "Where's the baby's momma?"

I was shocked. I hadn't broken any laws or ordinances. I immediately recalled the many times my father had given me "the talk." "The talk" in essence consisted of that conversation where a Black parent tells their Black child those things that are necessary to keep the child from danger.

"Dad, what do I do if I'm ever stopped by the police," I'd ask.

"Son, first thing is that it is not a matter of IF but WHEN you are stopped by the police. Don't talk back. Say yes sir and no sir—yes ma'am and no ma'am. Do what you are told. Make sure you keep your hands open and in plain sight at all times. Don't talk back."

And most importantly, he would say, "Make sure you live to survive another day."

I answered the officer with as much humility as I could muster. I smiled, lowered my shoulders, made sure not to give him too much direct eye contact or personality. It was the first time I felt completely vulnerable as your father, knowing that my ability to protect you was literally at the mercy of someone else. After I explained, he asked me for my driver's license and registration. I explained to him that I needed to reach into my back pocket to retrieve my license. As I gave him my license I also made sure to give him my active-duty military ID card. I had hoped that flashing him my military ID would humanize me to him. Employing the lessons I learned from your granny and pawpaw must have worked. He eventually let us go. I would feel completely vulnerable as your father a few more times throughout your young childhood, but never as reminded of that vulnerability as I was the day that I knew for sure that you realized and understood your Blackness in an American context. "Dad," you asked, "what do I do if I'm ever stopped by the police?"

August 2014

"Dad, what do I do if I'm ever stopped by the police?" you asked me one summer hot day. You stared inquisitively at me. The murder of teen and recent high school graduate Mike Brown by Darren Wilson was all over the news. I could tell that you were genuinely concerned. I was too. You were just fourteen years old, but I knew that to culturally incompetent people you would be seen as older and not as an innocent child. Seven. That is how old you were when you lost your innocence to some. I vividly remember coming to your second-grade parent-teacher conference at your suburban primary school and sitting across a table from your teacher, a White woman in her early to midtwenties. "Jamie hugs me a lot and I'm uncomfortable with it," she said coldly. "I've told him several times that he's at an age where he needs to ask permission to hug people and not just attack them." There is was. At seven years old, the person that I had entrusted to teach you reading, writing, and mathematics already viewed you as a hypersexualized brute who needed to be tamed as opposed to the innocent child you were, growing up without the presence of his mother in his daily life. While that moment was disappointing, it certainly was not surprising to me, and neither should it be for anyone.

What we know is that Black boys are disproportionately expelled or suspended in public schools for behaving similarly to their White male peers.[1] What we know is that Black boys as young as seven years of age on average are viewed as older, bigger, and less innocent than their White counterparts, and automatically guilty.[2] The most recent example that garnered national attention was the murder of Tamir Rice. Tamir was a twelve-year-old boy playing (like all children do) across the street from his home with a toy gun (like all children do) when a neighbor (a White woman) called 911 with concerns about "a man brandishing a weapon at the park." Only two seconds after the officer drove up, he shot and killed him. Speaking with his dispatcher he says "Shots fired . . . male down . . . maybe twenty." What we know is that most White boys raised in wealthy families will stay rich or upper-middle-class as adults, but Black boys raised in similarly rich households will not. What we know is that a Black man with a degree is more likely to be passed over for a job than is a White man who dropped out of high school AND has a criminal record![3] We also know that at as young as seven years of age, White children believe that

1. Black students, boys, and students with disabilities were disproportionately disciplined (e.g., suspensions and expulsions) in K-12 public schools, according to GAO's analysis of Department of Education (Education) national civil rights data for school year 2013–14, the most recent available (Government Accountability Office, "K–12 Education").

2. Goff et al., "Essence of Innocence."

3. Chetty, "Two Americas."

Black children are less capable of actually feeling physical pain.[4] Perhaps for this very reason Black children are likely to spend a longer period of time in an emergency room waiting area than White children are, and for this very reason Black children and are almost 40 percent less likely to be given pain medication in a situation when White children would receive it. We also know that the disparity in pain medication continues from childhood to adulthood for African Americans.[5] We know that Black men are disproportionately stopped by the police, arrested, convicted and issued stiffer fines, penalties, and longer confinement sentences.[6] We also know that white evangelical Christians continue to overwhelmingly believe that the criminal justice system treats people of color and Whites equally.[7] In almost every factor Black boys are worse off than their White peers. This is not merely coincidence or luck of the draw. This inequality is human made, maintained, and sustained. It is why Ta-Nehisi Coates defines being Black as "being at the bottom."[8] The examples of persisting inequality are not an exception to the status quo. They entail the epitome of the status quo. Despite the well-documented history of racial inequalities throughout society; despite all the empirically verified studies, data, documentaries, books, journals; interviews and testimonies, many still claim not to know that these inequalities exist.

What we know is that Black boys are under attack. Those under attack must find places of refuge and liberation. When I was your age, the Black church was that place for me. Today I worry that it may not be such a place for you.

The Black Church[9]

Sadly, many of our churches are distracted with pie-in-the-sky theology and the prosperity gospel, with denominationalism and dogma, and with

---

4. Hoffman et al., "Racial Bias in Pain Assessment," 113–16.

5. Green et al., "Unequal Burden of Pain."

6. Walsh, "Cost of Inequality."

7. Fowler, "Police Brutality Drove a Wedge."

8. Coates, *Between the World and Me*, 19.

9. "The Black church" is widely understood to include the following seven major Black Protestant denominations: the National Baptist Convention, the National Baptist Convention of America, the Progressive National Convention, the African Methodist Episcopal Church, the African Methodist Episcopal Zion Church, the Christian Methodist Episcopal Church, and the Church of God in Christ.

personal piety instead of public policy. Evangelical churches are easily entertained with so-called prophets who can tell you your name and the last digit of your Social Security number, and who engage in other sensational gimmicks. This religious sensationalism and entertainment is no different from that of a psychic. However, a biblical prophet is someone with the courage to speak truth to power. Even Pharaoh's prophets could turn water into blood, summon frogs, and turn sticks into snakes. What they could not or rather would not do was to tell Pharaoh that he was dead wrong for holding God's people as slaves and to demand that he let them go. A true prophet's role is not to entertain evangelical churches but to discern what the Lord has to say about what is happening in our local city halls, in our state governments, in the White House and in the world at large. What does the Lord have to say about racism and sexism, homophobia and hetero-sexism, capitalism and poverty, hunger and homelessness—to name a few types of oppression? True prophets speak truth to power. True prophets put their butts on the line. I suspect that many who call themselves prophets would more accurately be described as magicians, performing nothing more than magic tricks for entertainment in exchanged for an offering. In an era when our children are being educated in dilapidating schools until they're old enough to be shipped off to prisons, in an era when our children can be shot and killed and the perpetrator can go free, in an era when Black women earn at a minimum twenty-five cents less than Black men solely because they don't have a penis,[10] I echo Marvin A. McMickles's sentiment when he poetically and prophetically asks, "Where have all the prophets gone?"[11]

Conversely, progressive churches often are drowning in classism and elitism. One of the many examples of this snobbery is the question, often asked: where did you go to school? Often behind this question is not an attempt to get to know someone; rather the question is asked in order to determine how much respect to give the one who's asked. Interestingly enough, the higher the prestige of the school and the greater the accomplishment and status, the more the individual becomes "like family." Whether "that's my brother" or that's my "sister," depends on his or her qualifications, of course. The Black church of the '60s gave birth the civil rights movement, a movement that has been borrowed and copied many times domestically

10. Institute for Women's Policy Research, "Gender Wage Gap: 2017"; and Equal Rights Advocates, "Moving Women Forward."

11. McMickle, *Where Have All the Prophets Gone?*, 8.

and internationally by other marginalized groups. Our reality is that Black millennials have now caught up with White millennials and are leaving the church and organized religion at alarming rates[12]—so much so that Princeton University professor Eddie Glaude declared in an op-ed, "The Black church, as we have known it, is dead." If we are not careful, the modern-day church will not pass along anything living or lasting.

In Closing

Son, although you live a world that marginalizes you and insists that you are a minority, despite the fact that globally there are more people who look like you than there are those who believe themselves to be White, you are uniquely special. Even though you are my namesake, there will never be another you. You bear the imprimatur of the divine. You are my son. You are a walking sun. Your light shines bright. You have a fire that burns deep within you. Channel that fire to liberate the oppressed. Use it to speak up for the marginalized, the silenced, the disregarded, and the unheard. Know that wherever you go, you do not go alone. You are surrounded by a great cloud of witnesses. The blood of survivors, your ancestors who endured being kidnapped, being enslaved, and living under Jim and Jane Crow flows through your veins.

Your Black Life Matters!

Signed,

Forever your Dad,

The Talk Continued . . .

Derrick Floyd

> Then Jacob called his sons, and said: "Gather around, that I may tell you what will happen to you in days to come. Assemble and hear, O sons of Jacob; listen to Israel, your father." (Gen 49:1–2, NRSV)

---

12. See Kennedy, "Engaging Millennials through the Tradition."

Dear Son,

I'm sitting here thinking about our time together and all the great talks we so often have. I remember you asking me, why do we sit and have "the talk" after every situation in my life and every incident that becomes national news? I have often shared with you that my heart beats because of you. I will always protect you from any known or perceived threat. They are ever prevalent. My upbringing has governed why I do what I do with regard to you and our relationship. I grew up in the South, in a house of very loquacious people. I think we just loved to hear ourselves talk. It was refreshing. It still is. Moreover, the interesting dynamic was that we all had something to say. So we thought. Evenings were our favorite pastimes . We would clown with each other. We would level one put-down lovingly after another, but to hear my grandparents speak was the best. Seemingly the room stood still whenever they, my grandpa included, opened their mouths. It was always good, good words of wisdom. They would take a historically retrospective look through time. They would always take the time to remember whence they had come. It was almost prophetic to hear the things they had endured and the strides we had made as a country. It wasn't unusual for my grandmother to speak of great times, but in the same breath you would note the expressions of sadness that consumed her as she discussed where the world would end up. "Listen," my grandma would say with tears in her eyes, "Boy, you have to work twice as hard to be considered half as good. They ain't gone give you nuttin." And by "they," I knew she and they meant White people. As I got older, I suddenly realized that we were having "the Talk."

Many years had passed . . . I was sitting and thinking one day. A quote by author Carol Moseley-Braun had consumed me. She writes, "Defining myself, as opposed to being defined by others, is one of the most difficult challenges I face."[13] After sitting and contemplating what she said, much to my chagrin, I suddenly became ashamed. I gloated quite often about being "woke." I was one of the ones! In my mind, I understood the signs of the times. I knew what needed to happen, and I knew how to get it done. Somehow, Moseley-Braun's words annihilated what was, in times past, my prize possession. My wokeness! My fantasy world and the idea that I had been a beacon of light to my African American male peers in every area of their lives was now in question. I had somehow forgotten to have the talk with them that I had with you, and that my dad and grandfather had with

---

13 Quoted in D'Orio, *Carol Moseley-Braun*, 63.

me. As your dad, and the principal of a predominantly African American school, I've always wanted to be "the guy" for my son, and my extended sons. It is the source of my strength. The root that held me together. Unlike you, I knew these young men did not have fathers in the home, and I was intentional about being a father to them. I too watch many of them struggle with self-identity and self-worth. They had no inkling of their worth. They did not know they were kings. Royalty coursed through their veins. Other people always defined us. Societal norms, past and present, are the culprits. Consequently, for us, it was easier to accept who they say we are. I saw them, my Black males, acquiesce to ideas of promiscuity, rap artist, athletes, and criminal intentions as the sum total of who they were. This is not our legacy. Will this be our history? Of course not. I will die sharing with my sons who they are. This darker hue has always come with it's unique set of problems and assets. Carter Woodson says, "We should emphasize not Negro History, but the Negro in history. What we need is not a history of selected races or nations, but the history of the world void of national bias, race hate, and religious prejudice."[14]

In Genesis chapter 49 of the Bible, Jacob stops dying so he can speak into the lives of his sons. He gathers them together around his bedside. He did not want to sleep with his fathers until he had prophesied to his sons. There were things he needed them to know. Jacob needed to have the talk with his sons. He wanted to speak into their lives and tell them what they would become before society had an opportunity to tell them all they couldn't be. He longed to help his sons define themselves as opposed leaving that daunting task for someone else. He had to remind them of who their grandfather and great-grandfather were. Mickle in meaning, it was the nucleus of their existence. It parallels the father's role in a Jewish bar mitzvah. Traditionally the father speaks into the life of his son. He prays a blessing over him to protect him as he enters into this new phase of life. In essence, he is prescriptively having the talk with his son before a crowd of witnesses. If you read the text, Israel (Jacob) has decided what he will do to preserve the lives of his sons, but the second verse—"Assemble and hear, O sons of Jacob; listen to Israel your father"—provides instructions for the sons. When Jacob speaks, when he has the talk, they must be willing to listen to what he has to say. Beleaguered from past hurts, ideologies, stigmatizations, and stereotypes, it seems hard for us to persevere. "I am what time, circumstances, history, have made me, certainly, but I am also, much

14. Woodson, "Celebration of Negro History Week"

more than that. So are well all," writes James Baldwin.[15] This quote speaks to the mind-set of a population. In this quote, Mr. Baldwin says (without saying it) that we are products of our environment, but we are not prisoners to it. We are so much more than what "they" could ever imagine we would be.

We think about the efforts that have been made to ensure that we as a people would have equal footing—the civil rights era comes to mind. Twelve percent of African Americans were actively involved in the civil rights movement. By sheer addition and subtraction, this means 88 percent were watching from the sidelines. At a time in our history when things were do or die, sink or swim, even life or death. Only 12 percent of those directly impacted were in direct action. Do you know what that means? That means a few people can make a huge difference when they are of one mind and one heart. To the contrary, it also means that most people will stand back and let the few take the risks that will affect the masses. Sad, yes. I am glad to be in the 12 percent who is willing to make the sacrifice for our young men. I have come to realize that the talk is not an easy one to have. I also realize that if no one ever has it, then you, my son and my brothers, will forever live by the words of those who would rather us be paupers in a kingdom that belongs to us. Remember, the talk is one aspect, but the listen is the part that will cultivate change. Knowledge isn't power until it is applied.

What we have experienced in the past few hundred years has been a testament to the hearts of men. Fear and uncertainty have governed our nation. "They" never understood us nor desired too. W. E. B. DuBois, in *The Souls of Black Folk*, says, "Herein lies the tragedy of the age: not that men are all poor—all men know something of poverty; not that men are all wicked—who is good? Not that men are ignorant—what is truth? Nay, but that men know so little of men."[16] *The truth is marinated in this quote.* Men know so little of men. I want you to continue to move in faith and AC-TION. Move in the faith that I taught you. Not church faith. Church doesn't call for action but that we simply believe blindly that God will do it. This is not the lesson I teach. Not completely understanding what God and the universe is implementing in our lives, we trust. We trust that the actions we will use to overthrow ideas, customs, antiquated thought processes dripping with racism are sanctioned and supported by God. And if not, we use the advocate we have with the Father.

15. Baldwin, "Preface to the 1984 Edition," xii.
16. Du Bois, *Souls of Black Folk*, 226–27.

To you and to my brothers, the one constant we have is our commitment to each other as family, extended or otherwise. We may not all share the same, but we are family. Bereft of nothing, we have a unique bond that cannot be separated by time, distance, space, or the lack of understanding from others outside of our coalition. We support each other in good and bad times. We speak truth to each other, with the innate ability to call ourselves unto greatness. Iron sharpens iron. We speak truth to those who choose to believe the lie. We cultivate the man of valor that lies within. Prov 17:17 says, "A friend loveth at all times, but a brother is born for adversity."[17] We are morphing into a more excellent us. What I have you have. Your pain is my pain. Your joy is my joy. We bleed from the same vein and we drink from the same cup. Nothing shall ever divide us. What I am you are, and what you are I am. Am I my brother's' keeper? I am! Right now and always. We exist from this fiber. In Malcolm X's speech "Prospects for Freedom,"[18] he stood firmly and said, "You can't separate peace from freedom because no one can be at peace unless he has his freedom."[19] This fiber threads to the freedom of your mind. Be liberated in thought. Be liberated in deed. Be liberated in what you say. Jesus said, "It is the spirit that quickeneth; the flesh profiteth nothing: the words that I speak unto you, they are spirit, and they are life" (John 6:63, KJV). I am grateful I had the talk. I am grateful my fathers had the talk with me. It helped to shape what I would say to you and to my extended sons. Even though the talk was essential, I am even more thankful that I submitted to the listening. Jacob spoke well to his sons, but his sons also listened to what he had to say. It was because of the listen that I/we usually embraced the lesson.

Love,

Dad

17. Ibid.

18. X, "Prospects for Freedom."

19. Ibid., 152.

16

Changing the Subject

Creating Caring Communities
for Women Impacted by Abortion

KAREN WALKER-MCCLURE

During a women's Bible study one evening on the subject of forgiveness, one of the members (a middle-aged woman) said, "I can never ask God to forgive me for something I knew was wrong. I had two abortions when I was young, and I knew what I was doing. You can't ask for forgiveness when you know what you were doing is wrong." Her teacher (a woman minister) sat there flabbergasted and did not know how to respond to her statement. This is an excellent example which indicates that the church does not know how to respond to issues surrounding voluntary pregnancy termination, more commonly known as abortion. Maybe some ministers have preached from the pulpit that the Bible tells us, "Thou shalt not kill." Therefore women should not have abortions. Or we may hear the church take a side—as either pro-life or pro-choice—in the abortion argument.

However, the time has come to change the subject from whether or not one should have an abortion to how we minister to the millions of women who have had abortions and have kept a secret because they are ashamed of being judged, or because they believe they cannot ask for forgiveness because they "knew what they were doing."

When a child is stillborn, mothers are allowed to grieve. When a woman has a miscarriage, the parents are expected to grieve. When a baby lives for a short time and dies because of Sudden Infant Death Syndrome (SIDS), the mother is given sympathy and permitted to grieve. However, when a woman chooses to abort, some people think she does not have the right to grieve. Therefore she hides her pain and allows it to fester and manifest itself in many different ways. After experiencing abortion, some women feel that they are not worthy to be loved by a man. Some fear they will never have another child. Some feel that God is punishing them when bad things happen to them. In addition to the guilt, they also are holding shame and embarrassment.

Studies on both the pro-life and the pro-choice sides agree that trauma is associated with abortion.[1] The loss of a child is very traumatic. Studies have shown that women who have an abortion feel that they do not have the right to grieve because it was a decision they made. Therefore very few processes are in place to help a woman grieving from abortion. Many times, if a woman reaches out for help in dealing with grief to the clinic where her abortion was performed, she is told that her hormones are out of whack because of the procedure and that she will be fine in a few weeks. Or she may be told that she just has to live with the decision she made.

In her book *Forbidden Grief: The Unspoken Pain of Abortion*, coauthor Dr. Theresa Burke has said:

> Grief can be healing. It signals our living and feeling in connection with others. It represents our vulnerability, our humanity. When we remember and mourn our losses, we free our souls to move beyond the pain. This is the purpose of funerals. As difficult as they are, they provide a public expression of our grief, a way to say goodbye while surrounded by friends and loved ones, and a place to remember with dignity our lasting connections to one another. Women who undergo abortions are never permitted this social connection.[2]

Therefore because they have no way to publicly express grief over their lost child or to say goodbye, they must suffer in silence and in secret.

I chose a church setting as the place of my context because the church has been silent on the issue of abortion. The church may speak out against

---

1. See, e.g., Burke and Reardon, *Forbidden Grief*; and Babbel, "Post Abortion Stress Syndrome."
2. Burke and Reardon, *Forbidden Grief*, 64.

abortion and teach that abortion is sin, but no one tells a mother or father about what to do after the abortion. No one says, "Because we know that all have sinned and come short of the glory of God, this is how you can be helped even if you've done that. God loves you too." There is a need for a ministry to address this issue so that persons can be restored in their relationship with God, or be introduced for the first time into a relationship with God. Many times, persons who have experienced abortion feel that they cannot talk to anyone. They may experience guilt, fear, and disappointment. They may sometimes feel that God would not want to have a relationship with them because of what they have done. The church does not minister to these persons, either individually or in a group. So no one is able to work through the pain and guilt even when so many women in our churches have experienced it.

In my faith tradition, churches have ministries for those struggling with substance abuse and for those living with a substance abuser. They have ministries for single mothers, for children, and for men. Most recently there have been ministries popping up for women who are victims of domestic and sexual abuse. However, I do not know of any ministries that give women and men permission to grieve the loss of their aborted babies so they can be healed. Abortion is such a taboo subject; people are uncomfortable talking about it. Yet according to statistics one in four women have experienced an abortion, which means that a quarter of the women sitting in our congregations have had abortions.[3] Age does not matter. Some women have been carrying this guilt for over forty years, and some just recently had an abortion. Pastors have no problem providing pastoral care to persons who have lost a loved one; but when it comes to providing care to those who have had an abortion, women and men have few places to go to grieve the loss of their child so that healing can begin. How can they be restored to wholeness? The question is, how do we create safe places for persons to tell and retell their stories so they can be liberated from the secrecy, shame, and guilt they have carried around for many years?

On this explorative journey, it has been stated repeatedly, "You must address your secrets before you can be healed." The late Dr. Emma Justes addresses keeping secrets in her book *Please Don't Tell*. She discusses how secrets are often passed from generation to generation, and how damaging they can be. She indicates that the content of a secret is not the main problem; the problem is that keeping a secret can itself inflict damage on the one

3. Guttmacher Institute, "United States: Abortion."

guarding the secret. The whole premise is that once a secret is shared, it no longer has the destructive power over you that it once had. Secrets have a hidden power over us because if we keep secrets, we live in fear that they may one day come out and shame us or spoil our good name. However, secrets have no power over us once they are shared. Once a secret is shared, you never have to worry about someone finding out.[4]

Many women who had abortions have kept that secret for many years. Abortions can be swept under the rug and no one will ever have to know what happened. In fact, the primary reason women have abortions is so that no one will know they were ever pregnant. Women have abortions for many different reasons. Perhaps they wish to conceal a pregnancy resulting from an extramarital relationship. Maybe they are very young and feel that they cannot care for a child. Perhaps they have been raped. Maybe they are unmarried. Or they may be in an uncommitted relationship with a partner who is not in favor of having a child. Or they may already have children and do not feel that they can care for another child.

For instance, in the course of a conversation, one woman said, "You would be surprised at the number of women who are sitting in church every Sunday who have had abortions and are suffering in silence. I had an abortion, and I remember every time something bad happened to me I thought God was punishing me for murdering my child." Another woman said, "I had an abortion when I was a young woman, and now I've never had any children. I have often wondered if God didn't let me have any more children because he punished me for having the abortion." It is not God's intention that women should suffer because of their choices. God is a God of liberation, healing, and grace—not one who would desire that women live their lives in secrecy, shame, and guilt without the forgiveness of others or oneself. When we see how prevalent shame-held secrets are, and the pain with which they are held, we recognize the havoc these secrets create in the lives of individuals and families. Even church communities are not immune. "Kept secrets can deeply and negatively affect all the people they touch."[5]

The Bible has always been a source of comfort and hope for those in need. The Old Testament scripture I selected for my biblical foundation within my doctoral dissertation is 2 Sam 11:26–27; 12:24. This particular narrative was selected because as I read the story of Bathsheba, I observed

4. Justes, *Please Don't Tell*, 4.
5. Ibid.

that she suffered significant losses in a short time and could have experienced some issues of unresolved grief. She experienced an inordinate amount of grief and suffering during a short period of time. Bathsheba was married to a soldier named Uriah. While he was at war, she slept with King David, found out she was pregnant, and sent word back to the king. The king then had her husband murdered. After going through a brief period of grief, Bathsheba was then taken into the king's palace to be married to him. All in a matter of a few months or so.

What happens next is even more devastating. Second Samuel 11:27b lets us know that God was displeased with what David had done and sent the prophet Nathan to give King David a parable about a rich man taking a poor man's sheep. David thought the story was true and was incensed by the callousness of the rich man—only to find out the rich man represented himself and the poor man represented Uriah (Bathsheba's slain husband). God's punishment for the adulterous relationship and subsequent murder was that the child Bathsheba was carrying would die. David begged God not to take the baby's life, but after a seven-day illness the baby died. Though the text does not tell us how Bathsheba grieved the loss of her firstborn, 2 Sam 11:24 says, "Then David comforted his wife Bathsheba and he went to her and lay with her," indicating that she grieved the loss of her baby. It is my assertion that Bathsheba may have had to deal with unresolved issues of grief over losing her husband, marrying his murderer, and then losing her firstborn. Grief unresolved is unhealthy grief.

When ministering with women who have been impacted by abortion, this text will offer a biblical example of how circumstances that are shameful can be a stumbling block to healing. Although Bathsheba did not experience voluntary pregnancy termination, she had plenty of reasons to experience shame and guilt: These emotions could have easily arisen in response to her adulterous relationship, her pregnancy, the murder of her husband, her marriage to his murderer, or the loss of her child—or in response of all together. Anyone who had experienced such events as Bathsheba did without a faith community to aid in her healing could later experience unresolved grief, which might lead to unhealthy healing. Looking to a biblical example of someone who experienced shame and grief also shows us how many of our experiences that have brought us shame are also part of our biblical narrative.

Yet even in the midst of suffering is a word of liberation and hope to bring us healing. For this word we turn to the Gospel of Matthew. The

New Testament text is found in Matt 5:4 "Blessed are those who mourn for they will be comforted." This text is found in what is called the Sermon on the Mount. I have selected it because of my desire to illustrate through the word of God that even though we may mourn, we can still be blessed. This text gives hope to those who mourn and even calls them blessed. It demonstrates hope and healing as an example of how Jesus views those in mourning, with his blessings. Matt 5:4 directs us to the ability to hope in the Lord that we can be blessed even as we mourn. In his Sermon on the Mount, one thing I found interesting about Jesus' teaching is that those he says are blessed are not necessarily endowed with musical talent or artistic ability, they are not the highly intelligent or well educated. Those he is calling blessed are the poor in spirit, those who mourn. Those Jesus is calling blessed hardly seem to be blessed in this world's view. As we "change the subject," this text is a starting place from which to search of other biblical examples of how God loves, cares for, and forgives those whom others have deemed outcasts. This chapter, titled "Changing the Subject," highlights biblical examples of healing and hope for those who have lost the hope that they are loved and cared for by God or the church community.

As I began my research on this subject, I was surprised to find that abortions were practiced in ancient Greece and Rome. In antiquity, concerns about abortion were rarely, if at all regarding the fetus because the fetus was not considered a human. Concerns were more for the health and welfare of the mother and the father.

From the earliest days of ancient Greece and Rome; voluntary pregnancy termination was more common among the wealthy than among the poor. Motives for obtaining an abortion were no less varied in antiquity than they are today. However, many times rich women were motivated to have abortions because they did not want to share their wealth with "lower-class children" fathered illegitimately. Another motivation for rich women to abort was their desire to preserve their sex appeal, and not wanting to lose their figures by having babies.[6]

Methods for voluntary pregnancy termination also varied in antiquity. Some women took poisons, some took mixtures of herbs and alcohol; still others used mechanical methods to cause abortion. Some women chose to bind their bodies tightly around the womb while others struck the womb in an attempt to expel the fetus. Other methods used abortive instruments.[7]

6. Gorman, *Abortion & the Early Church*, 14.

7. Ibid., 15.

In 1973, the landmark *Roe v. Wade* decision impacted abortion laws in the United States. The law came into being as a result of a Texas woman who alleged that she had been raped and was denied the right to have a legal abortion. The case traveled from the Texas courts to the Supreme Court. However, the case took so long that as her pregnancy proceeded, she made the decision to have the baby. This case has had an impact on laws that are still in effect today. In *Roe v. Wade* the Supreme Court decided that during the first trimester of a pregnancy the state cannot prohibit abortion in any way. During the second trimester, the state can prohibit an abortion only if the procedure will endanger the health of the fetus or mother. In the third trimester, the Court said, the state can completely prohibit an abortion if the fetus is viable, in order to protect the fetus.[8]

History sets the tone in the evolution and dynamics surrounding issues specific to women. As individual women come to recognize that they are not the first to experience shame, guilt, and unforgiveness after having an abortion, together they will begin to build healing communities in which they can uncover and share their secrets and their shame in order to find wholeness. The God of hope and liberation brings us to our next section as we explore ways to change the subject from the God who judges and punishes to the God who liberates and heals.

It is my opinion that all too often women, especially African American women, who have voluntarily terminated their pregnancies, end up suffering needlessly because of the secrets, shame, and guilt associated with the sin of abortion preached, taught and lived out in many faith traditions. I believe the time has come to change the subject.

The question becomes, how do we create safe places for women to tell and retell their stories so they can be liberated from the secrecy, shame, and guilt that they have carried around for many years? I believe that it is not God's intention that women should suffer because of this choice they have made. God is a God of liberation, healing, and grace—not one who desires that women live their lives in secrecy, shame and guilt, without the forgiveness of others or of oneself.

The church has been our way to find liberation from our oppression and oppressors. Many men and women have found hope in the Black church when there was no other way. Yet the discourse of Black liberation, womanist, and confessional theology really set the framework for my theological position. My theological position has been influenced by the

---

8. Blanchard, *Anti-Abortion Movement*, 125.

voices of James Cone and Dwight Hopkins (liberation theologians), as well as womanist theologians Stephanie Mitchem, Alice Walker, and Linda Hollies. Finally, the voice of Dr. Frank Thomas, who introduced to me confessional theology—our faith seeking understanding as we admit and confess our faults one to another and so free ourselves up to openly acknowledge that we are not perfect. These theological discourses have helped me to develop my position. In addition to the voices of theologians, also the voices of grief counselors, therapists, and psychologists informed my theoretical foundation for this chapter.

Pastoral care professionals who are experts in grief counseling, therapists who have done extensive research on the subject of the unspoken pain of abortion and professionals who argue against any psychological or physical challenges associated with abortion also informed my project.

In the book titled *All Our Losses, All Our Grief*, the authors indicate that since no two occasions for grieving are exactly the same, grief is always a response to the particular loss of whatever the object is."[9] In other words, an individual's grief is primarily related to the particular loss, and though people grieve differently, some similarities emerge in the way people grieve.

In *Sisters of the Yam*, bell hooks notes the ways that African Americans experience death and shows how these differ from the ways Caucasians grieve. She observes from her life's experiences that death in Black culture was a time not only for grieving but for rejoicing. "The Home Going Celebration" is a time in which to celebrate the life of your loved one but also to openly grieve your loss. Dr. hooks also indicates that in the African American community, death is one of the rare moments when it is socially acceptable for folks to let go emotionally. Mourning a death we can break down and surrender to grief. Healthy grieving is important to the process of emotional healing after a loss.[10] That is why it is essential for persons impacted by voluntary pregnancy termination be given the opportunity to grieve.

Pastoral care professional Ed Wimberly in his book *Moving from Shame to Self-Worth*[11] recommends that telling our stories is one way to find healing, along with telling biblical stories and preaching. Wimberly indicates that changing views that people bring to events and relationships can be known through storytelling. Wimberly suggests that stories should

9. Mitchell and Anderson, *All Our Losses*, 53.

10. hooks, *Sisters of the Yam*, 101.

11. Wimberly, *Moving from Shame to Self-Worth*, 75.

be told in a way that grieving persons will be able to see themselves and their circumstances differently. He also indicated that biblical stories can assist in healing by presenting them in a way in which the hearer will be able to see themselves in the text.

Both clinical and pastoral care professionals have indicated that telling stories—biblical as well as personal—to grieving persons is an effective way of showing care. Consequently, each of these foundations has played a specific role in educating, as well as offering theological, biblical, and theoretical perspectives to significantly change the subject from guilt and shame to healing and hope for a future. These foundations offer a holistic approach to healing in mind, body, and spirit.

The setting chosen for my doctoral project was a weekend retreat. During the retreat, participants were encouraged to tell their stories of grief, shame, and guilt, and they were given the opportunity to hear biblical narratives that illustrated divine healing and transformation. While participants heard these biblical stories, they were guided to notice how they might find themselves or parts of their story within the ancient narratives. Finally, a memorial service provided retreat participants with a safe place to grieve and bring closure to their significant losses.

The impact of unresolved grief can be devastating over many years. I dedicate this chapter to the countless women and men who have been impacted by the guilt and shame of voluntary pregnancy termination and have kept it a secret. It is my prayer that God will point them in the direction of sharing their stories in a safe place where they can find divine healing and forgiveness on their journey together. It is also my desire that this chapter will compel readers to offer ministries within their churches in order to bring healing to those sitting in their congregations secretly suffering in silence.

PART 4

*Caring as Chaplains
within Institutional Settings*

17

Why CPE?

Ardella Gibson

Personal Constructs

I was five years old when I walked into an integrated classroom to attend kindergarten. In my first experience with integration, I played well with my new friends and I felt a strong sense of community when we were together. I must have had some trouble getting to sleep on the floor mats during nap time because my teacher picked me up and rocked me in her lap. I grew accustomed to her lap for nap time, so I claimed my place there each day until my mother picked me up from school one day. "Get down from there!" she snarled in a hushed tone. By that age I was able to discern that my mother's tone indicated some trouble that I had gotten myself into or that I had done something that needed explanation. After she got me into the car, I heard her rant over "what we can't do around them White folks" and what was not "acceptable" all the way home. Then she got on the phone to tell my grandmother where she found me. From that day forward, I tried the mats and never attempted to find comfort in the arms of another teacher, ever, especially not a White American.

This, an example of an early stimulus colored by a cultural dynamic in the synthesis of a cognitive style of interpretation, had long been a part of my subconscious processes by the time of my first Clinical Pastoral Education (CPE) unit. Unlike the Western alternative to interpretation, the African tendency to integrate experiences (in this case taught by someone who was an authority to me) in a style of interpreting the "inclusive whole"[1] formed my perspective of expectations. George Kelly called these expectations personal constructs.[2] That five-year-old's synthesis of her forty-two-year old mother's interpretation of a way of life was that something was wrong, different, maybe even deficient about me. My mother's seeming disapproval of me passed on a message from her historical reality. She assumed that I had crawled up into the teacher's lap without being invited, and that I was imposing an insistence on my teacher to be in her lap. Perhaps in my mother's historical reality Black American women took care of White-American children by holding them in their laps. I seemed to be reversing the rule. It was a violation of my family's personal construct that a Black person does not move toward White people without an invitation.

Born and raised in a racially divided America where the messages received from the cultural climate programmed both my parents, they learned to function in a microcosm of Black America's South. It was a South where Black Americans either managed to adhere to the law, the demoralizing cruelty of Jim Crow Laws, or face

> false and unjust accusations . . . and public, street beatings, extra judicial punishment, lynching, that followed . . . brutal, vicious beatings emasculation of Black American men . . . that included evil, inhumane beatings crosses burned in yards, church explosions, inciting terror in the Black American community . . . when beatings no longer soothed the criminal, *savage beast*.[3]

The cadence of this drumbeat is no longer in the distant past. The same types of injustices, still in operation today, continue to pervade every aspect of the Black American community. The atrocities of the past have only been hidden and now are being exposed in the age of technology. They reveal the same animals who continue to hunt Black blood. The caveat is of an all-too-familiar defense that is summarized in a simple feeling: I felt threatened. Police and other *trained* officials are not feeling safe when

1. Okeke et al., "Culture, Self, and Personality in Africa."
2. Kelly, *Theory of Personality*, 4.
3. See Okeke et al,, "Culture, Self, and Personality" (italics added).

confronting Black-American "perpetrators," but de-escalation is used for White American "suspects" who in too many instances (if not always) keep their lives—all because of a construct prompted by a feeling, which then informs the behavior. Is the feeling of the same level of threat not present for police officers any time there is a confrontation with White Americans?

While these injustices are not legal, our justice systems are scarcely addressing the underlying issues that remain after the protests are over and the emotions are no longer charged. How do personal constructs inform our approach to the irony of a justice system that continues to fail the Black American community? If George Zimmerman, a community-authorized neighborhood watchman in Sandford, Florida, can be told to stay in his vehicle and not to confront the "suspicious" individual he was reporting to the authorities, but Trayvon Martin dies, one is left to ask, what personal construct prompted Zimmerman to exit his vehicle? Then subsequently, what was the personal construct that prompted the Sandford police chief to hesitate to charge Zimmerman as he reported that there were no substantial grounds to disprove Zimmerman's story? Would implicit bias training prompt a different response, or is the power of the construct stronger than the need for the transformative reconstruction of the enforcers' perceptions? Still yet, what if the desire to spill Black American blood informs the bias?

The cadence is no longer in the distant past.

What construct informs resistance to the Black Lives Matter Global Network's call to action? What could be the construct of those who resist a Black man supporting the guiding principles of the Black Lives Matter movement, particularly as this man chooses to take his protests to visible stages? Is there not a cause, especially when a construct remains that makes kneeling for justice unpatriotic? Consider the contrast that Michael Frost draws between the (perceived) principles upon which Colin Kaepernick and other Black American NFL players kneel to protest social injustice, and the (perceived) principles upon which Tim Tebow shows commitment to his faith.[4] What constructs inform the perceptions of contradictions between Black American and White American athletes?

4. Frost, "Colin Kaepernick vs. Tim Tebow."

The Assumptions

George Kelly's theory of constructs posits that persons are scientists experimenting as they experience life. When the scientist forms a conclusion from a lesson gleaned from an experience, a construct emerges. Patterns of behavior derive from constructs that have been informed by one's perception of the conclusion. For example, a person's initial encounter with a dog may result in the terrified person being chased and then bitten by the dog. According to Kelly's theory, that person's next encounter with a dog (and possibly any other from then on) will likely prompt in the person the same feeling of terror and victimization that the person initially experienced. That is, constructs have emerged or are emerging for the person about any number of aspects of the initial encounter with a dog: a construct of dogs emerges, a construct of terror emerges, and a construct emerges of what circumstances may lead to another unwelcome meeting with a dog. Thus a pattern of behavior results from the construct created based upon the experience. Experience subsumes various factors that include but are not limited to environmental, societal or cultural influences—many of which are passed from one generation to the next.

The scientist may reevaluate constructs as the constructs continue to fit the application of this experience, but when those constructs do not work, the scientist forms new constructs. Experimentation is how people gain information about themselves and other events in their environment. Kelly's person-as-scientist[5] metaphor explains the philosophy behind constructs, which are representations of one's environment, lifted and tested against the reality of that environment. There is only one true reality, and it is experienced from a particular perspective, which is an alternative construction. As a construct flows through dynamic movements of the experience or significantly similar experiences, the concepts drawn from conclusions about those experiments are considered to be personal constructs. The new constructs could result in misguided generalizations. This is why I believe the dichotomy of "right versus wrong" has limited application when considered dynamically in matters of justice. But that's another chapter.

Each construct, then, is a perspective on the ultimate reality: a psychological process directed by successive construals of experiments, and constructs give an individual person his or her reality.[6] The process of ex-

5. Ibid.
6. Ibid.

perimentation is an organizing of stimuli based on the meaningful patterns of an individual's physical, social, and feeling (or inner) world. We organize our personal constructs into hierarchical fragments that, as verified, fit into place like pieces of a jigsaw puzzle.

Further, the formation of a construct occurs when an ordinary person like a scientist recognizes the similarities and differences from events with regard to the same features. Thus the construct is a "discrimination between events"[7] that occur in an individual's environment. Because views of reality do not remain static, a person develops as the view of reality changes and fosters development.[8] From the ground a mountain climber charts a course from the ground to the peak. After beginning the climb, reassessments (even critical assessment) with more tools becomes necessary as the climber's perspective changes. As the climber realizes a different perspective given the changing altitude, so an individual with a reality informed by experimentation recognizes a new perspective, first as results of a new position, and then as experimentation itself changes. What perspective of your reality informs conclusions on hidden discriminations?

What Is CPE?

Prior to understanding my mother's disapproval for napping in the teacher's lap, I functioned in community with my peers and my teacher, unaware of any need for adherence to social biases around race or ethnicity. Kelly's theory rings true to my experience: over the years I worked to *reconstruct* that perception by experimenting with evidence that either supported or disproved my stance. The evidence that I used to support a perspective was rarely impartial because the lens was colored by my construct. I had multiple ideas that attributed social phenomena to the ethnic expectations of a particular community. Those ideas came from my community of origin and are generally shared by my community as well.

When I began my first unit of CPE, most of my methodology for such experimentation with preconceived constructs was challenged. Particularly, the assumptions that informed my perceptions were out of the order necessary to make good use of *critical reflection*. Critical reflection is an essential part of the process of affording *reconstruction* of a construct. I use this idea as a basis of understanding the need for CPE. The definition of CPE as

7. Ibid.
8. Bannister and Fransella, *Inquiring Man.*

provided by the Association for Clinical Pastoral Education—the Standard (accrediting body) for Spiritual Care and Education reads as follows:

> Clinical Pastoral Education is interfaith professional education for ministry. It brings theological students and ministers of all faiths (pastors, priests, rabbis, imams and others) into [a] supervised encounter with persons in crisis. Out of an intense involvement with persons in need, and the feedback from peers and teachers, students develop new awareness of themselves as persons and of the needs of those to whom they minister. From theological reflection on specific human situations, they gain a new understanding of ministry. Within the interdisciplinary team process of helping persons, they develop skills in interpersonal and interprofessional relationships.[9]

My supervisory stance as an educator places the emphasis on the third sentence in this definition: the ACPE has found CPE to help the student "develop new awareness of themselves . . . [and a new awareness of] those to whom they minister." If one can consider the core educational process without the framework of ministry and a particular faith tradition, the substance left is simply the type of education that affords the student an emotional availability that comes from the *self*[10] awareness necessary to provide an empathic presence to the *other*.[11] Students usually (if not always) arrive in their first unit of CPE with constructs appropriate for the challenge of critical assessment, particularly if the methodology for arrival at a construct is introduced to new or different information. Could those terrorists in uniform—whose acts perpetuate the same systemic basis of rule that undergirded Jim Crow–like, discriminatory interpretations of the law—use a challenge to their constructs? If so, how does CPE lead the charge to perform this transformative work?

Care Consciousness

As we consider the applications of personal constructs around the care we provide for communities affected by the climate of this time, one can

9. ACPE, "For Prospective Students. Frequently Asked Questions."

10. The words *self* and *other* are italicized, referring to Martin Buber's concept of "I" for self and "Thou" for other in *I and Thou* (1958). Where *self* is italicized there is an emphasis placed on self-realization.

11. Ibid.

imagine a charge to be considered by professional caregivers, particularly chaplains. CPE is process education, built on a framework of integrating pastoral functioning with personal identity while strengthening the skills of the professional helper. Rev. Danielle J. Buhuro, DMin, provides a model for supervising CPE that addresses the prophetic role of the supervisor in educating students, preparing them to serve in multiple contexts and during this time in a world where the Black Lives Matter Global Network must exist.[12] She charges the educator (supervisor) to consider an approach that incorporates dynamic momenta relevant for various marginalized communities.

The missions and philosophies of our hospitals, educational institutions, churches and parachurch organizations, societies and social organizations guide our approach to service in the communities where we choose to locate them. Based on a theory of constructs, two underlying themes bring the prophetic model of supervision in harmony with the process of educating caregivers in the current climate (even if your institution does not directly serve the Black American population).

The first theme is the interconnective nature of the educational process with the present world in which we operate and with the climate of the nation. More of the messages we receive from those affected by present circumstances of gun violence and systemic oppression of legalized aggression offer the construct that "it is not our (non-Black American communities') problem." Further, this message is compounded by the classification of epidemics and aggressors of society that are addressed by the government, given a different name, and receive funding only as they have reached the White American communities as their affect has become a "crisis." The popular quote by Rev. Martin Luther King Jr., PhD, may be overused, but its relevance to this is still remarkable: "Injustice [oppression and depression of communities] anywhere is a threat to justice [immunity from oppression and depression of communities] everywhere."[13] Are we preparing professionals who are aware of those in our care? How is their narrative significant to our approach to provide an empathic presence? Do we partner with organizations outside our comfortable institutions to provide a pastoral or caregiving presence in an environment impacted by this reality?

The second theme is the capacity of each professional to make meaning of the significance and value of their construct at each stage evolution.

12. Buhuro, "Transforming Trauma to Trust."
13. King, "I Have a Dream."

During the migration of the construct with which one is experimenting, at each stage there is an opportunity to check meanings that arise from the information assimilated from experimentation—as there is progressive movement from one meaning to a deeper, more empathic understanding of the *other*. As a caregiver, the understanding that comes from useful and valued constructs is helpful, but they may have variations and hues of privilege. This will always *color* the care provided.

A pastoral caregiver will bring authority that comes with the skill of presence (including assessment and intervention). Yet the one who receives care has authority over their own reality. So as we provide pastoral care, we have an opportunity to try out a new construct—an interchanging authority. As pastoral caregivers, what do we need to relinquish so that we can clarify this new construct and better understand those for whom we care? Is your institution aware of the meaning made by providing professional pastoral care in a community underrepresented in the field of pastoral care? One may argue how much it matters that trained providers of pastoral care come from one's own racial and sociocultural community. Yet, how can the voice of a community's pastoral care needs be amplified and met without trained pastoral caregivers who know what these needs, and possible solutions, are?

18

... And the Truth Shall Set You Free

The Critical Need for CPE among African American Clergy in the Age of #BlackLivesMatter

Amber R. Coates and Mariela Janelle Gonzalez, Micheal Smith, and Terrance L. Thomas

For as long as it has existed, the African American church has been at the center of the various social and economic movements for liberation and equality within the Black community. From slavery to Reconstruction to the civil rights movement and Black power movements, African American clergy have galvanized their congregations from behind the sacred desk known as the pulpit to act in defense of the least of these. During these movements for justice, clergy such as Sojourner Truth, David Walker, Rev. Dr. Martin Luther King Jr., and Bishop Yvette Flunder all have used their prophetic voices to bring about social change. Even when African American clergy shifted their focus from more social engagement to personal transformation during the '80s, '90s, and early 2000s, clergy such as Rev. Dr. Michael Eric Dyson, Rev. Dr. Jeremiah Wright, and Rev. Dr. Johnnie Coleman all continued to raise the standard of justice within the African American church. However, in recent years, the need for more justice-minded clergy trained to engage social problems has emerged once again.

With the rise in deaths of African American men and women, including of Trayvon Martin, Sandra Bland, Rekia Boyd, and Mike Brown, at the hands of racist vigilantes and rogue police, there has been and continues to be an equally intense fight for human rights via the Black Lives Matter movement. Though initially hesitant to allow space for the traditional Black church because of that institution's previous positions on the criminal justice and on the humanity of those within the LGTBQ community, and because of oft times a too-cozy relationship with various government entities, eventually #BlackLivesMatter has come to settle on a power-sharing dynamic with progressive and justice-centered forces within the Black church. This shift in position though is not without its demands, and one of those demands is that clergy be not only educated but also trained to help identify and process the trauma inflicted during this present darkness. One of the ways this can be achieved is through the educational learning environment found within Clinical Pastoral Education (CPE). In this chapter, we will outline what CPE means to African American clergy, its benefits, and how ultimately CPE is a vital tool in caring for those within the parish and also for those in the community where the parish situates itself.

Therefore it is critical to look at what trauma encompasses and how it ties in to those persons who embark on the CPE journey. To be concise, *trauma* has been defined as "a deeply distressing or emotional experience."[1] These emotional experiences cause us to question and to experience feelings of immediate distress. Trauma in its authenticity creates moments of darkness and uncertainty. It's in these dark spaces where we want to see a glimmer of hope with the assurance that of light at the end of the tunnel; historically African Americans are renowned for having turned trauma into triumph. The day-to-day living of African Americans is an infinite reflection of ways we continue to rise above and to overcome traumatic situations. It has caused our hearts to stand in amazement with thanksgiving to the Creator as our souls look back to wonder how we got over.

CPE equips those whose hearts are turned towards chaplaincy to more clearly define strategies and interventions, ways to provide spiritual care for patients, families, and hospital staff experiencing immediate trauma. During the CPE journey we may be faced with responding to overhead pages, which could result in providing spiritual care to those who have lost a loved one, or in coming alongside family members when someone they love is

---

1. "What does *trauma* mean?" (Google Dictionary search): https://tinyurl.com/yyo8subl/.

being taken off life support. Our mission in those moments is to be present and authentic with the range of emotions that exists. CPE teaches us to be present with others but to manage our own traumas.

Three main types of trauma are **acute, chronic, and complex**. Acute trauma results from a single incident. Chronic trauma is repeated and prolonged, such as because of domestic violence or abuse. Complex trauma is exposure to varied and multiple traumatic events, often of an invasive, interpersonal nature.[2] Participants in the CPE journey are tasked with engaging in deep periods of reflection in order to become aware of what one's own triggers may be in light of trauma. Once self-awareness is established, helping others to be courageous and navigate difficult life experiences becomes easier. We assist patients and their family members as well as hospital staff by seeking to meet emotional, social, religious, and existential needs. Offering spiritual care is much more than reading a scripture, singing a hymn, or uttering a prayer; it is about meeting the deepest needs of the people in our community.

Working predominantly among African Americans, we are faced with trauma in different ways. It has been become the passion of CPE students and others to be intentional about journeying with those who encounter traumatic experiences and finding ways that we can equip our community to better handle trauma.

The paradox of two Americas continues—one White, and one increasingly Black and Brown. Notwithstanding gains by a small percentage of African Americans, a wide disparity persists between the two Americas in education, economic opportunities, healthcare access, and involvement with the criminal justice system. Of note is an increased incarceration rate after arrest for African American men, and African Americans are more likely than European Americans to be the victims of a violent crime. Within majority African American communities many residents have experienced physical, emotional, and social trauma, which contribute to an overall decrease in quality of life and life expectancy. The African American church and its clergy have most often been expected to address the physical, emotional, and social trauma of its community.

Historically, in the absence of a seminary education, for members of the clergy within the African American church providing pastoral care meant "showing the love of God in action."[3] In response to the question of

2. Missouri Department of Mental Health, "Early Childhood Mental Health."
3. In Johnson-Smith, ed., *Wisdom of the Ages*, 26.

how he or she would provide pastoral care, probable answers might sound like this: "I listen to the problem and pray with them"; "I don't make judgmental statements and share the word of God"; "advise them to meditate on the word," or "show how Christ can make a difference in his or her life." While not diminishing the vital role that faith can play for many receiving pastoral care, the essence of pastoral care is not prayer, Scripture reading, or promoting parochial language. Pastoral care must address a person's emotional, social, existential, and religious needs. Further, clergy who seek to provide pastoral care to congregants and members of the surrounding community are often also victims of the same physical, emotional, and social trauma as those who seek out their assistance. This is the paramount reason why African American clergy would benefit from CPE.

According to the Association for Clinical Pastoral Education, the accrediting agency for CPE, the focus of CPE is on self-awareness in ministry, which helps clergy become more aware of their own and others' needs. CPE assists a person (1) to identify and discuss major life events, relationships, social locations, cultural contexts, and social realities that impact personal identity as expressed in pastoral functioning, and (2) to demonstrate a range of pastoral skills, including listening and attending, empathic reflection, conflict resolution, transformation, confrontation, crisis management, and appropriate use of religious or spiritual resources.[4] In CPE, the entire life of a clergyperson (personal relationships and experiences) becomes focus points for study, reflection, and evaluation. In addition, CPE learning occurs within a group of other ministers—a group with an intentional diversity of gender, racial identity, sexual orientation, and faith tradition. A benefit of group process and learning is that each minister receives multiple perspectives, support, encouragement and feedback from other clergy in a safe and confidential environment. *The interpersonal interactions can provide individual ministers an opportunity to deepen their level of self-awareness and to learn how they relate to others.* Clergy are encouraged to give support and feedback to others, and to work with the reactions and responses that the contributions of others bring up for them.

"I am because we are." This African saying informs my CPE. In the CPE learning environment, an individual engages the reflection-action-reflection cycle within the context of the group. Our supervisor, Rev. Dr.

---

4. See Standards 311 and 312 of Outcomes of CPE Level I and II, *ACPE Standard Manual* (2016). https://www.manula.com/manuals/acpe/acpe-manuals/2016/en/topic/standards-311-312-outcomes-of-cpe-level-i-level-ii-programs/.

Danielle Buhuro, often reminds us, "I am because we are," or "Ubuntu."
She tells us that in the educational and professional environment set in
majority Black and Brown neighborhoods, we are a family. Her CPE model
rejects White, patriarchal pedagogy with its emphasis on competition and
individualistic ambition. In this CPE context, each person recognizes his
or her part in the whole. Even the leadership fully engages the group experience of teaching and learning. Leaders might approach learnings with
more wisdom about their strengths and growing edges due to experience;
nevertheless, power does not divorce anyone from the family. Those of us
who embrace the CPE learning covenant bring the particulars of our family
systems to this space and translate those nuances for a new group dynamic.
The Black feminist education method requires authentic engagement from
everyone. Together we grow. Because we are stronger, I am empowered.
Because I am self-aware, maximizing my strengths and growing edges, we
are stronger.

My colleagues have illustrated the importance of CPE. It is my privilege to add concluding thoughts, focusing on how CPE empowers within
community. This is my thesis: CPE empowers spiritual care providers to
liberate and heal communities, and the faith leaders themselves are uplifted
as part of the community.

In the CPE group setting, we explore learnings. Any person can contribute a possible learning when a member of the group presents a scenario.
We invite reflection from each other using the three-*e* method. Rev. Dr.
Buhuro introduces this at the beginning of each new CPE unit. The first *e*
is *empathy*, then move to *e* two, *education*, and end with *e* three, *empowerment*. This technique unhinges the Eurocentric method of critique. The
supervisor is not passing on rigid wisdom from a disconnected, lofty position. She does not emphasize an individual's mistakes, ask for a defense,
and then follow up with a teaching on the right way (or the supervisor's
way) to perform. She does not leave students bare, pondering the teaching
and feeling inadequate for moving forward. Rather, in empathy we show
understanding for one another. We invite one another to consider learnings
in education. Finally, we graciously encourage one another based on the
strengths we see in the empowerment moment.

The CPE student (a present and future faith leader), is uplifted in the
community through education because that education is surrounded by
empathy and empowerment. In this way there isn't shame or guilt associated with needing education. Also, consider the language Rev. Dr. Buhuro

uses. She purposely avoids language that opposes strengths to weaknesses, and instead describes strengths and growing edges. Yes, growing edges must be addressed, but not from a good-bad dichotomy. (Furthermore, dichotomous language tends to be unfriendly to people of color; some examples of such unfriendly language include the dichotomies of *light* and *dark*, *White* and *Black*, which are substituted in for *good* and *bad*.) Language highlighting strengths and weaknesses presents an either/or scenario: a student is either functioning competently as a chaplain, or that student is failing. That is not the case. Spiritual care providers act from who they are as whole persons, ideally maximizing their strengths and minimizing growing edges.

If "I am because we are" is true, then faith leaders know a both/and dynamic of receiving and providing spiritual care. We are both empathized with and empathetic, educated and educational, empowered and empowering. Having acted, we reflect through the three-*e* method, and—in learned ways—we act again. Education is not merely about adjusting behavior. Education is an adjustment of the whole person. As much as we cannot isolate an individual from the group, we cannot compartmentalize sections of a person. Who one is as a spouse impacts who one is as a CPE student, impacts who one is as a minister in community. Additionally, in the expression of who one is, everything matters—thoughts, words, actions, and intent or reasoning. Faith leaders are being made well in four areas: social, emotional, existential, and spiritual areas. Then our ministry flows from who we are—as being-made-well people—to other care recipients in those same areas.

Ministry from ministers trained in Afrocentric CPE is healing and liberating. First, liberation and healing occur from holistic care. We address four areas of the human experience—social, emotional, existential, and spiritual. Profound care happens when ministers prioritize social needs. For example, a person in prison may feel free in his spirit due to connection with sacred presence. And at the same time, that person literally benefits from good legal advice, and safe and humane prison conditions. Furthermore, care for social needs in community context is the work of social justice. In addition to acting for one person in the penal system, through community context, faith leaders may also address unfair, mass incarceration of African Americans.

Next, care providers and care recipients experience healing and liberation as they make adjustments using the three-*e* method. Through education, we are more our authentic selves, not less so, because we reject either/

184

or and good/bad dichotomy. We are empathetic, educated, and therefore empowered together. The togetherness is key. White supremacy is comfortable when people are othered and isolated (unless it is solidarity under Whiteness). This shows up on different sides of the issue of police brutality: A cop is described as one bad apple, and a news reporter emphasizes details in behavior or clothing of the person killed, in order to claim the issue is not systemic.

Ultimately, the faith leaders see themselves as in community, even as family, with spiritual care recipients, their congregants, their neighbors. I consider the question that Cain posed to God in the book of Genesis, "Am I my brother's keeper?" He already knew the answer. Cain could not be his brother's keeper, because he was his brother's killer. This calls me to consider the oppression killing of my Black and Brown brothers and sisters, and to think, how have I not been keeping care with my fellow humans? When we ask the divine if we are our brothers' keepers, we ask if we are responsible for each other. We ask are we in this together? The answer is a resounding yes! Ubuntu!

19

A Manifesto

Black Spiritual Care in American Hospitals

Karen Hutt

With the most concentrated Black population in America's most segregated city, Chicago is a perfect laboratory for research. The demographics provide the landscape for a cottage industry of social scientists, medical professionals, psychologists, economists, and political scientists seeking to examine and evaluate the full spectrum of Black life from birth to death. Universities, not-for-profits, and think tanks have thrived surveying, studying, interviewing, and assessing the conditions, behavior, and outcomes of being Black in Chicago for decades. The subjects of this research industry include the thirty-four-year-old Black man waiting for the bus on Seventy-Ninth Street to go job hunting; the kids leaving home on their way to school hungry, and the thousands of Black workers in retail, offices, and white-collar jobs throughout the metropolitan area who every day seek to survive, live, thrive, and prosper. Often these research studies reach conclusions that are reported in the media and become part of popular culture: "Obesity Rates for African Americans Linked to Consumption of Flamin' Hot Cheetos,"[1]

1. Eng, "Flamin' Hot Cheetos."

and "African American Men Are Disproportionately Profiled by Police."[2] No matter what academic discipline they fall under, most of these studies reach similar conclusions: "Black people are impacted in every aspect of their lives by discrimination and a lack of resources."[3] In other words, "It is Hard Out Here for Black Folks." Healthcare is often a well-funded part of the research industrial complex. As a result we are well aware of the health disparities that are killing Black people at an alarming rate.

After becoming immune to these horrific, unchanging statistics I was stunned when I discovered this simple zip code statistic. According to the Chicago Department of Health, the average life expectancy on the (largely White) North Side is eighty years, and it's sixty years on the (largely Black) South Side.[4] A few miles can lengthen or shorten your life by twenty years. This statistic was apparent in the daily census in all of the large major hospitals in the city.

As a chaplain in Chicago, I find that the data of community despair and structural inequality becomes real when Black people or someone they love is hospitalized. It is at this intersection of illness, Blackness, medical institutionalism, and public policy that the groundwork for racist behavior and stereotypic assumptions thwart the enterprise of care and healing for Black patients and families. Black patients are well aware that a hospitalization must be approached with vigilance. While some of the young millennial family members may not know the name of the experiment, they know that some white doctors did some bad stuff to the bodies of black males back in the day down south (the Tuskegee Experiment).[5]

For Black people, hospitalization ignites the hermeneutic of suspicion. Family members are summoned to take shifts *"to watch them"* as their loved ones receive care. Extra questions are asked about the medication regimens, large groups of family and community members take up residency in the family lounges to make sure *"Big Mama knows we are there with her."* The stress and anxiety of *hospitalization while Black* leads to many challenges and conflicts for hospital staff and family members. It is during these tense moments that the assistance of a chaplain or social worker could make all the difference in advocating for or simply listening to patients. Although a

2. Warren et al., "Driving While Black."

3. See Rios, *Punished.*

4 See Dubb, "Chicago West Side Residents." See also Hunt et al., Life Expectancy Varies."

5. Wikipedia, "Tuskegee Syphilis Experiment."

chaplain's presence may be helpful in such a situation, there are very few, if any, Black chaplains or social workers in major urban hospitals serving a sizable number of Black people according to the hospital census. As a result, the psychosocial and spiritual needs of Black people are often ignored, dismissed, or ridiculed by White hospital staff. This lack of care increases the anxiety of hospitalization and lessens favorable health outcomes for Black people.

Although no definitive link has been found between spiritual support and health, some studies suggest that chaplaincy plays an important role in helping patients cope with physical illness. In its accreditation of home care in the United States, the Joint Commission requires providers to respect the patient's "values, beliefs, and cultural preferences,"[6] and hospitals also must accommodate "the patient's right to religious and other spiritual services."[7] Contextual spiritual care can provide significant benefits to patients in a health crisis. When someone is ill and facing a life crisis, his or her belief system becomes fodder for daily exploration as the patient lies in bed waiting for the doctor or the test results. As a chaplain, I am concerned with the existential well-being of patients as I seek to provide with my listening ears and heart a container that can hold their feelings about their hospitalization. Although spirituality is a universal phenomenon, spiritual care in hospitals requires a nimble flexibility combined with authentic cross-cultural competencies that exceed the dictates of the latest list of cultural traits handout from a human resources seminar.

Often the training of chaplains in and the description of Black spirituality ignore the diversity of theologies, philosophies, and worldviews that help chaplains find meaning and purpose. As an educator of chaplains in my capacity as a clinical pastoral educator, I spend significant time exploring with White chaplains in training what it means to care for Black people in the hospital. Most of my students have no Black friends, grew up in segregated White areas, and are woefully ignorant of Black history, culture, and religiosity. This limitation in experience and the implicit bias that White supremacy creates reduce the opportunities for Black people to receive the type of care they deserve.

I served as a chaplain in six large teaching hospitals in Chicago and Minneapolis for over a decade, and I continue to work as a chaplain educator. Each day after making my rounds, I spent the remainder of the day

6. Joint Commission International, *Joint Commission International Accreditation*, 62.

7. Joint Commission International, "Crosswalk."

combing the census looking for Black patients. Weather they had sought a chaplain or not, I found them, introduced myself, and checked in on their well-being. Many times these patients were surprised to see a Black person enter their room who was not in a service uniform, since most Black workers in hospitals are cleaning floors or serving food. This surprise would often be followed by relief that they could "really talk" in an unfiltered manner about what they and their families were experiencing.

On one occasion a patient shared that she was extra stressed in the hospital because she was worried about losing her job—because if she didn't work, she would not get paid. I asked the patient if I could provide any assistance, and the patient asked if I could call her supervisor at McDonald's, because when the patient had told the supervisor she was sick, "he didn't believe me." I complied and smoothed the path for her to return to work. Another visit, with a gunshot survivor, turned into a conversation about the sacred texts of Tupac Shakur and Biggie Smalls. This conversation affirming the texts of the survivor's cultural context gave him permission to mourn the trauma he had experienced and was likely to experience again.

Sometimes these visits occurred during a security code call, when the medical team deemed it necessary to call hospital police to quell "potentially volatile or disruptive" patients and family members. I would often intervene as a bridge between the quiet and regimented hospital culture and a grieving family. Raised voices, loud prayers, large groups, and interrogating questions from the medical staff would often set off the Black alarm, and the medical team would begin to characterize Black patients as difficult or uncooperative in the electronic medical record, which minimized the concerns and the care of these patients.

A patient of mine recently shared a story with me about her visit to our emergency room a few years ago. She had a painful medical condition. The emergency room staff not only did not treat her pain, but she recounted, "They treated me like I was trying to play them, like I was just trying to get pain meds out of them. They didn't try to make any diagnosis or help me at all. They couldn't get rid of me fast enough."

Nothing in her history suggested that she was seeking pain medication because of an addiction. She is a middle-aged, churchgoing lady who has never had issues with substance abuse. Eventually she received a diagnosis and appropriate care somewhere else. She is convinced that she was treated poorly in that emergency room because she is Black.

A Black chaplain in a White institution has the added responsibility to explain Black people and protect Black people. This can be stressful, unpredictable, and job-threatening. In care conferences with the medical teams and the families, I have been the interpreter of Black religiosity; in another I served as a mediator in a conversation about how the spiritual needs of a family would be respected during an end-of-life ritual.

Traditionally, Black pastors assume multiple roles in the community, assisting their parishioners in navigating hostile or unfamiliar systems of power and authority. So when Black patients see a Black clergyperson in a hospital serving as a chaplain, they often expect that chaplain to be available to support them with advice and guidance that is culturally and spiritually specific. A patient once asked me to help her navigate how to talk to the social worker about needing family support services, because she was afraid that the interaction could take a turn, and she could have her children taken away from her. Another patient said she nodded her head like she understood what the doctor had been saying but was too afraid to ask questions because "they always think we are stupid." In one particularly egregious case, the medical team had to amputate the two hands of a homeless Black youth who had suffered frostbite, following the surgery he was told that he "wasn't going to do anything good with his hands anyway," so he should keep calm.

Cultural care is spiritual care for Black people who have been physically separated from their communities while facing life-threatening illnesses and complex medical decisions. Competent cultural care for the range of Black patients that present in the hospital means being cognizant that the religious and spiritual lives of Black people can manifest in many forms. Big Mama may be in church every week and be recognized as a church mother, while her son may be a Muslim and her daughter may be more of a cultural Christian who utilizes the constructs if African spirituality in her belief system. This diversity of the Black experience is rarely recognized by chaplains and often can cause stress to families, as the White chaplain's wide-eyed, gaping-mouthed curiosity and questions put genuine care on the backseat. Given the unleashed nature of White supremacy, Black people find little refuge in the existing spiritual care centers of most hospitals.

In the age of #BlackLivesMatter, our lives have to matter everywhere. They have to matter on the streets where we are hunted like prey by the police, and in the hospital room where "racism" could be typed onto death certificates, next to the cause. Our spiritual lives have to matter. The great writer and intellectual Audre Lorde said, "We were never meant to survive," and yet we do.[8] Our survival is rooted in the ever-evolving nature of our spirituality which has sustained us for centuries. Since the times of slave owners dropping Bibles down to shackled Africans who couldn't read or speak the English language, Black people have always developed a deeply personal definition of God and their spiritual identity. Enduring extreme persecution and exploitation, Black people took a template of Christianity and customized it to reflect their own interpretation of its teachings. As a result, spirituality became the soul of our artistry, the language of our existence, and the backbone of our communities. It instilled a sense of power and purpose within a race of people deemed powerless. For Black people, spirituality is about embracing who we are, developing own sense of belief, and walking boldly in the fullness of our potential. Our spirituality goes with us everywhere, and when we are facing health challenges, we seek the people places and resources in our lives where we can make sense of what is happening to us.

Without caring, culturally appropriate spiritual care in hospitals (where 40 percent of Blacks die, compared to 21 percent of Whites),[9] our humanity will continue to be diminished. The problems are clear, but what are the answers?

First, the few Black chaplains certified by the Association of Professional Chaplains (APC) as well as Black Clinical Pastoral Care Educators credentialed by the Association for Clinical Pastoral Education (ACPE) must demand that a nationwide three-pronged approach be developed to navigate spiritual care concerns in populations centers where the daily census of Black people is significant.

We demand institutional cultural humility.[10]

To practice cultural humility is to maintain a willingness to suspend what you know, or what you think you know, about a person based on generalizations about their culture. Rather, what you learn about your patients' culture stems from being open to what they themselves have determined

8. Lorde, "Litany for Survival," line 24 (page 255).

9. Zeng, et al., "Racial Disparities in in-Hospital Death and Hospice Use."

10. *Cultural humility* is a term that is widely used but was originally coined by Melanie Tervalon and Jann Murray-García, two African American doctors in the Bay Area. Cultural humility describes a way of infiltrating multiculturalism into their work as healthcare professionals. Replacing the idea of cultural competency, cultural humility centers on self-reflection and lifelong learning. See Tervalon and Murray-García, "Cultural Humility versus Cultural Competence."

is their personal expression of their heritage, their personal culture. This requires

Lifelong learning & critical self-reflection. To practice cultural humility is to understand that culture is first and foremost an expression of self and that the process of learning about each individual's culture is a lifelong endeavor, because no two individuals are the same; each individual is a complicated, multidimensional human being who can rightfully proclaim, "My identity is rooted in my history . . . and I get to say who I am."

Recognizing and challenging power imbalances for respectful partnerships. Although working to establish and maintain respect is essential in all healthy and productive relationships, the root of effective chaplaincy is acknowledging and challenging power imbalances inherent in our practitioner-patient dynamics.

Institutional accountability. Hospitals need to model these principles as well (from micro- to mezzo- to macropractice)

We demand better education for chaplains.

CPE programs are required learning for professional chaplains. Generally these programs do not require that didactics focus on the specific spiritual needs, history, and diversity of the Black religious experience. This education must be required where students will be coming in contact with a sizable population of Black patients. Where competent Black supervisors are not available to teach these lessons, community educators, pastors and seminary professors should be consulted to insure the quality and accuracy of the material being conveyed. These community-based educations—keepers and practitioners of Black culture—should be employed.

We demand more Black staff chaplains be hired in hospitals.

If you are a patient who speaks Spanish or Somali, the hospital provides you with an interpreter. If you are Catholic and you would like to receive a sacrament, a priest is sought. If you are a Muslim and you would like to speak with someone about your family's concern around death and dying, and imam is summoned. If you are Jewish and you would like to talk with a rabbi about a family matter, the hospital complies and calls a rabbi to visit. In all these scenarios the cultural and religious context of the patents and their families is respected and considered. Yet, when African Americans may request African American spiritual support, their requests fall on def ears, and the "regular staff chaplain" who is almost always White, arrives. Given the historical, systemic, and long-term collective trauma Black people have experienced at the hands of White medical professionals and ancillary staff, it is critical that staff chaplains reflect the census of their patients. If half the census is African American, than half the staff chaplains should be African American to ensure that quality, culturally specific care is provided.

Our health, our well-being, our sanity, and our lives depend on it.

20

Pastoral and Spiritual Care to African Americans in the United States Armed Forces

Joseph Yao-Kotay

2 Before you engage in battle, the priest shall come forward and speak to the troops, **3** and shall say to them: "Hear, O Israel! Today you are drawing near to do battle against your enemies. Do not lose heart, or be afraid, or panic, or be in dread of them; **4** for it is the LORD *your God who goes with you, to fight for you against your enemies, to give you victory.*" (Deut 20:2–4, NRSV)

To have the certainty that God will go with you and even fight for you against your enemies seems to be a wonderful practice to maintain—not to mention having an intermediary to comfort, care for, assure, and support you amid your fear and anticipatory grief. Readers should not be surprised that in a theocracy the priest is the first person who comes forward to speak to the troops before they go off to war. The ancient Israelites adhered to this style of government before the establishment of a monarchy.

Who speaks first within the United States Armed Forces? What is required or is expected for its service members to hear and experience before going off to war? What role does God play in the United States Armed Forces? What is the pastoral or spiritual care provided to African American or Black service members in preparation for war and after returning from war?

In this chapter, I will attempt to address these questions. If nothing else, simply be curious about the inquiries. I will share my own personal experience as a combat veteran in the United States Army. In addition, I will offer my point of view as a clergyperson who provided pastoral care to service members.

The United States of America is not a theocracy. A *theocracy* (noun) is: 1. *A form of government in which God or a deity is recognized as the supreme civil ruler, the God's or deity's laws being interpreted by the ecclesiastical authorities. 2. A system of government by priests claiming a divine commission. 3. A commonwealth or state under such a form or system of government.*[1] Rather than a theocracy, the federal government of the United States is organized and divided into three branches: the legislative branch (Congress) makes laws; the executive branch (the president, the vice president, the cabinet members, and the agencies they lead) carries out the laws. The judicial branch (the Supreme Court and other, lower courts) evaluates laws. The United States is not governed by God, and God is not mentioned in its Constitution, though the Constitution does protect citizens' rights to practice religion.

The president of the United States, as commander-in-chief, speaks first by providing orders for the United States Armed Forces. Faith in God is not a requirement as commander-in-chief. Even as many U.S. citizens prefer that the president be a person of faith (while some citizens do not hold this preference), service members look to the president (or at least to the presidency) as to a moral compass. Today the United States of America and its military is rich in diversity. Both claim to be pluralistic, tolerant, and inclusive despite their rich history of oppression. Nevertheless, the United States may benefit from this ancient Israelite practice to first seek God for guidance and comfort before going off to war. If words of motivation, comfort, and support do not come from the commander-in-chief, presumably such care comes from the chaplain.

The United States military once recognized just over one hundred religions. Now a new list has grown, with up to 240 religions, "to include the earth-based faiths, such as heathens and Asatru, and an additional eight Protestant groups, including the International Communion of the

---

1. *Dictionary.com*, s.v. "theocracy (*n.*)," https://www.dictionary.com/browse/theocracy.

Charismatic Christian Church. Jewish servicemen and -women may now choose among Orthodox, Conservative and Reform instead of just 'Jewish.'" Also included are agnostics, atheists, and the nonreligious. What does this mean? It means that servicemen and -women who are members of small faith groups are now guaranteed the same rights, privileges, and protections granted to their peers who are members of larger faith groups.[2]

This is good news if you are a person who is nonjudgmental and does not buy into any one of the mainstream religions that practices exclusion. The issue is the expectation that each chaplain will serve only his or her faith group—that Roman Catholic chaplains will only care for Roman Catholic service members, or that Jewish chaplains will serve only Jews. It is this writer's opinion that all chaplains should be educated to serve all service members regardless of each service member's faith, nonfaith, ethnicity, or sexual orientation. At the same time, chaplains should also be empowered to practice their own faith. Historically, military chaplains have not always been able to serve in this capacity.

For instance, Alan Cooperman, a staff writer for the *Washington Post*, wrote,

> The tradition of chaplains in the U.S. military goes back to George Washington, who first sought a minister for his Virginia regiment in 1756. In the early days of the republic, commanders simply chose a chaplain who shared their beliefs. But with the expansion of the military in World War II, the armed services set quotas for chaplains of various faiths, attempting to match the proportion of each denomination in the general population."
>
> In a class-action lawsuit filed in 1999 in U.S. District Court for the District of Columbia and still in the discovery, or evidence-gathering, stage—more than fifty Navy chaplains contend that the formula became a rigid and discriminatory "thirds rule": one-third Catholics, one-third mainline Protestants and one-third everybody else.
>
> According to Hum, the military abandoned numerical targets about twenty years ago, partly for legal reasons and partly because the proliferation of religious groups made the system unworkable. Although chaplains are paid by the armed services, they must be ordained and "endorsed," or nominated, by religious organizations. The number of endorsers has grown from about ten denominations in 1945 to more than 240 groups today. Like college

2. Winston, "Defense Department."

admissions officers, Pentagon officials now say they seek diversity without using quotas.[3]

God plays a significant role in the lives of Black service members. If pastoral care is not provided by the chaplain, it comes from those within the ranks, often enlisted, who serve as prophets, elders, ministers, deacons, and evangelists within their local churches. The Black church is significantly underrepresented in the United States Armed Forces. This is primarily because most Black service members are enlisted. They have limited resources compared to officers. Moreover, the military chaplains from other faith traditions are not prepared to provide pastoral and spiritual care to service members of color. These chaplains primarily are from the mainstream denominations. For example, chaplains are Roman Catholic, and from Protestant denominations, including Methodism, Presbyterianism, and Baptist. In addition, there is a growing number of Jewish and Muslim chaplains. Readers should keep in mind that the ratio of chaplain to service member is relatively high. For example, only one chaplain maybe assigned to a battalion, which consists of anywhere between three hundred and eight hundred troops. Now imagine the diversity of those troops compared to a chaplain with an exclusive, intolerant faith tradition. Do not get me wrong: there are some outstanding chaplains working hard to meet the pastoral and spiritual needs of service members and their families. Here is where I put a plug for Clinical Pastoral Education (CPE). CPE is a wonderful adult education program offered for both civilian and military chaplains to help them become competent caregivers to all people.

How do you minister to a service member who, like me, entered the United States Army after receiving his General Education Diploma at the age of nineteen? My only option, having grown up poor in the "Wild, Wild Hundreds" of Chicago's famed South Side was to enlist in the military (in the army specifically). Before I was a minister, I was a warrior. Surviving in the gang-infested streets and poverty prepared me for the military. I learned how to fight well before I raised my right hand and swore an oath to protect and defend the Constitution of the United States. The army taught me valuable skills to survive and fight. Moreover, rooted in my learning to become a warrior was the education of love and grace taught by my parents and my religious tradition as a Baptist. If you can imagine, I was always in conflict with myself—a disorienting dilemma, if you will, between what is good versus what was bad . . . right versus wrong . . . to kill or to let live.

3. Cooperman, "Military Struggles."

When I received orders and briefings that I was going to war, I was afraid to die. In fact, I was concerned with ensuring the protection of the men and women in my charge and bringing them all back home safely. Not being able to competently lead my troops, and not returning them home with all their "fingers and toes" was my fear. I remember the first thing that I did was call my mother. I shared with her some of the details. As she cried, I tried to console her as she had done for me so many times in my life. I shared how competent my training had been, and how sophisticated the military was compared to the enemy. It did not work; she still cried. Despite my arrogant confidence, she wept. However, true to form, during her tears my momma said, "Baby, don't forget to pray about it." As scary as it was for my momma to hear that her oldest son was going off to fight a war in a foreign country, with not knowing what to do or say, she knew enough to pray and to seek God for instruction.

Prayer was the best advice my mother could give me; in fact it was her way to make the priestly pronouncement, "It is the LORD your God who goes with you, to fight for you against your enemies, to give you victory." I always wondered why my mother's initial response to me was always, "Son pray about it." I determined that when we as human beings do not know what to do amid trauma and despair, prayer is a way to establish hope. However, for my mom I think it was more than hope. Her suggestion to pray came out of deeply rooted experiences that suggested, if I ask God for what I needed, God will provide and honor my request. Pray is what I did. Prayer is rooted in my faith tradition and culture as an African American.

Truth be told, that when you are fighting a war, sometimes you forget to pray. It is a broad assumption, I know, but it rings true for me. I relied on my friends' and family's ability to pray. And I needed more. Where is the priest? In this case, where is the chaplain?

African Americans are a nation within a nation. If this is true, then we are a military within a military, with needs specific to our culture. Like the ancient Israelites, we practice our faith trusting in a God who will protect us against our enemies. Within Black culture there is a connection greater than that of our religious affiliations. Far greater than our citizenship as Americans and our cultural identities as Africans, South Americans, Caribbean, Aborigines, and others. We are connected spiritually and divinely through the ancestors and God.

The Black church is composed of the mainstream denominations. However, what are known as "reformations and fellowships" also exist.

Many of these reformations and fellowships are offspring of mainstream denominations, often calling themselves nondenominational. For the most part, these reformations and fellowships are formed with buy-in from a collection of churches that has broken away and has promised its pastor consecration as a bishop or a significantly important place within the reformation and fellowship.

Many of these churches are charismatic in nature; they combine high church and low church in their litany. Whether you believe in the existence of these churches or not, one thing is certain: Black parishioners attend these churches in large numbers. And these parishioners are entering the military.

In the two conflicts in which I was ordered to serve, the chaplains assigned to my units could not adequately care for the African Americans. I was asked by the service members to provide Bible study and a weekly worship service for our Black soldiers, because I was a minister outside of the army, in my personal life. I did not know how to be a chaplain, but the troops wanted a taste of home to get them through the difficult days. We build pews, altars, and chairs in designated tents. Or we gathered near a Humvee or truck to pray and read scriptures. We sang hymns. We cried. We reminisced. We loved each other. It was great for morale. Yet, there were always those individuals who complained because they were fearful or too proud to be inclusive, and requested we stop.

I have the certainty that God will go with you and even fight for you against your enemies. Seeking God's guidance is a wonderful practice to maintain. Moreover, it is comforting to have family, friends, or comrades comfort you amid your fear and anticipatory grief. This writer hopes that you are no longer surprised that in a theocracy, the priest is the first person who comes forward to speak to the troops before they go off to war—and that in the absence of a priest, God can utilize a kid from the "Wild, Wild Hundred" to provide care.

In this chapter, I have attempted to address these questions. If nothing else, simply be curious of the inquiries: Who speaks first within the United States Armed Forces? What is required or expected for its service members to hear and experience before going off to war? What role does God play in the United States Armed Forces? What is the pastoral or spiritual care provided to service members in preparation for war and postwar—specifically for Blacks or African Americans? I have shared my personal experience as a combat veteran in the United States Army, and I've shared my point of view as a clergyperson who provided pastoral care to service members. Ashe!

Bibliography

Abrams, Jasmine A., et al. "Carrying the World with the Grace of a Lady and the Grit of a Warrior: Deepening Our Understanding of the 'Strong Black Woman' Schema." *Psychology of Women Quarterly* 38 (2014) 503–18.

Abel, Godard. "What McDonald's Can Teach Us about Selling." Insider. *The Next Web*, May 9, 2015. https://thenextweb.com/insider/2015/05/09/what-mcdonalds-can-teach-us-about-selling.

ACPE. "Information "For Prospective Students. Frequently Asked Questions." On ACPE website. https://www.acpe.edu/ACPE/_Students/FAQ_S.aspx.

Adetiba, Liz, and Anna Almendrala. "Watching Videos of Police Brutality Can Traumatize You, Especially If You're Black." Black Voices. *Huffington Post*, July 8, 2016. https://www.huffingtonpost.com/entry/watching-police-brutality-videos_us_577ee9b3e4b0344d514eaa5d.

African American Domestic Peace Project. Website. https://www.aadpp.org/.

Alexander, Michelle. *The New Jim Crow: Mass Incarceration in the Age of Colorblindness.* New York: New Press, 2010.

Allen, Argie J., et al. "Being Examples of the Flock: The Role of Church Leaders and African American Families Seeking Mental Health Care Services." *Contemporary Family Therapy* 32 (2010) 117–34. https://link-springer-com.turing.library.northwestern.edu.

American Civil Liberties Union (ACLU). "Fuel the Fight: Become an ACLU Member." *ACLU* (website). https://action.aclu.org/give/fuel-fight-7.

American Psychiatric Association Foundation, and Mental Health and Faith Community Steering Committee. *Mental Health: A Guide for Faith Leaders.* Arlington, VA: American Psychiatric Association Foundation, 2016.

American Psychological Association. Psychology Help Center. "Coping with a Diagnosis of Chronic Illness." https://www.apa.org/helpcenter/chronic-illness.

Arroyo, Julia, et al. *Crossover in Median Age at First Marriage and First Birth: Thirty Years of Change.* Family Profiles. Bowling Green, OH: National Center for Family & Marriage Research, 2013.

Awosan, Christiana I., et al. "Understanding the Experience of Black Clients in Marriage and Family Therapy." *Journal of Marital and Family Therapy* 37 (2011) 153–68.

Babbel, Susanne. "Post Abortion Stress Syndrome (PASS)—Does It Exist?" *Psychology Today* (blog), October 24, 2010. https://www.psychologytoday.com/us/blog/somatic-psychology/201010/post-abortion-stress-pass-does-it-exist.

Baldwin, James. "Preface to the 1984 Edition." In *Notes of a Native Son*, ix–xvi. Beacon Paperback 39. Boston: Beacon, 1984.

Bambara, Toni Cade. *The Salt Eaters*. 1st Vintage Contemporaries ed. New York: Vintage, 1992.

Bannister, Don, and Fay Fransella. *Inquiring Man: The Psychology of Personal Constructs*. 3rd ed. London: Taylor & Francis, 2003. Kindle.

Barnes, Donna Holland. "Suicide." In *Handbook of African American Health*, edited by Robert L. Hampton et al., 444–60. New York: Guilford, 2010.

Bell, Yvonne R., et al. "Afrocentric Cultural Consciousness and African-American Male-Female Relationships." *Journal of Black Studies* 21 (1990) 162–89.

Bentancourt, Joseph R., et al. "Defining Cultural Competence: A Practical Framework for Addressing Racial/Ethnic Disparities in Health and Health Care." *Public Health Reports* (2016) 293–302.

Bertocchi, Grazielle, and Dimico Arcangelo. "The Racial Gap in Education and the Legacy of Slavery." *Journal of Comparative Economics* 40 (2012) 581–95.

Black AIDS Institute. Website. https://blackaids.org.

Black, M. C., et al. *The National Intimate Partner and Sexual Violence Survey (NISVS): 2010 Summary Report*. Atlanta: National Center for Injury Prevention and Control, Centers for Disease Control and Prevention, 2011.

Blanchard, Dallas A. *The Anti-Abortion Movement and the Rise of the Religious Right—From Polite to Fiery Protest*. Social Movements Past and Present. New York: Twayne, 1994.

Borum, Valerie. "African American Women's Perceptions of Depression and Suicide Risk and Protection: A Womanist Exploration." *Affilia* 27 (2012) 316–27.

Boulware, Ebony L., et al. "Race and Trust in the Health Care System." *Public Health Reports* 118 (2016) 358–65.

Braxton, Brad. *No Longer Slaves: Galatians and African American Experience*. Collegeville, MN: Liturgical, 2002.

Brewer, Rose M. "Theorizing Race, Class, and Gender: The New Scholarship of Black Feminist Intellectuals and Black Women's Labor." In *Theorizing Black Feminisms: The Visionary Pragmatism of Black Women*, edited by Stanlie M. James and Busia P. A. Abena, 13–30. New York: Routledge, 1993.

Brown, Michael Joseph. *What They Don't Tell You: A Survivor's Guide to Biblical Studies*. Louisville: Westminster John Knox, 2000.

Buber, Martin. *I and Thou*. 2nd ed. Translated by Ronald Gregor Smith. New York: Scribner, 1958.

Buhuro, Danielle J. "Transforming Trauma to Trust: A Prophetic Model of CPE Supervision in an Age of #BlackLivesMatter." *Reflective Practice: Formation and Supervision in Ministry* 38 (2018) 154–64. http://journals.sfu.ca/rpfs/index.php/rpfs/article/view/527/510.

Burke, Theresa Karminski, and David C. Reardon. *Forbidden Grief: The Unspoken Pain of Abortion*. Springfield, IL: Acorn, 2007.

Burrell-Jackson, Carol V. "Black Christians' Use of Ministers in Times of Distress: An Exploration of Congregant and Clergy Responses, and Review of Back Clergy Referral Attitudes and Practices." PhD diss., Michigan State University, 2008.

Capelouto, Susanna. "Eric Garner: The Haunting Last Words of a Dying Man." CNN, December 8, 2014. https://www.cnn.com/2014/12/04/us/garner-last-words/index.html.

Catalano, Ray, et al., "Disproportionate Use of Psychiatric Emergency Services by African Americans." *Psychiatric Services* 60 (2009) 1664–71.

Centers for Disease Control and Prevention (CDC). National Center for Chronic Disease Prevention and Health Promotion. "African American Health." In *Vital Signs*. https://www.cdc.gov/vitalsigns/aahealth/index.html.

———. "HIV among African Americans." https://www.cdc.gov/hiv/group/racialethnic/africanamericans/index.html.

———. "HIV among Women." https://www.cdc.gov/hiv/group/gender/women/index.html.

Chambers, Anthony L., and Aliza Kravitz. "Understanding the Disproportionately Low Marriage Rate among African Americans: An Amalgam of Sociological and Psychological Constraints." *Family Relations* 60 (2011) 648–60.

Chang, Patricia M. Y., et al. "Church-Agency Relationships in the Black Community." *Nonprofit and Voluntary Sector Quarterly* 23 (1994) 91–105.

Chapman, Kevin L., and Michael F. Streger. "Race and Religion: Differential Prediction of Anxiety Symptoms by Religious Coping in African American and European American Young Adults." *Depression and Anxiety* 27 (2010) 316–22.

Charles, Kerwin Kofi, and Ming Ching Luoh. "Male Incarceration, the Marriage Market, and Female Outcomes." *Review of Economics and Statistics* 92 (2010) 614–27.

Cheng, Amrit. "Fact-Checking Family Separation." *ACLU* (blog), June 19, 2018. https://www.aclu.org/blog/immigrants-rights/immigrants-rights-and-detention/fact-checking-family-separation.

Cherlin, Andrew J. "American Marriage in the Early Twenty-First Century." *Future of Children* 15 (2005) 33–55.

Chetty, Raj, et al. "Two Americas: Upward Mobility for White vs. Black Children." *Portside* (website), March 25, 2018. https://portside.org/2018-03-25/two-americas-upward-mobility-white-vs-black-children.

Chödrön, Pema. *The Wisdom of No Escape: And the Path of Loving-Kindness*. Shambhala Library. Boston: Shambhala, 2010.

Coates, Ta-Nehisi. *Between the World and Me*. New York: Spiegel & Grau, 2015.

———. "This Is How We Lost to the White Man: The Audacity of Bill Cosby's Conservatism." *Atlantic* 30/4 (May 2008) 52–62. https://www.theatlantic.com/magazine/archive/2008/05/-this-is-how-we-lost-to-the-white-man/306774.

Cone, James H. *A Black Theology of Liberation*. 40th anniversary ed. Maryknoll, NY: Orbis, 2010.

Conference on Crimes against Women. Website. http://www.conferencecaw.org/.

Cooperman, Alan. "Military Wrestles With Disharmony among Chaplains." *Washington Post*, August 30, 2005. https://tinyurl.com/y359cjfz.

Cooper-Patrick, Lisa, et al. "Identification of Patient Attitudes and Preferences Regarding Treatment of Depression." *Journal of General Internal Medicine* 12 (1997) 431–38.

Coppock, Vicki, and Bob Dunn. *Understanding Social Work Practice in Mental Health*. Los Angeles: Sage, 2010.

Cowan, Megan. "The Role of Stillness in Mindfulness." Posted in Implementation Stories. *Mindful Schools* (website), June 15, 2012. https://www.mindfulschools.org/implementation-stories/the-role-of-stillness-in-mindfulness.

Cox, Sue, et al. "Trust Relations in High-Reliability Organizations." *Risk Analysis* 26 (2006) 1123–38.

Curtin, Sally C., et al. "Suicide Rates for Females and Males by Race and Ethnicity: United States, 1999 and 2014." National Centers for Health Statistics, Centers for Disease Control and Prevention (website). https://www.cdc.gov/nchs/data/hestat/suicide/rates_1999_2014.htm.

Davey, Maureen P., and Marlene F. Watson. "Engaging African Americans in Therapy: Integrating a Public Policy and Family Therapy Perspective." *Contemporary Family Therapy* 30 (2008) 31–47.

Davis, Sharon Ellis. *Battered African American Women: A Study of Gender Entrapment.* Lewiston, NY: Mellen, 2014.

Dempsey, Keith, et al. "Black Churches and Mental Health Professionals: Can This Collaboration Work?" *Journal of Black Studies* 47 (2016) 73–87.

Desmond, Matthew, et al. "Police Violence and Citizen Crime Reporting in the Black Community." *American Sociological Review* 81 (2016) 857–76.

Dill, Bonnie Thornton, et al. "Fictive Kin, Paper Sons, and Compadrazgo: Women of Color and the Struggle for Family Survival." In *Families in the U.S.: Kinship and Domestic Politics*, edited by Karen V. Hansen and Anita Ilta Garey, 431–45. Women in the Political Economy. Philadelphia: Temple University Press, 1998.

D'Orio, Wayne. *Carol Moseley-Braun.* African-American Leaders. Philadelphia: Chelsea House, 2004.

Douglas, Kelly Brown. "Black and Blues: God-Talk/Body-Talk for the Black Church." In *Womanist Theological Ethics: A Reader*, edited by Katie Geneva Cannon et al., 113–31. Library of Theological Ethics. Louisville: Westminister John Knox, 2011.

Downs, Kenya. "When Black Death Goes Viral, It Can Trigger PTSD-Like Trauma." Nation. *PBS News Hour*, July 22, 2016. https://www.pbs.org/newshour/nation/black-pain-gone-viral-racism-graphic-videos-can-create-ptsd-like-trauma.

Dubb, Steve. "Chicago West Side Residents and Hospitals Aim to Close 16-Year Life Expectancy Gap." *Nonprofit Quarterly*, February 28, 2018. https://nonprofitquarterly.org/2018/03/05/chicago-west-side-residents-hospitals-aim-close-16-year-life-expectancy-gap.

Du Bois, W. E. B. *The Souls of Black Folk.* New York: Fawcett, 1961.

Early, Kevin. *Religion and Suicide in the African-American Community.* Contributions in Afro-American and African Studies 158. Westport, CT: Greenwood, 1992.

Elkin, Elizabeth, and Emily Smith. "What Is the Flores Settlement?" *CNN*, July 10, 2018. https://www.cnn.com/2018/07/10/politics/flores-settlement-history/index.html.

Eng, Monica. "Flamin' Hot Cheetos Inspire Fanatic Loyalty among Kids." *Chicago Tribune*, October 11, 2012. https://www.chicagotribune.com/entertainment/ct-xpm-2012-10-11-chi-20yearold-snack-with-high-levels-of-salt-and-fat-inspires-fanatic-loyalty-among-kids-20121011-story.html.

Equal Rights Advocates. *Moving Women Forward: On the 50th Anniversary of Title VII of the Civil Rights Act; A Three-Part Series.* "Part One: Sexual Harassment Still Exacting a Hefty Toll." https://www.equalrights.org/wp-content/uploads/2014/11/ERA-Moving-Women-Forward-Report-Part-One-Sexual-Harassment-Oct-2014.pdf.

Farrakhan, Louis. "The Million Man March: Past, Present, and Future." Interview by the *Final Call*, November 4, 2003. http://www.finalcall.com/artman/publish/Minister_Louis_Farrakhan_9/The_Million_Man_March_Past_Present_and_Future_1099.shtml.

Ferdman, Roberto A. "The Disturbing Ways That Fast Food Chains Disproportionately Target Black Kids." Economic Policy. November 12, 2014. https://www.

washingtonpost.com/news/wonk/wp/2014/11/12/the-disturbing-ways-that-fast-food-chains-disproportionately-target-black-kids.

Feuer, Alan, and Matt Apuzzo. "With Prosecutors at Odds, U.S. Inquiry into Eric Garner's Death Drags On." *New York Times*, July 11, 2016. https://www.nytimes.com/2016/07/12/nyregion/with-prosecutors-at-odds-us-inquiry-into-eric-garners-death-drags-on.html.

Fowl, Stephen. *Engaging Scripture: A Model for Theological Interpretation*. Challenges in Contemporary Theology. Malden, MA: Blackwell, 2000.

Fowler, Anthony, Jr. "Police Brutality Drove a Wedge between Me and My Church." Commentary, April 11, 2018. *The Marshall Project* (blog). https://www.themarshallproject.org/2018/04/11/police-brutality-drove-a-wedge-between-me-and-my-church.

Frame, Marsha W., et al. "Counseling African Americans: Integrating Spirituality in Therapy." *Counseling and Values* 41 (1996) 16–28.

Freedenthal, Stacey. *Helping the Suicidal Person: Tips and Techniques for Professionals.* New York: Routledge, 2018.

Frost, Michael. "Colin Kaepernick vs. Tim Tebow: A Tale of Two Christians on Their Knees." On Faith. Perspective. *Washington Post*, September 24, 2017. https://www.washingtonpost.com/news/acts-of-faith/wp/2017/09/24/colin-kaepernick-vs-tim-tebow-a-tale-of-two-christianities-on-its-knees.

Gaffney, Ebony. "African American Clergy's Attitude toward Professional Mental Health Services." PhD diss., Walden University, 2016.

Gagnon, John, et al. "The National Health and Social Life Survey" (NHSLS). In *The Social Organization of Sex: Sexual Practices in the United States*, 549–678 (appendixes B and C). Chicago: University of Chicago Press, 1994.

Gardner, Connie C. "Stigma and the Acceptability of Depression Treatments among African American Baptist Clergy." PhD diss., Liberty University, 2013/.

Gearing, Robin, and Dana Lizardi. "Religion and Suicide." *Journal of Religion and Health* 48 (2009) 332–41.

General Practice Alliance (South Gippsland, Australia). *Self Care: A Workbook.*

Giger, Joyce Newman, et al. "Church and Spirituality in the Lives of the African American Community." *Journal of Transcultural Nursing* 19 (2008) 375–83.

Gilkes, Cheryl Townsend. "'Liberated to Work Like Dogs!': Labeling Black Women and Their Work." In *The Experience and Meaning of Work in Women's Lives*, by Hildreth Y. Grossman and Nia Lane Chester, 179–202. London: Psychology Press, 2013.

Glaude, Eddie, Jr. "The Black Church Is Dead." *Huffington Post*, April 26, 2010. Updated August 23, 2012. https://www.huffpost.com/entry/the-black-church-is-dead_b_473815.

Goff, Phillip Atiba, et al. "The Essence of Innocence: Consequences of Dehumanizing Black Children." *Journal of Personality and Social Psychology* 104 (2014) 526–45. https://www.apa.org/pubs/journals/releases/psp-a0035663.pdf.

Goldman, Noreen, et al. "Demography of the Marriage Market in the United States." *Population Index* 50 (1984) 5–25.

Gorman, Michael J. *Abortion & the Early Church: Christian, Jewish & Pagan Attitudes in the Greco-Roman World*. New York: Paulist, 1982.

Government Accountability Office. "K–12 Education: Discipline Disparities for Black Students, Boys, and Students with Disabilities." March 2018. https://www.gao.gov/assets/700/690828.pdf.

Green, Carmen R., et al. "The Unequal Burden of Pain: Confronting Racial and Ethnic Disparities in Pain." *Pain Medicine* 4 (2003) 277–94.

Greenstein, Laura. "I Stop Stigma By . . ." *NAMI Blog*, November 16, 2016, https://www.nami.org/Blogs/NAMI-Blog/November-2016/I-Stop-Stigma-by%E2%80%A6/.

Gullotta, Daniel N. "Among Dogs and Disciples: An Examination of the Story of the Canaanite Woman." *Neotestamentica* 48 (2014) 325–40.

Guttmacher Institute. "United States: Abortion"(webpage). https://www.guttmacher.org/united-states/abortion.

Halford, W. Kim, et al. "Strengthening Couples' Relationships with Education: Social Policy and Public Health Perspectives." *Journal of Family Psychology* 22 (2008) 497–505.

Hanson, Rick. "What Makes You Feel Threatened? Bring Mindful Awareness to How Your Brain Reacts to Feeling Threatened." Your Wise Brain. *Psychology Today*, January 18, 2016. https://www.psychologytoday.com/us/blog/your-wise-brain/201601/what-makes-you-feel-threatened.

Harrison-Quintana, Jack, et al. *Injustice at Every Turn: A Look at Black Respondents to the National Transgender Discrimination Survey*. Washington, DC: National Black Justice Coalition, National Center for Transgender Equality, and Gay and Lesbian Task Force, 2011. https://www.transequality.org/sites/default/files/docs/resources/ntds_black_respondents_2.pdf.

Head, Tom. *Absolute Beginner's Guide to the Bible*. Absolute Beginner's Guide. Indianapolis: Que, 2006.

Henley, William Ernest. "Invictus." *Poetry Foundation* (website). https://www.poetryfoundation.org/poems/51642/invictus/. Originally published in *Book of Verses*. London: Life and Death Echoes, 1888.

Hennessy-Fiske, Molly. "'Prison-Like' Migrant Youth Shelter Is Understaffed, Unequipped for Trump's 'Zero Tolerance' Policy, Insider Says." *Los Angeles Times*, June 14, 2018. https://www.latimes.com/nation/la-na-border-migrant-shelter-20180614-story.html.

Herman, Judith. *Trauma and Recovery: The Aftermath of Violence from Domestic Abuse to Political Terror*. New York: Basic Books, 1997.

Hernandez, Tony. "A Brief History of Anti-immigrant Propaganda." In *Immigrant Archive Project Blog*, 2016/17. https://immigrantarchiveproject.org/brief-history-anti-immigrant-propaganda.

"Herstory." *Black Lives Matter* (website). https://blacklivesmatter.com/about/herstory/.

Hill, Shirley A. "Marriage among African American Women: A Gender Perspective." *Journal of Comparative Family Studies* 37 (2006) 421–40.

Hines, Paulette Moore, and Nancy Boyd-Franklin. "African American Families." In *Ethnicity & Family Therapy*, edited by Monica McGoldrick et al., 87–100. 3rd ed. New York: Guilford, 2005.

HIV.gov/ (website). "U.S. Statistics." https://www.hiv.gov/hiv-basics/overview/data-and-trends/statistics/.

Hoffman, Kelly M., et al. "Racial Bias in Pain Assessment and Treatment Recommendations, and False Beliefs about Biological Differences between Blacks and Whites." *Proceedings of the National Academy of Sciences* 113 (2016) 113–16.

Holloway, Karla F. C. *Passed On: African American Mourning Stories; A Memorial*. Durham, NC: Duke University Press, 2002.

hooks, bell. *Sisters of the Yam: Black Women and Self-Recovery*. Boston: South End, 1993.

Horsley, Scott. "Fact Check: Trump, Illegal Immigration, and Crime." Special Series: Fact Check. National Public Radio, June 22, 2018. https://tinyurl.com/yd6phdbu.

Hughes, Michael, and Bradley R. Hertel. "The Significance of Color Remains: A Study of Life Chances, Mate Selection, and Ethnic Consciousness among Black Americans." *Social Forces* 68 (1990) 1105–20.

Hunt, Bijou R., et al. "Life Expectancy Varies in Local Communities in Chicago: Racial and Spatial Disparities and Correlates." *Journal of Racial and Ethnic Health Disparities* 2 (2015) 425–33. https://link.springer.com/article/10.1007/s40615-015-0089-8.

Institute for Women's Policy Research. "The Gender Wage Gap: 2017." March 2018. Fact Sheet. IWPR C464. https://iwpr.org/wp-content/uploads/2018/03/C464_Gender-Wage-Gap-2.pdf.

Jackson, Imani J. "The Trauma of Police Brutality: Column." *USA Today*, September 2, 2016. https://www.usatoday.com/story/opinion/policing/spotlight/2016/09/02/trauma-police-brutality-column/89019122.

Jackson, Jesse. Interview by Henry Louis Gates Jr. "The Two Nations of Black America. *Frontline*. Original airdate: February 10, 1998. DVD. Alexandria, VA: PBS Home Video, 2008. https://tinyurl.com/y52znwmb.

Jeffrey, Courtland. "School Shootings in the U.S.: When, Where Each Shooting Has Occurred in 2018." News. Data. ABC-15, February 1, 2018. Updated May 25, 2018. https://www.abc15.com/news/data/school-shootings-in-u-s-when-where-each-shooting-has-occurred-in-2018.

Jennings, Mary, preparer. *Community of Practice in Building Referral Systems for Women Victims of Violence*. UNRWA Gender Series 1. United Nations Relief and Work Agency for Palestine (UNRWA) (2010). https://www.unrwa.org/userfiles/2010081854458/.pdf.

Johnson, Jason. "Why White People Call the Police on Black People in Public Spaces." Interview by Ari Shapiro. *All Things Considered*, NPR, May 15, 2018. Audio: 4:35. https://www.npr.org/2018/05/15/611389765/why-white-americans-call-the-police-on-black-people-in-public-spaces.

Johnson, Kecia R., and Karyn Loscocco. "Black Marriage through the Prism of Gender, Race, and Class." *Journal of Black Studies* 46 (2015) 142–71.

Johnson-Smith, Robert, II., ed. *Wisdom of the Ages: The Mystique of the African American Preacher*. Valley Forge, PA: Judson, 1995.

Joint Commission International. "Crosswalk of the National Standards for Culturally and Linguistically Appropriate Services (CLAS) in Health and Health Care to The Joint Commission Hospital Accreditation Standards." Prepared by the Joint Commission, with assistance from the Health Determinants & Disparities Practice at the Society of Research Administrators (SRA) International. July 2014. https://tinyurl.com/yyd8ve4a.

———. *Joint Commission International Accreditation Standards for Home Care*. 1st ed. Effective 1 July 2012. Oakbrook Terrace, IL: Joint Commission Resources Inc., 2012.

Justes, Emma J. *Please Don't Tell: What to Do with the Secrets People Share*. Nashville: Abingdon, 2014.

Kabat-Zinn, Jon. *Wherever You Go, There You Are: Mindfulness Meditation in Everyday Life*. New York: Hyperion, 1994.

Kelly, George Alexander. *A Theory of Personality: The Psychology of Personal Constructs*. Norton Library. New York: Norton, 1963.

Kennedy, Jason D. "Engaging Millennials through the Tradition of the Holy Spirit and Mission of the Assemblies of God." DMin diss., George Fox University, 2018. https://www.digitallcommons.georgefox.edu/dmin/265.

King, Anthony E. O., and Terrence T. Allen. "Personal Characteristics of the Ideal African American Marriage Partner: A Survey of Adult Black Men and Women." *Journal of Black Studies* 39 (2009) 570–88.

King, Deborah K. "Multiple Jeopardy, Multiple Consciousnsess: The Context of a Blank Feminist Theology." *Signs* 14 (1988) 42–72. https://www.jstor.org/stable/3174661/.

King, Martin Luther, Jr. "Beyond Vietnam." Delivered on April 4, 1967. Stanford University: The Martin Luther King, Jr. Research and Education Institute. https://kinginstitute.stanford.edu/king-papers/documents/beyond-vietnam.

———. "I Have a Dream." In *I Have a Dream: Writings and Speeches That Changed the World*, edited by James M. Washington, 101–6. San Francisco: HarperSanFrancisco, 1992.

———. "Letter from Birmingham City Jail." In *A Testament of Hope: The Essential Writings and Speeches of Martin Luther King, Jr.*, edited by James M. Washington, 289–302. New York: HarperCollins, 1991.

———. *I Have a Dream: Writings and Speeches That Changed the World.* Edited by James M. Washington. San Francisco: HarperSanFrancisco, 1992.

Krug, Etienne G., et al., eds. *World Report on Violence and Health.* Geneva: World Health Organization, 2002. https://www.who.int/violence_injury_prevention/violence/world_report/en.

Larkman, Connie. "UCC Leaders Join National Call to End 'Cruel' Immigration Policy, Keep Families Together." June 1, 2018. News. *United Church of Christ News. United Church of Christ* (website). http://www.ucc.org/news_ucc_leaders_join_national_call_to_end_cruel_immigration_policy_keep_families_together.

Lawrence, Ryan, et al. "Religion as a Risk Factor for Suicide Attempt and Suicide Ideation among Depressed Patients." *Journal of Nervous and Mental Disease* 204/11 (2016) 845–50.

Lopoo, Leonard M., and Bruce Western. "Incarceration and the Formation and Stability of Marital Unions." *Journal of Marriage and Family* 67 (2005) 721–34.

Lorde, Audre. "A Litany for Survival." In *The Collected Poems of Audre Lorde*, 255–56. New York: Norton, 1997.

Loveless, Tom. "Racial Disparities in School Suspensions." Brown Center Chalkboard (blog). Brookings Institution, March 24, 2017. https://www.brookings.edu/blog/brown-center-chalkboard/2017/03/24/racial-disparities-in-school-suspensions.

Males, Mike. "White People Should Be More Afraid of Other Whites Than They Are of People of Color." Opinion. *Los Angeles Times*, August 3, 2017. https://www.latimes.com/opinion/op-ed/la-oe-males-white-americans-violence-sanctuary-cities-20170803-story.html.

McDaniel, Anne, et al. "The Black Gender Gap in Educational Attainment: Historical Trends and Racial Comparisons." *Demography* 48 (2011) 889–914.

McMickle, Marvin A. *Where Have All the Prophets Gone? Reclaiming Prophetic Preaching in America.* Cleveland: Pilgrim, 2006.

McMinn, Mark R., et al. "Psychologists Collaborating with Clergy." *Professional Psychology: Research and Practice* 29 (1998) 564–70.

Mendoza, Cynthia "Muffy." "Mindful Meditation Should Be Required for Black Kids." *Brown Mamas Blog*, June 17, 2014. https://brownmamas.com/mindful-meditation-should-be-required-for-black-kids.

Messner, Steven F., and Robert J. Sampson. "The Sex Ratio, Family Disruption, and Rates of Violent Crime: The Paradox of Demographic Structure." *Social Forces* 69 (1991) 693–713.

Missouri Department of Mental Health. "Early Childhood Mental Health." https://dmh.mo.gov/healthykids/about.html.

Mitchell, Kenneth R., and Herbert Anderson. *All Our Losses, All Our Griefs: Resources for Pastoral Care.* Philadelphia: Westminster, 1983.

Moran, Michael, et al. "A Study of Pastoral Care, Referral, and Consultation Practices among Clergy in Four Settings in the New York City Area." *Pastoral Psychology* 53 (2005) 255–66.

Movement Advancement Project. *LGBT Policy Spotlight: HIV Criminalization Laws.* December 2016. http://www.lgbtmap.org/policy-and-issue-analysis/policy-spotlight-HIV-criminalization.

Moyer, Justin Wm. "Researchers Unclear Why Suicide Is Increasing among Black Children." *Chicago Tribune*, March 8, 2018. https://www.chicagotribune.com/lifestyles/health/ct-black-childrens-suicide-20180308-story.html.

Nadeem, Erum, et al. "Does Stigma Keep Poor Young Immigrant and U.S.-Born Black and Latina Women from Seeking Mental Health Care?" *Psychiatric Services* 58 (2007) 1547–54.

National Coalition against Domestic Violence. *NCADV.org* (website), "Statistics; National Statistics." https://ncadv.org/statistics?gclid=EAIaIQobChMIi8vP87KR4QIVjrSzCh2uKQi5EAAYASAAEgI8e_D_BwE.

National Institute of Mental Health, National Institute of Health. "Suicide" (webpage). https://www.nimh.nih.gov/health/statistics/suicide.shtml.

NBC-5 Chicago News. "Chicago Senator, Kids Make Cards for Children Separated from Parents at Border." *NBC-5 Chicago* (website), Ward Room, June 25, 2018. https://www.nbcchicago.com/blogs/ward-room/Durbin-Cards-to-Give-to-Children-Separated-From-Parents-at-Border-486469761.html.

Nhat Hanh, Thich. *Creating True Peace.* New York: Free Press, 2003.

Okeke, Barnabas I., et al. "Culture, Self, and Personality in Africa." In *Personality and Person Perception across Cultures*, edited by Yueh-Ting Lee et al., 139–62. Mahwah, NJ: Erlbaum, 1999.

Oppenheimer, Julie E., et al. "A Comparative Analysis of the Psychological Literature on Collaboration between Clergy and Mental-Health Professionals-Perspectives from Secular and Religious Journals: 1970–1999." *Pastoral Psychology* 53 (2004) 153–62.

Osborne, Samuel. "Brewer Become Most Educated Group in U.S." *Independent*, June 3, 2016. https://www.independent.co.uk/news/world/americas/black-women-become-most-educated-group-in-us-a7063361.html/.

Oxford Living Dictionaries: English (website). "Iconography." https://en.oxforddictionaries.com/definition/iconography.

Payne, Jennifer S. "'Saints Don't Cry': Exploring Messages Surrounding Depression and Mental Health Treatment as Expressed by African-American Pentecostal Preachers." *Journal of African American Studies* 12 (2008) 215–28.

————. "Variations in Pastors' Perception of the Etiology of Depression by Race and Religious Affiliation." *Community Mental Health Journal* 45 (2009) 355–65. https://link.springer.com/article/10.1007%2Fs10597-009-9210-y.

Pettit, Becky, and Bruce Western. "Mass Imprisonment and the Life Course: Race and Class Inequality in U.S. Incarceration." *American Sociological Review* 69 (2004) 151–69.

Phillips, Amber. "'They're Rapists': President Trump's Campaign Launch Speech Two Years Later, Annotated." The Fix. *Washington Post*, January 6, 2017. https://www.washingtonpost.com/news/the-fix/wp/2017/06/16/theyre-rapists-presidents-trump-campaign-launch-speech-two-years-later-annotated.

Pinderhughes, Elaine B. "African American Marriage in the 20th Century." *Family Process* 41 (2002) 269–82.

Poussaint, Alvin F., and Amy Alexander. *Lay My Burden Down: Suicide and the Mental Health Crisis among African Americans*. Boston: Beacon, 2000.

Priest, Naomi, et al. "A Systematic Review of Studies Examining the Relationship between Reported Racism and Health and Wellbeing for Children and Young People." *Social Science & Medicine* 95 (2013) 115–27.

Qualls, Sara Honn. "What Social Relationships Can Do for Health." *Generations: The Journal of the Western Gerontological Society* 38 (2014) 8–14.

Raifman, Julia, et al., "Difference-in-Differences Analysis of the Association between State Same-Sex Marriage Policies and Adolescent Suicide Attempts." *JAMA Pediatrics* 171 (2017) 350–56.

Richie, Beth. *Arrested Justice: Black Women, Violence, and America's Prison Nation*. New York: New York University Press, 2012.

Rickwood, Deborah, and Kerry Thomas. "Conceptual Measurement Framework for Help-Seeking for Mental Health Problems." *Psychology Research and Behavior Management* 5 (2012) 173–83.

Rios, Victor M. *Punished: Policing the Live of Black and Latino Boys*. New Perspectives in Crime, Deviance, and Law Series. New York: New York University Press, 2011.

Rothman, E. F., et al. "How Employment Helps Female Victims of Intimate Partner Violence: A Qualitative Study." *Journal of Occupational Health Psychology* 12/2 (2007) 136–43. http://dx.doi.org/10.1037/1076-8998.12.2.136.

Saar, Malika Saada, et al. *The Sexual Abuse to Prison Pipeline: The Girls' Story*. Washington DC: Human Rights Project for Girls and Georgetown Law Center on Poverty and Inequality, 2015.

Sahgal, Neha, and Greg Smith. "A Religious Portrait of African-Americans." *Pew Forum on Religion & Public Life*, 30 January 2009. http://www.pewforum.org/2009/01/30/a-religious-portrait-of-african-americans.

Sampson, Robert J. "The Effect of Male Joblessness and Family Disruption." *American Journal of Sociology* 93 (1987) 348–82.

Sanchez, Ray. "Choke Hold by Cop Killed NY Man, Medical Examiner Says." CNN, August 2, 2014. https://www.cnn.com/2014/08/01/justice/new-york-choke-hold-death/index.html.

Sassler, Sharon. "Partnering across the Life Course: Sex, Relationships, and Mate Selection." *Journal of Marriage and Family* 72 (2010) 557–75.

Schram, Jamie, et al. "NYPD Chokehold Death Ruled a Homicide." New York Post, August 1, 2014. https://nypost.com/2014/08/01/staten-island-chokehold-victim-death-ruled-a-homicide.

Segal, Corinne. "Same-Sex Marriage Laws Linked to Fewer Youth Suicide Attempts, New Study Says." Health. *PBS News Hour*, February 20, 2017. https://www.pbs.org/newshour/health/same-sex-marriage-fewer-youth-suicide.

Segovia, Fernando. "The Bible as a Text in Cultures: An Introduction." In *The Peoples' Bible: New Revised Standard Version with the Apocrypha*, edited by Curtiss Paul DeYoung et al., 23–30. Minneapolis: Fortress, 2009.

Shakur, Assata. *Assata: An Autobiography*. London: Zed, 1987.

Shear, Michael D., et al. "Trump Retreats on Separating Families, but Thousands May Remain Apart." *New York Times*, June 20, 2018. https://www.nytimes.com/2018/06/20/us/politics/trump-immigration-children-executive-order.html.

Sheppard, Phillis Isabella. *Self, Culture, and Others in Womanist Practical Theology*. Black Religion/Womanist Thought/Social Justice. New York: Palgrave Macmillan, 2011.

Sherman, Francine T. *Detention Reform and Girls: Challenges and Solutions*. Pathways to Juvenile Detention Reform 13. Baltimore: Annie E. Casey Foundation, 2005.

Sherman, Francine T., and Annie Balck. *Gender Injustice: System Level Juvenile Justice Reform for Girls*. In partnership with the National Crittenton Foundation and the National Women's Law Center, and with support from the Public Welfare Foundation, Novo Foundation, and the Boston College Law School. Boston: Boston College Law School, 2015. http://www.nationalcrittenton.org/wp-content/uploads/2015/09/Gender_Injustice_Report.pdf.

Shockley, Grant, et al. "Christian Education and the Black Church." In *Christian Education Journey of Black Americans: Past, Present, Future*, compiled by Charles R. Foster et al., 1–18. Nashville: Discipleship Resources, 1985.

Shopshire, James Maynard. "A Sociological Perspective." In *Perspectives on Suicide*, edited by James T. Clemons, 22–40. Louisville: Westminster John Knox, 1990.

Skloot, Rebecca. *The Immortal Life of Henrietta Lacks*. New York: Crown, 2010.

Smith, John David. "'I Was Raised Poor and Hard as Any Slave': African American Slavery in Piedmont, North Carolina." *North Carolina Historical Review* 90 (2013) 1–25.

Solis, Marie. "Six Anti-Muslim Comments That Could Haunt Trump in Supreme Court Travel Ban Case." U.S. *Newsweek*, April 24, 2018. https://www.newsweek.com/tk-trumps-anti-muslim-comments-could-come-back-haunt-him-travel-ban-supreme-898086/.

Spates, Kamesha. *What Don't Kill Us Makes Us Stronger: African American Women and Suicide*. New Critical Viewpoints on Society Series. New York: Routledge, 2016.

Spates, Kamesha, and Brittany C. Slatton. "I've Got My Family and My Faith: Black Women and the Suicide Paradox." *Socius: Sociological Research for a Dynamic World* 3 (4 December 2017). https://doi.org/10.1177%2F2378023117743908.

Smith, Llewellyn, et al., dirs. *Race: The Power of an Illusion*. Produced by Larry Adelman et al. TV series (3 episodes). DVD. San Francisco: California Newsreel, 2003.

Stack, Steven. "The Relationship between Culture and Suicide: An Analysis of African Americans." *Transcultural Psychiatry* 35 (1998) 253–69.

Stanford, Matthew S. "Demon or Disorder: A Survey of Attitudes toward Mental Illness In the Christian Church." *Mental Health, Religion & Culture* 10 (2007) 445–49.

Stanley, Scott M., et al. "Community-Based Premarital Prevention: Clergy and Lay Leaders on the Front Lines." *Family Relations* 50 (2001) 67–76.

Sullivan, John, et al. "Nationwide, Police Shot and Killed Nearly 1000 People in 2017." *Washington Post*. January 6, 2018. https://www.washingtonpost.com/

investigations/nationwide-police-shot-and-killed-nearly-1000-people-in-2017/2018/01/04/4eed5f34-e4e9-11e7-ab50-621fe0588340_story.html?utm_term=.a7941710af3c.

Summer, Donna, with Marc Eliot. *Ordinary Girl: The Journey.* New York: Villard, 2003.

Taylor, Robert J., et al. "Mental Health Services in Faith Communities: The Role of Clergy in Black Churches." *Social Work* 45 (2000) 73–87.

Tervalon, Melanie, and Jann Murray-García. "Cultural Humility versus Cultural Competence: A Critical Distinction in Defining Physician Training Outcomes in Multicultural Education." Guest Editorial. *Journal of Health Care for the Poor and Underserved* 9 (1998) 117–25. https://melanietervalon.com/wp-content/uploads/2013/08/CulturalHumility_Tervalon-and-Murray-Garcia-Article.pdf.

Thornton, Amber. "The Reality of Suicide in the Black Community." *Dr. Amber Thornton* (website/blog), July 20, 2017. https://www.dramberthornton.com/blog/the-reality-of-suicide-in-the-black-community.

Thurman, Howard. *Jesus and the Disinherited.* 1949. Reprint, Boston: Beacon, 1996.

Trader-Leigh, Karyn, and the Joint Center for Political and Economic Studies Health Policy Institute. *Understanding the Role of African American Churches and Clergy in Community Crisis Response.* Washington DC: Joint Center for Political and Economic Studies, Inc., 2008. http://jointcenter.org/sites/default/files/UnderstandingRoleofChurches.pdf.

Trible, Phyllis. *Texts of Terror: Literary-Feminist Readings of Biblical Narratives.* Overtures to Biblical Theology. Philadelphia: Fortress, 1984.

Truman, Jennifer L., and Rachel E. Morgan. "Nonfatal Domestic Violence, 2003–2012." Special Report, April 2014. Washington DC: Bureau of Justice statistics, Office of Justice Programs, U.S. Department of Justice, 2014.

Umberson, Debra, and Jennifer Karas Montez. "Social Relationships and Health: A Flashpoint for Health Policy." *Journal of Health and Social Behavior,* 1 suppl. (2010) S54–S66.

United Nations Population Fund (UNFPA) Regional Office for Eastern Europe and Central Asia, et al. *Strengthening Health System Responses to Gender-Based Violence in Eastern Europe and Central Asia: A Resource Package* (2014). https://eeca.unfpa.org/sites/default/files/pub-pdf/WAVE-UNFPA-Report-EN.pdf.

Vitali, Ali, et al. "Trump Referred to Haiti and African Nations as Shithole Countries." *NBC News,* January 11/12, 2018. https://www.nbcnews.com/politics/white-house/trump-referred-haiti-african-countries-shithole-nations-n836946.

Waite, Linda J., and Evelyn L. Lehrer. "The Benefits from Marriage and Religion in the United States: A Comparative Analysis." *Population and Development Review* 29 (2003) 255–76.

Walker, Alice. "Preface." In *In Search of Our Mothers' Gardens: Womanist Prose,* xi–xii. A Harvest Book. San Diego: Harcourt Brace Jovanovich, 1983.

Walker-Barnes, Chanequa. "The Burden of the Strong Black Woman." *Journal of Pastoral Theology* 19 (2009) 1–21.

———. *Too Heavy a Yoke: Black Women and the Burden of Strength.* Eugene, OR: Cascade Books, 2014.

Walsh, Colleen. "The Costs of Inequality: A Goal of Justice, a Reality of Unfairness." *Harvard Gazette,* February 29, 2016. https://news.harvard.edu/gazette/story/2016/02/the-costs-of-inequality-a-goal-of-justice-a-reality-of-unfairness.

Wang, Phillip S., et al. "Recent Care of Common Mental Disorders in the United States: Prevalence and Conformance with Evidence-Based Recommendations." *Journal of General Internal Medicine* 15 (2000) 284–92. http://www.ncbi.nlm.nih.gov/pmc/articles/PMC1495452.

Warren, Patricia, et al. "Driving While Black: Bias Processes and Racial Disparity in Police Stops." *Criminology* 44 (2006) 709–38.

Weaver, Andrew J., et al. "Marriage and Family Therapists and the Clergy: A Need for Clinical Collaboration, Training, and Research." *Journal of Marital and Family Therapy* 23 (1997) 13–25.

Weaver, Vesla Mae. "Why White People Keep Calling the Cops on Black Americans." Vox, May 17–19, 2018. Updated May 29, 2018. https://www.vox.com/first-person/2018/5/17/17362100/starbucks-racial-profiling-yale-airbnb-911.

Weems, Renita J. *Battered Love: Marriage, Sex, and Violence in the Hebrew Prophets.* Overtures to Biblical Theology. Minneapolis: Fortress, 1995.

———. "Reading Her Way through the Struggle: African American Women and the Bible." In *Stony the Road We Trod: African American Biblical Interpretation*, edited by Cain Hope Felder, 57–77. Minneapolis: Fortress, 1991.

West, Traci C. *Disruptive Christian Ethics: When Racism and Women's Lives Matter.* Louisville: Westminster John Knox, 2006.

———. *Wounds of the Spirit: Black Women, Violence, and Resistance Ethics.* New York: New York University Press, 1999.

Western, Bruce, and Christopher Wildeman. "The Black Family and Mass Incarceration." *Annals of the American Academy of Political and Social Science* 621 (2009) 221–42.

White, Evelyn C. *Chain, Chain, Change: For Black Women in Abusive Relationships.* New Leaf Series. Seattle: Seal, 1985.

White House Council on Women and Girls. "Advancing Equity for Women and Girls of Color." November 2015. https://obamawhitehouse.archives.gov/sites/whitehouse.gov/files/documents/ADVANCING_EQUITY_FOR_WOMEN_AND_GIRLS_OF_COLOR_REPORT.pdf.

White Katz, Maude. "She Who Would Be Free—Resistance." *Freedomways* 2 (Winter 1962) 60–71.

"Why Mindfulness Is Needed in Education." Mindful Schools (website). https://www.mindfulschools.org/about-mindfulness/mindfulness-in-education.

Wikipedia, "Tuskegee Syphilis Experiment." https://en.wikipedia.org/wiki/Tuskegee_syphilis_experiment.

Williams, David R., and Steven Mazzle. "Tackle Problems of Policing, Racism as Public Health Issue." *USA Today*, January 2, 2017. https://tinyurl.com/y5jw54jt.

Wilmoth, Joe D., and Abigail D. Blaney. "African American Clergy Involvement in Marriage Preparation." *Journal of Family Issues* 37 (2016) 855–76.

Wimberly, Edward P. *Moving from Shame to Self-Worth: Preaching and Pastoral Care.* Nashville: Abingdon, 1999.

Winston, Kimberly. "Defense Department Expands Its List of Recognized Religions." *Religion News Service*, April 21, 2017. https://religionnews.com/2017/04/21/defense-department-expands-its-list-of-recognized-religions/.

Woodson, C. G. "The Celebration of Negro History Week, 1927." *Journal of Negro History* 12 (1927) 103–9.

World Health Organization. *Mental Health: A State of Well-Being.* Updated August 2014. http://www.who.int/features/factfiles/mental_health/en.

Wormwood, Jolie. "How Feelings Guide Threat Perception." *Emotion News*, December 22, 2014. http://emotionnews.org/feelings-and-threat-perception/.

Wright, Almeda M. *The Spiritual Lives of Young African Americans*. New York: oxford University Press, 2017.

X, Malcolm. "Prospects for Freedom." Speech delivered on January 7, 1965. In *Malcolm X Speaks: Selected Speeches and Statements*, edited with prefatory notes by George Breitman, 147–56. London: Secker & Warburg, 1966.

Yalom, Irvin D. *Love's Executioner, and Other Tales of Psychotherapy*. New York: Basic Books, 2012.

Zheng, Nan Tracy, et al. "Racial Disparities in In-Hospital Death and Hospice Use Among Nursing Home Residents at the End-of-life." *Medical Care* 49 (2011) 992–98.

Zeng, Zhen. *Jail Inmates in 2016. Bureau of Justice Statistics Bulletin*, NCJ 251210, February 2018. U.S. Department of Justice, Office of Justice Programs, Bureau of Justice Statistics, 2016. https://www.bjs.gov/content/pub/pdf/ji16.pdf.

Index

Aaron, Hank, 103
abortion
   about, 160
   laws on, 166
   ministries supporting grief from,
      162
   secrecy of, 162–63
   statistics on, 162
   throughout history, 165–66
   trauma associated with, 161
accountability, domestic violence
      and, 45
activism. *See also* Black Lives Matter
      movement
   Black Lives Matter movement
      compared to traditional,
      faith-based, 23
   burnout and, 24
   churches and, 25
   racism rallies, 27
   sustainable, 24
acute trauma, 181
"Advancing Equity on Women and
      Girls of Color" report, 48–49
adversarial, as a self object need, 83
adverse childhood experiences
      (ACEs), trauma and, 51–52
advocacy
   domestic violence and, 45–47
   on the macro level, 20
   spiritual care of Black advocates,
      111–12
African American Christian
      education, racism in, 73–76

African American church. *See* Black
      Church
African Americans
   barriers to accessing mental
      health for, 92–101
   health problems and, 6–7
   importance of image to, 93
   importance of perception to,
      93–94
   importance of trust to, 97
   self-care steps for, 7–8
African Methodist Episcopal Church,
      153n9
African Methodist Episcopal Zion
      Church, 153n9
Alexander, Amy, 122
Alexander, Michelle
   *The New Jim Crow: Mass
      Incarceration in the Age of
      Colorblindness,* 41–42
Ali, Mohammed, 103
all or nothing thinking, as a self-care
      intervention, 130
All Our Losses, All Our Grief, 167
American Civil Liberties Union
      (ACLU), 21
antiviolence, 30–32
apostolic (mid) level, of response, 19,
      20–21
Arnett, Benjamin W., 138
*Arrested Justice: Black Women,
      Violence and America's Prison
      Nation* (Richie), 52
Assatta's Daughters, 34

Association for Clinical Pastoral
Education (ACPE), 175–76,
182, 191
Association of Professional Chaplains
(APC), 191
Association of Theological Schools,
25
assumptions, in United States Armed
Forces, 174–75
asylum seekers, demonization of,
15–22

Baldwin, James, 113, 157–58
Bambara, Toni Cade
The Salt Eaters, 100–101
Banneker, Benjamin, 138
Barnes, Donna Holland, 122
Battered African American Women: A
Study of Gender Entrapment
(Davis), 40
batterer, accountability for the, 40,
41–45
Belafonte, Harry, 113
Bell, Sean, 4
"Beyond Vietnam" speech (King,
Jr.), 19
Bible
issues in the practice of ministry,
72–73
reading of the, 71–72
slavery interpretations in the,
73–74
stories of couples in the, 142–43
Black advocates
spiritual care of, 111–12
Black allies
spiritual care and, 110–11
Black Church
circular leadership and, 34–35
creating a culture of safety in the,
48–57
denominations in the, 198–99
Hawley on, 153–55, 153n9
historical and sociological context
of the, 73–76
homosexuality in the, 75

interpretations of the Bible in the,
72–73
mental health and, 84, 87–88
the movement and, 27–29
safe space and, 53–54, 91
underrepresentation of in United
States Armed Forces, 197
Black liberation theology, hope of,
109
"Black Life Matters Ride," 5
Black Lives Matter Global Network,
177
Black Lives Matter movement, 180
Black Church and, 27–29
compared to traditional, faith-
based activism, 23
creation of, 39n2, 138
initial trending of
#BlackLivesMatter, 4–5
self-care and, 24
Black respectability, HIV/AIDS and,
107–8, 110–11
Black shame, HIV/AIDS and, 108–9
Black trauma, self-care for, 7–8
Black Youth Project (BYP100), 34
Bland, Sandra, 4, 106, 150, 180
boycotting, on the macro level, 20
Boyd, Rekia, 180
Braxton, Brad, 76, 79
Brown, James, 113
Brown, Michael, 4–5, 11, 76, 105,
106, 142
Brown, Mike, 4, 151–52, 180
Buber, Martin, 176n10
Buhuro, Danielle J., 177, 183–84
bullying, 58–59
Burke, Theresa
Forbidden Grief: The Unspoken
Pain of Abortion, 161
burnout, activism and, 24

capitalism, participation of churches
in, 26
care consciousness, 176–78
caregivers
in hospitals, 177–78

micropractice/pastoral work done
by direct, 21–22
Castile, Philando, 4, 5, 142
*Chain, Chain, Change: For
Black Women in Abusive
Relationships* (White), 41
chaplains
in hospitals, 186–93
in United States military, 196–97
Chödrön, Pema, 66
Christian education, secular
education *versus,* 79–80
Christian Methodist Episcopal
Church, 153n9
chronic illnesses, mental health
services for, 130, 131
chronic trauma, 181
Church of God in Christ, 153n9
churches. *See also* Black Church
activism and, 25
leadership models of, 32–34
nonviolence and, 31–32
participation in capitalism of, 26
self-care and, 24
circular leadership, 34–35
circular power, 34
citizenship, 17
civil rights movement, 154–55, 158
clergy
critical need for CPE among
African American, 179–85
as a spiritual resource for mate
selection, 144–45
Clinical Pastoral education (CPE)
about, 85, 175–76
assumptions in, 174–75
care consciousness in, 176–78
critical need for among African
American clergy, 179–85
focus of, 182
importance of, 183, 197
personal constructs and, 171–73
trauma and, 180–1
A Clockwork Orange (film), 24
Close to Home program, 57
Coates, Ta-Nehisi, 153
Coleman, Johnnie, 179

complex trauma, 181
Cone, James H., 108–9, 112, 166–67
Conference on Crimes against
Women (CCAW), 37–38
congregations, role of in suicide
prevention, 116–17
Cooperman, Alan, 196–97
Cooper-Patrick, Lisa, 88
Cornelius, Don, 115
Cosby, Bill, 107, 108
Cowan, Megan, 64
Creating Circles of Peace program,
62–63, 67–68
Creating True Peace (Nhat Hanh), 59
criminal and juvenile justice systems
adverse childhood experiences
(ACEs) and, 51–52
justice and domestic violence,
45–47
statistics on women/girls entering
the, 48–49, 57
trauma and, 51–52
victimization and, 49–50
criminalization, HIV, 105
critical reflection, 175–76
Crutcher, Terence, 5–6
Cullors, Patrisse, 4, 5, 39n2
cultural care, as spiritual care, 190–91
cultural humility, 191–92, 191n10

Davis, Sharon Ellis
*Battered African American
Women: A Study of Gender
Entrapment,* 40
Deferred Action for Childhood
Arrivals, 17
"Demon or Disorder: A Survey of
Attitudes toward Mental
Illness in the Christian
Church," 82
*Detention Reform and Girls:
Challenges and Solutions*
study, 49
Diallo, Amadou, 4
discipline, in schools, 152–53, 152n1
disqualifying the positive, as a self-
care intervention, 130

INDEX

Disruptive Christian Ethics: When Racism and Women's Lives Matter (West), 46
domestic violence
    advocacy and, 45–47
    justice and, 45–47
    pastoral care and, 37–47
    statistics on, 43
    victim safety and, 40, 41–45
    young women/girls and, 50
Dorhauer, John, 20
Douglas, Kelly Brown, 87
Douglass, Frederick, 103
Dream Act, 17
drug wars, 41–42
DuBois, W. E. B., 103
    The Souls of Black Folk, 158
Durbin, Dick, 21–22
Dyson, Michael Eric, 179

Early, Kevin E.
    Religion and Suicide in the African-American Community, 121
Easter, Ethel, 98
Ebenezer Baptist Church, 27–28
education
    Christian *versus* secular, 79–80
    on the macro level, 20
    statistics on African American levels of, 74n9, 138
    in three-*e* method, 183–84
educational attainment, as a barrier to mate selection, 138–39
efficacy, as a self object need, 83
emancipation proclamation, 17
emotional reasoning, as a self-care intervention, 131
empathy, in three-*e* method, 183–84
empowerment, in three-*e* method, 183–84
ethic of resistance, young women/girls in prison nation and, 56–57
Eurocentric method of critique, 183
European Americans
    bias of, 10–13

paranoia of, 13–14
executive branch, of federal government, 195

faith healing, as a barrier to accessing mental health, 94–95
family separations, 18, 20
Farrakhan, Louis, 107, 108
federal government, branches of, 195
First Baptist Church, 28
Flores Settlement, 17, 21
Floyd, Derrick, letter to son by, 155–59
Flunder, Yvette, 179
food oppression, in the Black community, 127–32
Forbidden Grief: The Unspoken Pain of Abortion (Burke), 161
forgiveness, domestic violence and, 44–5
Fowl, Stephen, 76–77
Franklin, Benjamin, 15
Frazier, E. Franklin
    The Negro Church in America, 28
Freedenthal, Stacey, 123–24
Frost, Michael, 173

Garner, Eric, 3–4, 5, 106
Garvey, Marcus, 113
Garza, Alicia, 4, 39n2
Gearing, Robin, 120
gender
    educational differences in, 138
    suicide statistics based on, 118–19
Gender Informed Practice Assessment (GIPA), 51–52
gentrification, 149
Glaude, Eddie, 155
Goff, Phillip Atiba, 7
grief, importance of healthy, 167

Hanson, Rick, 10
Hathaway, Donny, 115
Hawley, Jamie D., letter to son by, 149–55
healing

in Black spiritual tradition,
112–13
as pastoral care, 21–22
health disparities, between African
Americans and other races,
129
health ministries, 129–30
Henley, William Ernest, 65
historical-critical method, of
interpretation, 77–78
HIV criminalization, 105
HIV/AIDS
racial bias in, 106
respectability and, 107–8, 110–11
spiritual care and, 102–13, 110
statistics on, 104–5
Hollies, Linda, 166–67
Homeland Security Act, 16
homophobia, 75
homosexuality
HIV/AIDS and, 103–5
statistics on, 75
hooks, bell
Sisters of the Yam, 167
Hopkins, Dwight, 166–67
hospitals, Black spiritual care in,
186–93
Hyman, Phyllis, 115

iconography, 103
idealizing, as a self object need, 83
image, importance of to African
Americans, 93
immigrants, demonization of, 15–22
immigration quota laws, 17
The Immortal Life of Henrietta Lacks,
97–98
In Search of Our Mother's Gardens:
Womanist Prose (Walker),
43–44
incarceration
as a barrier to mate selection, 141
statistics on, 141, 181
victimization and, 49–50
institutional accountability, cultural
humility and, 192
integration, between races, 171

interpretations
of the Bible in the Black Church,
72–73
methods of, 77–80
theological implications of
Biblical, 76–77
interpretive tools, for spiritual care,
71–80
"Invictus" (poem), 65

Jackson, Jesse, 99, 103, 110
Jackson, Robert, 15
Japanese Americans, 15–16
Jim Crow, 129n9
Johnson, Jason, 12, 14
Johnson, Magic, 102–13
judicial branch, of federal
government, 195
jumping to conclusions, as a self-care
intervention, 130–31
Justes, Emma
Please Don't Tell, 162–63
juvenile justice systems. See criminal
and juvenile justice systems

Kabat-Zinn, Jon, 61, 66
Kaepernick, Colin, 173
Katz, Maude White, 88–89
Kelly, George, 172, 174–75
King, Martin Luther, Jr., 19, 26, 33,
68, 103, 177, 179
kinship/twinship, as a self object
need, 83
Kohut, Heinz, 82–83
Korematsu v. the U.S., 15–16

labeling and mislabeling, as a self-
care intervention, 131
language, use of in CPE, 183–84
law enforcement. See policing
leadership
circular, 34–35
models of, for churches, 32–34
legislative branch, of federal
government, 195
Let Us Breathe, 34
LGBQT, domestic violence and, 47

life expectancy statistics, 187
lifelong learning, cultural humility
    and, 192
Lizardi, Dana, 120
lobbying, on the macro level, 20
Lorde, Audre, 190–91

macro (prophetic) level, of response,
    19–20
Magic Johnson, 102–13
magnification, as a self-care
    intervention, 131
Malcolm X, 103, 110, 159
Males, Mike, 13
Mandela, Nelson, 65
marriage market, 137. See also mate
    selection
marriage statistics, 137
Martin, Trayvon, 4, 106, 110, 142,
    173, 180
mate selection
    about, 135–36
    barriers to, 138–41
    current state of, 137–38
    history of, 143–44
    spiritual premarital counseling
        and, 145–46
    spiritual resources and, 144–45
    spirituality and, 142–43
    therapeutic interventions and,
        142–43, 146–47
Maxwell, Peter, 65
McMickle, Marvin A., 154
Meadows, Bresha, 50
medical/psychiatric model, of suicide,
    122, 123
meditation. See mindfulness
Mendoza, Cynthia, 63–64
mental filter, as a self-care
    intervention, 130
mental health
    about, 81
    barriers to accessing, 92–101
    in the Black Church, 84, 85,
        87–88
    consequences of untreated
        distress in, 82

referrals for, 89
services for chronic illness, 130,
    131
stigmatization of, 88
micro (pastoral) level, of response,
    19, 21–22, 58–68
mid (apostolic) level, of response, 19,
    20–21
military. See United States Armed
    Forces
The Million Man March, 107
Mindful Schools/Curriculum, 64,
    66–67
mindfulness
    as a pastoral response, 58–68
    rise in popularity of, 66–67
ministry issues, 72–73. See also
    specific topics
mirroring, as a self object need, 83
Mitchem, Stephanie, 166–67
Moeller, Susan, 7
Moore, Darnell, 5
moral communities, 56–57
moral safety, for young women/girls
    in prison nation, 55
Moseley-Braun, Carol, 156
Moving from Shame to Self-Worth
    (Wimberly), 167–68
Moyer, Justin, 115

National Baptist Convention, 153n9
National Baptist Convention (of
    America), 153n9
National Council of Churches, 27
National LGBTQ Task Force, 114
National Organization of People of
    Color against Suicide, 114–15
National Suicide and Black Church
    Conference, 114–15
nationalism, 17
Naturalization Act (1790), 17
The Negro Church in America
    (Frazier), 28
Nelson, Rashon, 9–10
New Age Christian congregations, 76

The New Jim Crow: Mass Incarceration in the Age of Colorblindness (Alexander), 41–42
Nhat Hanh, Thich
   Creating True Peace, 59
nonviolence, violence *versus,* 29–32

Obama, Barack
   citizenship of questioned, 18
   Deferred Action for Childhood Arrivals, 17
   Dream Act, 17
   ICE under administration of, 17
   legacy of King, Jr. and, 33
obesity, 127–8
Olivet Baptist Church, 27
overgeneralization, as a self-care intervention, 130
Owens, Jesse, 103

Pantaleo, Daniel, 4
paranoia, of white people, 9–10
Parker, Pat, 42–43
particularities, 38–40
pastoral care
   to African Americans in the United States Armed Forces, 194–200
   domestic violence and, 37–47
pastoral caregivers, 177–78
pastoral (micro) level, of response, 19, 21–22, 58–68
perception
   as a barrier to accessing mental health, 93–94
   of contradictions between Black and White athletes, 173
   importance of to African Americans, 93–94
personal constructs, 171–73, 174–75
personal racism valets, white people's view of police as, 12
personalization, as a self-care intervention, 131
Please Don't Tell (Justes), 162–63
policing
   about, 151

experience of African Americans vs European Americans, 11–12
   police brutality highlighted on social media, 5–8
   racial bias in, 106
posttraumatic stress disorder (PTSD), racism and, 6
Poussaint, Alvin, 122–23
power imbalances, cultural humility and, 192
premarital counseling, 145–46
PrEP (Pre-exposure prophylaxis), 113
prison nation, Black women/girls and, 52, 53–54. *See also* incarceration
Progressive National Convention, 153n9
prophetic (macro) level, of response, 19–20
psychiatric/medical model, of suicide, 122, 123
psychological model, of suicide, 122, 123
psychological safety, for young women/girls in prison nation, 54

racial bias, in policing *versus* HIV/AIDS, 106
racial hoaxes, 12
racism, posttraumatic stress disorder (PTSD) and, 6
reader-response method, of interpretation, 79
"Reading Her Way through the Struggle" (Weems), 73n2
referral network
   establishing for young women/girls in prison nation, 55–56
   for mental health, 89
reformations and fellowships, in the Black Church, 198–99
refugees, demonization of, 15–22
Reign, April, 6–7
relationships, between church members and clergy, 89–91

"The Relationship Between Culture and Suicide: An Analysis of African Americans" study, 121

Religion and Suicide in the African-American Community (Early), 121

religions
as a positive factor in suicide prevention, 119–22
recognized by United States military, 195–96

residential treatment center (RTC), 49–50

respectability, HIV/AIDS and, 107–8, 110–11

respite space, 57

Rice, Tamir, 4, 142, 152

Richie, Beth E.
Arrested Justice: Black Women, Violence and America's Prison Nation, 52

Robinson, Donte, 9–10

Roe v. Wade, 166

Roof, Dylan, 11

Roosevelt, Franklin D., 15

Russell-Brown, Katheryn, 12

safe space, 91

safety
Black Church as a place of, 53–54, 91
creating a culture of in the Black Church, 48–, 54–55

The Salt Eaters (Bambara), 100–101

Satcher, David, 122–23

Scottsboro case, 12

scripture, methods for interpreting, 77–80

secular education, Christian education *versus,* 79–80

self object needs, 83

self-awareness in ministry, as a focus of CPE, 182

self-care
interventions in, 130–31
the movement and, 24

self-reflection, cultural humility and, 192

Sessions, Jeff, 20

sexual orientation, suicide and, 120

The Sexual Abuse to Prison Pipeline: The Girls' Story report, 49

shame
abortion and, 163–64
HIV/AIDS and, 108–9

Sharpton, Al, 110

Shelby, Betty Jo, 5–6

shelters, domestic violence, 44

Sheppard, Phillis Isabella, 83

Sherman, Francine T., 49

Shockley, Grant, 73–74

Shopshire, James M., 121–22

"should" statements, as a self-care intervention, 131

Simone, Nina, 113

Sisters of the Yam (hooks), 167

Sixteenth Street Baptist Church, 27

Siyonbola, Lolade, 9

slavery
Biblical interpretations of, 73–74, 112
drug wars and, 41–42
growth of, 99–100
literacy during, 138
mating practices and, 143–44

Smith, Susan, 12

social justice
as apostolic care, 20–21
as prophetic care, 19–20

social media, as a resource, 5–8

social safety, for young women/girls in prison nation, 54–55

sociological model, of suicide, 122–23

sons, raising, 148–59

The Souls of Black Folk (DuBois), 158

Southern Christian Leadership Conference (SCLC), 33

spiritual care
for African Americans in the United States Armed Forces, 194–200
for Black advocates, 111–12

Black allies and, 110–11
for Black people living with HIV/
    AIDS, 110
cultural care as, 190–91
in hospitals, 186–93
interpretive tools for, 71–80
opportunity for, 19
Spiritual Care and Education
    standard, 175–76
spiritual premarital counseling,
    145–46
spirituality, mate selection and, 142–
    43, 144–45
Stack, Steven
    "The Relationship Between
    Culture and Suicide:
    An Analysis of African
    Americans" study, 121
statistics
    on abortion, 162
    on African American education
        levels, 138
    on Black suicide, 118–19
    on domestic violence, 43
    on education of African
        Americans, 74n9
    on HIV/AIDS, 104–5
    on homosexuality, 75
    on incarceration, 141, 181
    on life expectancy, 187
    on marriage, 137
    on suicide, 115, 118–19
    on violence, 43, 181
    on white safety and voting
        patterns, 13
"Stay Woke," 23–24
Sterling, Alton, 4, 5
stigmatization, of mental health, 88
storytelling, for dealing with grief,
    167–8
strength, as a barrier to accessing
    mental health, 95–96
stress, violence and, 60–61
Stress Reduction and Relaxation
    Program, 61

strong Black woman (SBW), as a
    barrier to mate selection,
    139–40
substance abuse, ministries
    supporting, 162
suicide
    rate of among world religions,
        120
    sexual orientation and, 120
    statistics on, 115, 118–19
suicide intervention and prevention
    about, 114–17
    identifying signs of potential
        victims, 122–25
    religion as a positive factor in,
        119–22
    role of congregations in, 116–17
    terminology for, 117
Summer, Donna, 115–16
SuperKids for Peace, 67–8
suspicion
    as a barrier to accessing mental
        health, 96–101
    hospitalization and, 187–88
sustainable activism, 24

Tebow, Tim, 173
theocracy, 195
theological clarity, domestic violence
    and, 44
theological interpretive implications,
    76–77
theology, of Black shame, 108–9
therapeutic interventions, mate
    selection and, 142–43, 146–47
Thomas, Frank, 44, 44n14, 167
threats, occurrence of, 10–13
three-e method, 183–84
Tometi, Opal, 4, 39n2
trauma
    adverse childhood experiences
        (ACEs) and, 51–52
    defined, 180
    types of, 181
Trump, Donald, 17–18
trust, importance of to African
    Americans, 97

Truth, Soujourner, 179
Tubman, Harriet, 113
Tuskegee syphilis experiment, 97
twinship/kinship, as a self object
    need, 83

United States Armed Forces, pastoral
    and spiritual care to African
    Americans in the, 194–200
U.S. Immigration and Customs
    Enforcement (ICE), 16–17

vicarious trauma, 6
victim safety, domestic violence and,
    40, 41–45
victimization, incarceration and,
    49–50
violence. *See also* domestic violence
    as a barrier to mate selection,
        140–41
    nonviolence *versus*, 29–32
    statistics on, 181
    stress and, 60–61

Walker, Alice, 166–67
    *In Search of Our Mother's
    Gardens: Womanist Prose*,
    43–44
Walker, David, 179

Walker-Barnes, Chanequa, 90
War on Terror, 16
Washington, Booker T., 107, 138
weathering effect, 6
Weaver, Vesla Mae, 11–13
Weems, Renita J.
    "Reading Her Way through the
        Struggle," 73n2
West, Traci C., 56, 57
    *Disruptive Christian Ethics: When
    Racism and Women's Lives
    Matter*, 46
White, Evelyn
    *Chain, Chain, Change: For
    Black Women in Abusive
    Relationships*, 41
Williams, Monnica, 6
Wilson, Darren, 4–5, 11, 151–52
Wimberly, Ed
    Moving from Shame to Self-Worth,
    167–68
womanism, 43–44
Women's Justice Institute (WJI),
    51–52
Woodson, Carter, 157
Wright, Jeremiah, 179

Zimmerman, George, 4, 173

Made in the USA
Monee, IL
02 September 2020